MENTORING HISTORY TEACHERS IN THE SECONDARY SCHOOL

Mentoring History Teachers in the Secondary School supports mentors to develop the knowledge, skills and understanding essential to the successful mentoring of beginning history teachers who are undertaking their initial teacher training or being inducted into the profession as early career teachers. The authors critically explore models of mentoring and place subject specificity at the heart of every chapter, offering practical mentoring strategies rooted in the best evidence and research from the history teaching community.

This book is a vital source of encouragement and inspiration for all those involved in developing the next generation of history teachers, providing accessible summaries of history-specific thinking on a range of topics alongside mentoring support. Key topics include:

- Understanding what being a subject-specific mentor of beginning history teachers involves.
- Establishing a dialogic mentor-mentee relationship.
- Supporting beginning teachers to develop the substantive and disciplinary knowledge they need to become excellent history teachers.
- Guiding beginning history teachers through the lesson planning process.
- Conducting subject-specific lesson observations and pre- and post-lesson discussions.
- Supporting beginning history teachers to consider the purpose of history education and how they can navigate this in relation to values education, the use of ICT, and the teaching of controversial and sensitive issues.

Mentoring History Teachers in the Secondary School offers an accessible and practical guide to mentoring beginning history teachers, with ready-to-use strategies to support and inspire both mentors and beginning teachers alike.

Victoria Crooks is Assistant Professor in History Education and the Subject Lead of the Secondary History PGCE course at the University of Nottingham.

Laura London is a lecturer in education in the School of Education and Lifelong Learning at the University of East Anglia.

Terry Haydn is Emeritus Professor of Education at the University of East Anglia.

MENTORING TRAINEE AND EARLY CAREER TEACHERS

Series edited by: Susan Capel, Trevor Wright, Julia Lawrence and Sarah Younie

The **Mentoring Trainee and Early Career Teachers** Series are subject-specific, practical books designed to reinforce and develop mentors' understanding of the different aspects of their role, as well as exploring issues that mentees encounter in the course of learning to teach. The books have two main foci: first, challenging mentors to reflect critically on theory, research and evidence, on their own knowledge, their approaches to mentoring and how they work with beginning teachers in order to move their practice forward; and second, supporting mentors to effectively facilitate the development of beginning teachers. Although the basic structure of all the subject books is similar, each book is different to reflect the needs of mentors in relation to the unique nature of each subject or age phase. Elements of appropriate theory introduce each topic or issue, with emphasis placed on the practical application of material. The chapter authors in each book have been engaged with mentoring over a long period of time and share research, evidence and their experience.

We hope that this series of books supports you in developing into an effective, reflective mentor as you support the development of the next generation of teachers.

For more information about this series, please visit: https://www.routledge.com/Mentoring-Trainee-and-Early-Career-Teachers/book-series/MTNQT

Titles in the series

Mentoring Teachers in the Primary School
Edited by Kristy Howells and Julia Lawrence, with Judith Roden

Mentoring Geography Teachers in the Secondary School
Edited by Grace Healy, Lauren Hammond, Steve Puttick and Nicola Walshe

Mentoring Teachers in Scotland
Edited by Sandra Eady, Jane Essex, Margaret McColl and Kay Livingston

Mentoring Religious Education Teachers in the Secondary School: A Practical Guide
Edited by Helen Sheehan

Mentoring History Teachers in the Secondary School
Terry Haydn, Victoria Crooks and Laura London

'With this book, Healy et al. have launched a giant into the relatively empty space of literature that exists on effective mentoring of geography teachers. The passionate theme that courses through the chapters is of the importance of subject specificity (geography) in approaches to mentoring to ensure that beginning teachers are inducted, not only into generic principles of teaching and learning, but into those which lead to exceptional teachers of geography. The book contextualises the broader picture of contemporary geography education in which mentors find themselves, which addresses the knotty issue of how that could inform approaches to mentoring and highlights the opportunities effective geography mentoring can offer not just the mentee, but importantly and often forgotten, the mentor. Included throughout are strategies, tasks and discussion questions to support readers, particularly geography mentors, to reflect and apply the principles to their own practice. This is a must-read for every geography teacher educator from novices to experts and will be sure to give rise to critical reflection of mentoring practice and productive discussions of ways in which mentoring of beginning teachers can continue to improve.'

Elizabeth Butler, Lead Geography Consultant, Harris Federation

'There has been a welcome knowledge-turn in our schools and with it an increased awareness of the differences between subject disciplines. However, until now, there has been little thought given to the considerations that are needed when mentoring people who are becoming teachers of those distinct subject disciplines. *Mentoring Geography Teachers in the Secondary School* changes that. This book takes a rigorously academic, whilst still practical, look at how we can support people in becoming teachers who are teachers of geography first and foremost. All aspects of the mentor's role is given comprehensive consideration, from the day-to-day such as observing lessons and holding mentoring conversations, to the bigger picture of what sort of geography education these teachers will be providing. I have no doubt that this book will be a valuable guide for anyone who is taking on the role of mentor or those who have been mentoring for some time but without the subject-specific guidance necessary to truly support the next generation of geography teachers entering the profession.'

Mark Enser, Head of Geography and Research Lead and author of
Powerful Geography: Curriculum with Purpose in Practice

'As the political landscape rightly shifts to focus increasingly on the role of mentoring, this book makes a timely and important contribution. It is well grounded in the existing research literature and yet asks the questions of the moment. Bringing together authors who are at the forefront of supporting mentors and mentees, the book firstly develops critical stances around what it means to be a mentor within geography education, bringing questions of disciplinary knowledge and identity to the fore. The book then explores a variety of lived perspectives on the theory and practice of mentors, offering readers ways to consider their own practices. It then supports mentors to draw on research in offering ways to develop geography teachers through processes which develop mentors, mentees and students. In this way the book manages to be both practical and ambitious, enabling all involved in geography education to have agency in a highly dynamic world.'

Dr Mark Hardman, Associate Professor, Centre for Teachers and Teaching Research, UCL Institute of Education, UK

'*Mentoring Geography Teachers in the Secondary School* is an innovative and insightful must-read. Ideal for new and experienced ITE and ECT mentors, the book encapsulates all aspects required to fully excel in the role of the geography mentor, including lesson observations, subject knowledge, and well-being for both the beginning teacher and mentor. The book is divided into three sections: mentoring in geography education, perspectives and experiences in geography mentoring, and being a geography mentor, taking the reader on a journey of excellence in the realm of geography mentoring. The chapters are deeply rooted in research and pedagogy, posing a variety of typologies and frameworks for success for the reader to interpret how they wish. The book is guaranteed to leave the reader feeling inspired and upskilled in the role of the geography mentor to help shape a new wave of well-rounded and impactful beginning geography teachers.'

Simran Jouhal, Senior Teacher responsible for New and Beginning Teachers and former Head of Geography, The Archer Academy, North London, UK

'The implementation of the Early Career Framework, which articulates increased expectations for school-based subject mentors, means that *Mentoring Geography Teachers in the Secondary School* is both much needed and timely. It provides a comprehensive exploration of what it means to be a geography mentor in a secondary school, which is grounded in both personal experiences and the wider policy landscape. While the authors draw extensively on the research literature and write in an authoritative tone, the chapters are, without exception, highly accessible for busy teachers. Discussion questions, suggestions for further reading and practical tasks punctuate the chapters, combining theory with practice and encouraging readers to take their thinking further. Whether you intend on dipping in or reading cover to cover, this book is an essential text for all those involved in the mentoring of geography teachers in secondary schools.'

Dr Rebecca Kitchen, CPD, Curriculum and Marketing Manager, Geographical Association

'Questioning what "identity" can encompass for teachers and mentors is a theme that runs throughout. This resonated with me since being not just a teacher or a mentor, but also a learner, is key to my identity. This collection of provocative, thoughtful and example-based insights reminds mentors that we will always be learners and that it is through community and collaboration where we can get the best out of early career teachers in our care. I found reading this a cause for deep introspection and somewhat unsettling, and to quote Palombo and Daly in Chapter 14, "indeed it should be". This book is also timely and relevant, not fearing to weave in current affairs and controversial issues. John Morgan's chapter is particularly punchy and necessarily so. After all, tackling contemporary issues is one thing that Geography does best, right?'

Kit Rackley, freelance educator and Associate ITE Tutor and former geography school teacher and mentor based at the University of East Anglia, UK

'This is a book every geography mentor and anyone involved in their training should read. It recognises the complexity and challenges of the role of mentor and is ambitiously wide-ranging in its scope and scale, from the global context to the detailed planning of lessons. The book draws on an impressive range of literature and theoretical thinking and also gives voice to the experiences and views of mentors, tutors and, illuminatingly, of mentees. Throughout the book there is an emphasis on the need for geography mentors to be concerned with what is being taught, how and why. There are practical examples of how a focus on geography can be used to support lesson planning, classroom observation, post-lesson discussion and marking pupils' work. Mentors are encouraged to challenge assumptions and to consider the implications of different ways of conceptualising the important mentor/mentee relationship. The questions for discussion, suggestions for further reading and a range of tasks provide excellent support for professional development helping both mentors and mentees to learn from the process of mentoring.'

Margaret Roberts MBE, former Senior Lecturer in Geography Education, University of Sheffield, UK

'Mentors and the work of mentoring form a vital part of Initial Teacher Education and ongoing teacher professional development. This book provides a comprehensive and rich consideration of mentoring teachers in the context of secondary school geography, bringing together perspectives from both school and university settings. This is a valuable and timely contribution which will be essential reading for both mentors and mentees within and beyond secondary school geography.'

Dr Elizabeth Rushton, Lecturer in Geography Education, King's College London, UK

'This edited volume addresses the complexities of mentoring beginning teachers through the lenses of policy, theory, research and practice, at a range of scales. Acknowledging the pivotal role of subject identity and knowledge(s) in mentoring geography teachers, many of the chapters are also uniquely geographical in orientation. This book is a godsend to geography teacher mentors the world over, given its strong theoretical and empirical underpinnings, and applicability to a range of contexts.'

Dr Tricia Seow, Senior Lecturer, National Institute of Education, Nanyang Technological University, Singapore

'As the role of mentoring in schools seemingly comes to the fore, this is a timely publication. This book will serve as a much-needed addition to the literature – particularly given its consideration of mentoring through a uniquely geographical lens. Reading as a teacher and PGCE mentor, this book provided me with plenty of food for thought through its combination of theoretical underpinnings, discussion of empirical findings and links to implications for classroom practice. With an unashamed focus on mentoring teachers to be the very best *geography* teacher possible, this is a must-read for experienced and new mentors alike.'

Kate Stockings, Head of Geography, Hampstead School

'This excellent and very timely publication offers a detailed analysis of the role of the subject-specialist mentor in schools and very effectively highlights and examines the complex context within which ITE operates. The text helps teachers recognise and adapt to the enhanced profile that mentoring now attracts and offers a thorough grounding in its character, role, challenge and value. It is written in a very personal and engaging style, carefully and thoughtfully guiding the reader to examine and critically reflect upon the pivotal role that the geography mentor undertakes.'

Justin Woolliscroft, former PGCE Programme Director and Lecturer in Education (Geography), University of Hull, UK

MENTORING HISTORY TEACHERS IN THE SECONDARY SCHOOL

A Practical Guide

Victoria Crooks, Laura London and Terry Haydn

LONDON AND NEW YORK

Designed cover image: Getty Images/Johnny Greig

First published 2024
by Routledge
4 Park Square, Milton Park, Abingdon, Oxon OX14 4RN

and by Routledge
605 Third Avenue, New York, NY 10158

Routledge is an imprint of the Taylor & Francis Group, an informa business

© 2024 Victoria Crooks, Laura London and Terry Haydn

The right of Victoria Crooks, Laura London and Terry Haydn to be identified as authors of this work has been asserted in accordance with sections 77 and 78 of the Copyright, Designs and Patents Act 1988.

All rights reserved. No part of this book may be reprinted or reproduced or utilised in any form or by any electronic, mechanical, or other means, now known or hereafter invented, including photocopying and recording, or in any information storage or retrieval system, without permission in writing from the publishers.

Trademark notice: Product or corporate names may be trademarks or registered trademarks, and are used only for identification and explanation without intent to infringe.

British Library Cataloguing-in-Publication Data
A catalogue record for this book is available from the British Library

Library of Congress Cataloging-in-Publication Data
Names: Crooks, Victoria, author. | London, Laura (Educator), author. | Haydn, Terry, 1951- author.
Title: Mentoring history teachers in the secondary school : a practical guide / Victoria Crooks, Laura London, Terry Haydn.
Description: New York, NY : Routledge, 2024. | Includes bibliographical references and index. | Summary: "Mentoring History Teachers in the Secondary School supports mentors to develop the knowledge, skills and understanding essential to the successful mentoring of beginning history teachers"–Provided by publisher.
Identifiers: LCCN 2023026188 (print) | LCCN 2023026189 (ebook) |
    ISBN 9781032121901 (hbk) | ISBN 9781032121918 (pbk) | ISBN 9781003223504 (ebk)
Subjects: LCSH: History–Study and teaching (Secondary) | Mentoring in education. | Teachers–Professional relationships.
Classification: LCC D16.2 .C766 2024 (print) | LCC D16.2 (ebook) |
    DDC 907.1–dc23/eng/20230821
LC record available at https://lccn.loc.gov/2023026188
LC ebook record available at https://lccn.loc.gov/2023026189

ISBN: 978-1-032-12190-1 (hbk)
ISBN: 978-1-032-12191-8 (pbk)
ISBN: 978-1-003-22350-4 (ebk)

DOI: 10.4324/9781003223504

Typeset in Interstate
by Apex CoVantage, LLC

Thank you to those who have mentored us throughout our careers and helped us to understand why mentors matter.

CONTENTS

List of illustrations	xiii
List of case studies	xv
List of tasks	xvi
Foreword	xviii
Acknowledgements	xx
List of contributors	xxi
An introduction to the series: mentoring trainee and early career teachers	xxii

1 **Mentoring beginning history teachers**   1
Victoria Crooks

2 **Supporting beginning history teachers to develop their subject knowledge**   18
Terry Haydn

3 **Supporting beginning teachers to understand and utilise substantive and disciplinary historical concepts**   39
Victoria Crooks

4 **Helping beginning history teachers to plan, deliver, and evaluate lessons**   72
Victoria Crooks and Laura London

5 **Working with beginning history teachers to support all pupils' learning**   96
Victoria Crooks

6 **Developing beginning teachers' reflective practice through lesson observation and feedback**   118
Laura London

7 **Exploring the relationship between values and history education**   136
Terry Haydn

8 **Supporting beginning history teachers to teach controversial and sensitive issues**   153
Laura London and Victoria Crooks

| 9 | **Supporting beginning teachers' use of ICT in the history classroom** | **176** |

Terry Haydn

| 10 | **Continuing Professional Development for beginning history teachers and mentors** | **194** |

Laura London

Index 212

ILLUSTRATIONS

Boxes

8.1	Question 1: disclosing personal views	169
8.2	Question 2: spontaneous controversial remarks	170
8.3	Question 3: the respectful use of photographs and films	170
8.4	Question 4: developing subject knowledge	171
9.1	Some Twitter feeds and blogs	183

Figures

2.1	The importance of footnotes and references	29
3.1	The different forms of historical substantive knowledge	41
3.2	Concept categories covered in a simple definition of the Reformation	45
3.3	Concept map for the Reformation	45
4.1	Staged process for planning shown as a continuing sequence of stages in a circular flow	82
4.2	A worked example of circular planning for the George Africanus enquiry	84

Tables

1.1	Summary of approaches to teachers' professional learning, developed from model expressed in the work of Winch, Oancea, & Orchard (2015)	7
1.2	Example of spiral approach to subject-specific mentoring developed drawing on the work of Stanford (2019) and Burnham and Crooks (2022)	8
3.1	Table derived from Haenen and Schrijnemakers' (2000) taxonomy for substantive concepts (p. 24)	42
4.1	Approaches to lesson evaluations	91
6.1	Questions to support mentors to focus on historical learning during lesson observations developed drawing on UEA History PGCE course materials (London, 2022)	122
6.2	Structure for feedback conversations following the lesson observation	125
6.3	Example of written lesson observation feedback	127

10.1	Opportunities for history-specific CPD	199
10.2	A stepped approach to curricular planning with your mentee	203
10.3	Personal statement checklist	206
10.4	Potential questions for interview	207

CASE STUDIES

5.1	Simone's new class	96
5.2	Leila's support for a pupil with dyslexia	112
5.3	Adeel's targets	112
5.4	Paul's support of newly arrived refugee children	113
10.1	Theo's subject-specific gaps	205
10.2	Rachel's planning challenge	205

TASKS

1.1	Preconceptions of the mentoring role	2
1.2	Balancing the demands of mentoring	5
1.3	Considering starting points	9
1.4	Reflecting on what it means to be a history teacher and mentor	12
2.1	'Chapter and verse': expert views on the importance of secure substantive subject knowledge	23
2.2	Learning how to distil overall subject knowledge into an effective introduction to a topic, and learning to formulate clear learning objectives for the topic to be taught	25
2.3	Learning to ask historical questions	29
2.4	Suggested readings on assessment at Key Stage 3	32
3.1	Conceptual expositions	41
3.2	Identifying substantive concepts	42
3.3	Key substantive concepts	43
3.4	Concept mapping	46
3.5	Articulating the disciplinary content of your own curriculum	49
3.6	Understanding the relationship between enquiry questions and their disciplinary focus	50
3.7	Exploring the disciplinary concepts	65
3.8	Progression in disciplinary understanding	66
4.1	Practical approaches to support beginning teachers to understand the interplay between historical rationale and planning	74
4.2	Identifying and generating effective enquiry questions	78
4.3	The takeaways test	81
4.4	Supporting beginning teachers to see their lesson plan as a 'working document'	83
4.5	Modelling planning from an existing departmental plan or resource	87
4.6	Supporting beginning teachers with assessment	90
5.1	Preparation for teaching a new class	101
5.2	Exploring the curriculum	103
5.3	Considering planning	107
5.4	Thinking about questioning	109

5.5	Reviewing visual images	110
5.6	Storytelling	111
6.1	Pre-lesson observation activities for mentors	120
6.2	Mentor reflection: history-specific observations	124
6.3	Mentor reflection: providing subject-specific written feedback	129
6.4	Mentor reflection: what to do if your mentee is not responding to feedback	131
6.5	How to support other members of the department to work with your mentee	133
7.1	Discussing the Department for Education's (DfE) advice for promoting Fundamental British Values (FBV) with your mentee	137
7.2	'Opening up' values issues in the history curriculum	142
7.3	What constitutes 'good history'?	145
7.4	The International Baccalaureate learner profile	146
7.5	Finding time for 'truth' in the history classroom	148
8.1	Exploring your history curriculum with your mentee	157
8.2	Understanding curricular rationale	158
8.3	Considering your own teaching of controversial and sensitive issues	160
8.4	Reviewing curriculum content	161
8.5	Reviewing textbook presentations of controversial and sensitive issues	167
8.6	Planning and creating resources for teaching controversial and sensitive issues	168
8.7	Mentor reflection: answering beginning teachers' questions about teaching controversial and sensitive issues	171
9.1	Thinking about what it means 'to be good at ICT' in history teaching	181
9.2	Reviewing the extent to which ICT agendas have been considered in the course of the placement	186
9.3	Guiding mentees towards showing initiative in the harvesting of high-quality resources	187
9.4	Talking about and sharing some impact resources for the history classroom	188
9.5	Supporting your mentee with remote teaching	190
10.1	Reflecting on your own Continuing Professional Development (CPD)	195
10.2	A reflection for mentors: the history teaching community	201
10.3	Mentor reflection on curriculum planning	204
10.4	Supporting a mentee's professional development	205
10.5	Supporting your mentee to do well at interview	207

FOREWORD

For the past 25 years, the professional journal *Teaching History* has included a 'problem page' intended to support history mentors in the vital work that they do. Each focuses on a particular scenario and includes an outline of the challenge that the history mentor faces in that situation, along with two or three extracts from documents that illustrate the issue from different perspectives. All the scenarios are fictionalised, but the problem at the heart of each one is always based on a real issue. When I took on the role of editing 'Move Me On' – constructing the scenario and inviting history mentors (working in different contexts) to write a reply outlining how they would respond – I had little idea that the feature would still be running a quarter of a century later. The fact that it is still going strong makes clear just how valuable this book is and how much it has to cover.

The value of the book arises first from the fact that for any beginning teacher, regardless of their particular route into teaching, their mentor will be the most important source of encouragement and guidance. While there is much that can be learned from beyond the classroom – from rigorous research conducted in multiple, diverse contexts; from rich, contextualised accounts of teachers' curricular thinking and classroom experimentation shared in a professional journal such as *Teaching History*; from role-play and rehearsals – beginning teachers ultimately need to develop their own knowledge for practice. It is, therefore, only in practice that all the other sources of knowledge on which they might draw come together and acquire meaning for them. And it is the person who can regularly be with them in that practice – not just in the classroom, but in the planning and preparation and in the reflection and review that leads into the next planning cycle – who plays a crucial supporting role. Indeed, not just one role but many, as the first chapter of the book makes clear.

Most fundamental is the educative work that mentors need to do: structuring and sequencing beginning teachers' learning effectively to enable them to master the range of knowledge bases on which they need to draw – consciously and deliberately at first, but with increasing fluency and confidence over time. Inescapably linked to that educative role are responsibilities for pastoral care and for assessment, which can be difficult to balance effectively yet have to be achieved together when inducting a new colleague into the teaching profession. Without care, sensitivity, and encouragement, learning to teach is a very daunting process; without focus and rigour in ongoing assessment (always rooted in consideration of how the new teachers' practice is promoting pupil leaning), the process is not one of professional preparation.

This book has much practical advice to share in relation to each of these roles and how they can be effectively combined; but beyond this, its value lies in its subject-specific focus – particularly at a time when teacher education in England has been subject to a wave of reform that has threatened to obscure (or even obliterate) the fundamental importance of attending to the subject that is being taught. While there is undoubtedly much to be learned about effective teaching from empirical research findings and observations that encompass many different subjects, these insights need to be interrogated in light of the particular nature and demands of the subject being taught. It was Lee Shulman's (1986) study of expert practice that first gave us the term 'pedagogical content knowledge', used to capture the integration of general knowledge about effective pedagogy with specific knowledge related to the subject being taught; it is this integrated form of professional knowledge that characterises high-quality subject teaching.

Pedagogical content knowledge is distinct from rich knowledge of the content being taught – essential as that is – and distinct from knowledge of the curriculum and assessment structures within which that knowledge is taught. It is an understanding of the subject that has been reconceptualised for teaching. It is rooted in the distinctive practices of the subject discipline and in the purposes that such knowledge serves. It involves recognition of the fundamental building blocks that serve as the bases for building further knowledge and conceptual understanding. But it also implies a subject-specific understanding of young people and of the kinds of questions that they may bring to the classroom. It requires familiarity with the sorts of subject-specific misconceptions that young people might hold and with strategies by which such misconceptions can first be elicited and then effectively overturned – all without undermining young people's confidence or enthusiasm! This is the kind of knowledge that experienced and skilful teachers possess, and that they need to make accessible to beginners if those beginners too are to become experts.

This book's distinctive contribution lies in its thorough understanding of the importance of pedagogical content knowledge. It is because of its thorough understanding of what it means to reconceptualise history for teaching, as well as the ways in which it has made this understanding accessible to mentors and the strategies that it offers for helping beginners to develop this kind of understanding that it will prove so valuable to new and experienced mentors.

In encouraging readers to read and return regularly to the advice offered here, I will draw once more on the Move Me On feature with which I began this foreword. The guidance that I give to mentors writing a response to the problem scenarios always includes the stipulation that they should offer at least one suggested reading that might help the mentor or that the mentor might encourage their mentee to read. I am confident that each of the chapters in this book will appear regularly among those recommendations – and that taken together they might finally make the feature itself redundant!

Katharine Burn PGCE Course Director, University of Oxford

ACKNOWLEDGEMENTS

A book only exists because of the support extended to the authors during the writing period.

We would like to thank our families for their support and forbearance during the writing process, especially amazing grandparents who helped provide much-needed space for writing.

In addition, we would like to thank the many people who supported us by acting as response readers during the editing process. Your thoughtful and incisive comments helped to make us better. Thanks go to Sally Burnham, Vicky Christoforatou, Caleb Crooks, Colin Crooks, Kerryn Dixon, Alex Ford, Esther Fulton, Chris Gilmore, Teni Gogo, Swerupa Gosrani, Sylvia Green, Fleur McCole, Ali Messer, Gary Mills, Sophie Vauzour, and Chris Weight.

CONTRIBUTORS

Victoria Crooks is Assistant Professor in History Education and the Subject Lead of the Secondary History PGCE course at the University of Nottingham. Before moving into ITE she taught history and humanities for 10 years in East Midlands schools, where she was also involved in sixth form leadership and mentored beginning teachers. Victoria's current research interests include subject-specific mentoring. She has presented her work nationally and internationally and writes a blog to support teacher-mentors in their role. Victoria is co-Chair of the History Teacher Educators' Network (HTEN).

Laura London is a lecturer in education in the School of Education and Lifelong Learning at the University of East Anglia, where she is the leader of the Secondary History PGCE course. Prior to this she was a history teacher and ITE mentor and worked for 15 years in 11-18 secondary schools in East Anglia. Laura's current research interests include mentoring in history ITE, and she has presented her work nationally and internationally. Laura is also co-Chair of the History Teacher Educators' Network (HTEN).

Terry Haydn is Emeritus Professor of Education at the University of East Anglia. He worked as a history teacher for 19 years in an inner-city school in Manchester before moving to work in teacher education at the Institute of Education, University of London, and the University of East Anglia. His research interests are in the purposes of school history, the use of new technology in history teaching, and the working atmosphere in the classroom.

The authors are also Honorary Fellows of the Historical Association.

AN INTRODUCTION TO THE SERIES: MENTORING TRAINEE AND EARLY CAREER TEACHERS

Mentoring is a very important and exciting role. What could be better than supporting the development of the next generation of subject teachers? A mentor is almost certainly an effective teacher, but this doesn't automatically guarantee that he or she will be a good mentor, despite similarities in the two roles. This series of practical workbooks covers primary mentoring and most subjects in the secondary curriculum. They are designed specifically to reinforce mentors' understanding of different aspects of their role, for mentors to learn about and reflect on their role, to provide support for mentors in aspects of their development and enable them to analyse their success in supporting the development of beginning teachers (defined as trainee, newly qualified and early career teachers). This book has two main foci: first, the focus is on challenging mentors to reflect critically on theory/research/evidence, on their own knowledge, how they work with beginning teachers, how they work with more experienced teachers and on their approaches to mentoring in order to move their practice forward. Second, the focus is on supporting mentors to effectively facilitate the development of beginning teachers. Thus, some of the practical activities in the books are designed to encourage reflection, whilst others ask mentors to undertake activities with beginning teachers.

This book can be used alongside generic and subject books designed for student and newly qualified teachers. These books include *Learning to Teach in the Secondary School: A Companion to School Experience*, 9th edition (Capel, Leask, Younie, Hidson and Lawrence 2022) which deals with aspects of teaching and learning applicable to all subjects. Further, the generic books are complemented by three series: *Learning to Teach (subject) in the Secondary School: A Companion to School Experience*; and *A Practical Guide to Teaching (subject) in the Secondary School*; and *Learning to Teach in the Primary School*. These books are designed for student teachers on different types of initial teacher education programmes (and indeed a beginning teacher you are working with may have used/currently be using them). However, these books are proving equally useful to tutors and mentors in their work with student teachers, both in relation to the knowledge, skills and understanding the student teacher is developing and some tasks which mentors might find it useful to support a beginning teacher to do.

It is also supported by a book designed for newly qualified teachers, *Surviving and Thriving in the Secondary School: The NQT's Essential Companion* (Capel, Lawrence, Leask and Younie, 2019). These titles cover material not generally needed by student teachers on an initial teacher education course, but which is needed by newly qualified teachers in their school work and early career.

The information in this book should link with the information in the generic text and relevant book in the three series in a number of ways. For example, mentors might want to refer a beginning teacher to read about specific knowledge, understanding and skills they are focusing on developing, or to undertake tasks in the book, either alone or with their support, then discus the tasks. It is recommended that you have copies of these books available so that you can cross-reference when needed.

In turn, the books complement a range of resources on which mentors can draw (including other mentors of beginning teachers in the same or other subjects or age phase, other teachers and a range of other resources including books, research articles and websites).

The positive feedback on *Learning to Teach* and the related books above, particularly the way they have supported the learning of student teachers in their development into effective, reflective teachers, encouraged us to retain the main features of that book in this series. Like teaching, mentoring should be research and evidence-informed. Thus, this series of books introduce theoretical, research and professional evidence-based advice and guidance to support mentors as they develop their mentoring to support beginning teachers' development. The main focus is the practical application of material. Elements of appropriate theory introduce each topic or issue, and recent research into mentoring and/or teaching and learning is integral to the presentation. Tasks are provided to help mentors identify key features of the topic or issue and reflect on and/or apply them to their own practice of mentoring beginning teachers. Although the basic structure of all the books is similar, each book is different to reflect the needs of mentors in relation to the unique nature of each subject.

The chapter authors in the books have been engaged with mentoring over a long period of time and are aiming to share research/evidence and their experience. We, as series editors, are pleased to extend the work in initial teacher education to the work of mentors of beginning teachers. We hope that this series of books supports you in developing into an effective, reflective mentor as you support the development of the next generation of subject teachers.

Susan Capel, Julia Lawrence, and Sarah Younie, June 2023

1 Mentoring beginning history teachers

Victoria Crooks

Introduction

> [Mentoring] allows you to think about your own teaching as well and not just about the trainee. And when you come up with a history-specific target each week, you kind of reassess your own teaching once again and think: Am I doing this? Am I giving this appropriate attention?
>
> **History Mentor of Beginning Teachers**

Mentoring is the bedrock of effective teacher development. From Initial Teacher Education (ITE) to continuing professional development at middle and senior leadership levels, teachers' growth is enabled by the support of those who mentor them. This 'passing on of the baton' from one generation of teachers to the next comprises an essential part of the 'practical theorising' (McIntyre, 1995, p. 377) in which teachers must engage to grow in confidence and competence in their role. The very act of mentoring also prompts the mentor to engage in reflection upon their own teaching practice. As the mentor's reflection above demonstrates, when mentoring is prioritised, it can be a key driver for improvement within schools and the education system at large.

Mentoring with a history-specific focus is powerful not only for beginning and early career teachers but also for mentors themselves; however, to do it well requires specialised understanding of what it means to be a history teacher specifically. The role of a history mentor is therefore multi-faceted, bridging both the disciplinary and the affective domains. Mentors support not only the development of the mentee's subject and pedagogical content knowledge (Shulman, 1986) but also their growing understanding of professionalism (including their induction to the profession, well-being, and preparedness for the responsibilities of the role). It is a crucial and joyous responsibility – effective mentoring ensures the ongoing health of history as a school subject and provides the individual mentor with opportunities for their own growth.

Objectives

At the end of this chapter, you should be able to:

- Understand the crucial role of the mentor in developing beginning and early career history teachers.

- Reflect on the different approaches underpinning beginning and early career teacher development.
- Understand the distinctive nature of subject-specific mentoring.

Task 1.1 Preconceptions of the mentoring role

- What was your own experience of being mentored as a beginning and early career teacher?
- What aspects of a mentee's development should a mentor seek to support?
- What do you understand as being the key difference between being a *mentor* and being a *history mentor*?

What is mentoring?

Mentoring plays a key role in the process of learning to teach and, since the 1980s, there has been recognition of mentors' importance in the preparation of beginning and early career teachers (Little, 1990; McIntyre & Hagger, 1996). From 2010, early career teacher development in the English context has undergone a period of significant diversification, yet throughout these changes the role of the mentor has remained central (CooperGibson Research, 2019). Indeed, the mentor-mentee relationship can have the greatest influence upon their beginning teacher's emerging teacher identity (Izadinia, 2015; 2016), and will undoubtedly have shaped your own conceptions of the role (as illustrated in Task 1.1). Quite simply, mentors really matter.

Mentoring can take several different forms in school practice, for example peer mentoring (Cornu, 2005) or group mentoring (Mitchell, 1999). However, for the purposes of this book, mentoring is defined as one-to-one support provided to a novice, beginning, or early career teacher (referred to hereafter as mentee or beginning teacher) by a more experienced school-based colleague (mentor). Mentoring in this context is multi-dimensional. It recognises that 'issues such as reflection, emotions, beliefs, dispositions, agency, professional values, etc. are key in developing as a teacher along with robust knowledge' (La Velle & Flores, 2018, p. 524). Thus, mentoring support seeks to prepare the beginning teacher for independent classroom practice by:

1. **Inducting into the profession:** enabling the mentee to manage the professional demands of their role through inducting them into the specific contexts and environment in which they will teach.
2. **Offering pastoral support:** providing pastoral support which is concerned for the wellbeing of the beginning teacher as they become an independent practitioner.
3. **Acting as a guide into teaching the discipline:** preparing the mentee for classroom teaching by helping them to develop the necessary pedagogical content knowledge to teach their subject.
4. **Assessing their competencies against teacher standards:** assessing the mentee's readiness for independent practice outside of their ITE or early career induction programme.

In this context, therefore, mentoring is regarded as a situation in which professional expertise is a distinct form of professional knowledge. Mentors understand that they are critical agents in novice teacher development, prepared to 'see themselves as teacher educators willing to plan for the learning of a novice' (Feiman-Nemser & Buchman, 1985, p. 64). Just because someone is an effective or even inspirational classroom teacher, it does not mean they will automatically be a good mentor. Mentoring requires professional commitment to developing the skills and dispositions of a mentor. A model for mentoring can be seen in the four domains of mentoring support, which are explained more fully below. Task 1.2 will give you the opportunity to consider how these domains fit into your own understanding of the mentoring role.

A model for mentoring: the domains of mentoring

Domain 1: mentor as inductor into the profession

Mentors are often seen by their mentees as arbiters of professional understanding – colleagues with insight into how the beginning teacher should conduct themselves and fulfil the wider responsibilities of the teaching role. Most beginning teachers enter the classroom either trying to emulate the 'style' of teachers they knew and admired or aiming to avoid the approach of a teacher they associate with negative learning experiences (Borg, 2004). At the start of their ITE year, beginning teachers often view teaching purely in terms of the final performance on the classroom stage. Mentors are critical in helping beginning teachers to look behind the curtain and understand the breadth of their new responsibilities, including the backstage and front-of-house roles teachers adopt. As Hobson et al. (2009) assert, mentors 'play an important role in the socialisation of novice teachers, helping them to adapt to the norms, standards and expectations associated with teaching in general and with specific schools' (p. 209). In turn, they support the beginning or early career teacher to develop professional relationships with colleagues and pupils, understand their statutory and school-specific responsibilities and, most importantly, help them as they navigate the creation of their own teacher persona (Crooks, 2019b). Invariably, this aspect of the role requires patience and understanding on the part of the mentor, but in taking such an approach the mentee is led to greater autonomy and an understanding of professional obligations. This aspect of a mentee's development is often a primary concern in the initial phases of the mentoring relationship, when expectations are being established.

Domain 2: mentor as pastoral support

The variety of roles assumed by teachers mean it is common for beginning teachers to struggle to manage their well-being and workload as they gradually adopt the role of teacher and try to develop a sustainable work-life balance (Worth & Van Den Brande, 2019). A critical aspect of the mentor's role is therefore to provide pastoral support. To do this effectively, the mentor needs to develop a 'trusting personal relationship' with their mentee early on in their placement (Adey, 1997). To achieve this, it is important the mentor is non-judgemental, and able to empathise with the mentee, with a 'willingness and ability to take an interest in beginning teachers' work and lives' (Tomlinson, Hobson, & Malderez, 2010). Effective mentors, therefore, provide support, where beginning teachers trust that making mistakes will be respected as part of the learning process, affording opportunities to review and rethink and get better. They also adopt a position of watchful concern for their mentee's well-being and resilience, particularly as they ride the wave of observation feedback; they know when to push their mentee on and when to pull back on the demands and 'carve out some space . . . [for the mentee] to reset [their] understanding' (Crooks, 2019a, p. 13). Beginning teachers need support to continually reframe their teacher personas as their understanding of pedagogy and the subject discipline grows, and in turn they develop their teacher identities (Korthagen & Kessels, 1999; Izadinia, 2016). Mentors do, however, need to be careful to ensure this aspect of a mentee's development does not subsume all others. Professional boundaries are equally important for the mentor, and it is important that mentors feel able to draw on the support of departmental colleagues, ITE tutors, and programme leaders, especially where there are significant emerging pastoral needs.

Domain 3: mentor as guide into teaching the discipline

Mentors also play a crucial role in supporting beginning teachers to develop their appreciation of their subject's substantive and disciplinary uniqueness and the pedagogical methods required to support pupil understanding. They encourage their mentees to engage in a continual process of subject-knowledge enhancement, with a focus upon developing approaches for teaching the conceptual frameworks of the subject. Mentoring which has this subject-specific focus can critically set the tone of the mentee's entire conception of what it means to be a teacher of history. Mentors therefore need to possess (or be prepared to develop) the ability to deconstruct and articulate pedagogical approaches or curricular thinking in a manner that is accessible to a novice teacher. Mentees need their mentors to facilitate practice-based experiences that deepen the beginning teacher's understanding of the connections between theory and practice. In this way, mentors provide insights into the process of history curriculum design, the planning of sequences of lessons, the selection of appropriate curriculum materials, and the evaluation of teaching impact via appropriate assessment structures. Through observation of their mentee's teaching, they also provide the beginning teacher with development targets which necessarily have a focus upon the enaction of the lesson or the planning underpinning it. The *Carter Review of Initial Teacher Training* (ITT) in England identified an important aspect of a mentor's role as understanding subject-specific issues. Indeed, a key recommendation of the report was that 'Issues in subject-specific pedagogy should be part of a framework for ITT content' (Carter, 2015, p. 8).

The premise of this book is that a subject-specific approach to mentoring is critical for the effective development of beginning history teachers (Fordham, 2016; Lambert, 2018; Healy, Walshe, & Dunphy, 2020). Yet, increasingly, mentoring is being reframed as a generic endeavour which is so devoid of sensitivity to context and subject that it is failing to meet the needs of beginning teachers (Murtagh et al., 2022; TeacherTapp, 2022). The subsequent chapters of this book will therefore seek to establish how mentors can support beginning teachers in the development of historical subject knowledge for teaching, historical thinking, and curricular understanding (Loughran & Menter, 2019).

Domain 4: mentor as assessor

In ITE and the induction of early career teachers, a conflict of interest often presents itself, as mentors are usually required to be the assessor of their mentee as well as their primary source of support and development. The need for mentors to undertake an assessment of their mentee's ability to meet teacher standards or criteria can create tensions with the more reciprocal and nurturing aspects of the role (Jones, 2001; Hobson & Malderez, 2013). This is an aspect that many mentors find difficult and can lead to a reluctance to speak with candour when making interim assessments about the mentee's progress. Being able to identify and communicate the progress the beginning teacher is making, to enable them to meet the summative standards by which they will be judged at the end of the course, is an important mentoring responsibility. However, it is vital that assessment does not become the primary focus of all mentoring interactions. Effective mentoring creates space for the mentee to experiment without the need to constantly justify approaches against mechanistic criteria designed for the purposes of summative assessment. In doing so, it frees the beginning teacher to try and fail, and learn from their mistakes without the constant threat of failure hanging over them.

Task 1.2 Balancing the demands of mentoring

- Consider the four different domains of mentoring outlined here, and reflect on how much time you allocate in your mentoring to explore each different domain with your mentee.
- What do you find difficult about balancing these different aspects of the role?

Teacher development and mentoring approaches

All beginning teachers are engaged in an act of creation: the process of becoming a teacher is not innate, it is carefully constructed and practised. Mentors rarely witness the full harvest of the seeds sown during their time with their mentee. The best teachers hone their skills over the course of their whole career. Consequently, the goal of ITE, or any teacher induction programme, should be a beginning teacher who is competent to practice independently (within a supportive department) and has the capacity for continued growth and improvement.

Beginning teachers are on a journey from being entirely focused upon themselves, preoccupied with their own development and ability to meet the assessment criteria to enable them to practice (the teacher focus), to being primarily concerned with the pupil learning occurring in their classrooms (the learning focus). Mentors therefore need to approach their mentees with an awareness of their need to spiral back through the different domains of development as this shift in perspective takes hold (La Velle & Flores, 2018).

It is also important mentors recognise that beginning teachers are unlike any other learners they support. They are novices in this new endeavour of becoming history teachers, but they are not novice 'learners', nor do they come to the process as a blank slate. As adult learners they arrive with their own preconceptions of the classroom and what it means to teach history well. They bring experience and expertise in their previous field – whether from prior academic studies or the world of work (Koehler et al., 2014). It is also possible that for many, the process of becoming a teacher will be the first time they have encountered failure, as their command over the variables which combine to achieve a successful classroom environment slips away at various points. Understanding this mindset is crucial, as one of the greatest challenges for a mentor is learning to support alongside their mentee, rather than imposing their own approaches and perspectives. Some mentees find it disconcerting to be challenged to analyse and deconstruct these preconceptions, but it is a necessary step before they can truly begin to see new school contexts, understand how and why to employ different pedagogical approaches, and appreciate the building blocks of their subject disciplines (Crooks, 2021a). The outcomes of this aspect of the mentor role are less tangible. These outcomes are foundational and underpin the dispositions required for a long-term teaching career (Osguthorpe, 2013; Korthagen, 2017).

As I've noted before (Crooks, 2021b), working alongside beginning teachers quickly reveals their desire for quick solutions to today's problems. They find it hard to look beyond their short-term development and need their mentors to help them to think outside of their limited range of experience. Mentoring which prioritises the adoption of instrumental technicist approaches, which are then practised and employed in the classroom, will meet their need for immediate solutions to their classroom dilemmas. However, as Winch and Orchard (2015) assert, 'Professionals do not require protocols setting out in detail what to do in every conceivable situation. Rather, a set of guiding principles is developed and agreed over time and the kinds of attitudes and dispositions that help teachers to reach the right decisions are fostered during their training' (p. 18). They need their mentors to look beyond 'craft' and 'executive technician' approaches (see Table 1.1), to avoid developing mindsets which see teacher knowledge – content, curriculum, pedagogical content knowledge, and practice knowledge (Shulman, 1986) – as an inert and given canon. Beginning teachers need to be developed as thinking practitioners who engage with their craft as a professional endeavour. They need to engage with research in situations where they are supported to develop criticality, enabling them to exercise their own judgement as to the relevance of that research to their own phase/subject domain and school context (Crooks, 2021b).

The preparation of excellent beginning teachers looks beyond short-term solutions and aims to equip the student for the long term. The more beginning teachers see subject, pedagogical, and practice knowledge as passive and given, the more their continued professional growth is hindered. A core aspect of a mentor's role, therefore, is to draw their mentee into the process of reflection as a tool for self-improvement, supporting the beginning teacher's abstract conceptualisation or 'sense making' of their experiences in the classroom.

Clarke and Hollingsworth's (2002) 'Interconnected Model' of teacher development demonstrates the complexity of the task confronting mentors of beginning teachers. The model sets out the four domains of influence that lead to changes in the beginning teacher's conception of their endeavour: 'the personal domain (teacher knowledge, beliefs and attitudes), the domain of practice (professional experimentation), the domain of consequence (salient outcomes), and the external domain (sources of information, stimulus or support)' (p. 950). It also rejects the idea that teacher development is linear. Instead, it recognises

Table 1.1 Summary of approaches to teachers' professional learning, developed from model expressed in the work of Winch, Oancea, & Orchard (2015).

Craft	Executive technician	Professional endeavour
Common-sense apprenticeship model. Emphasises situated professional knowledge. Understanding of students and approaches is developed through observation and practice. No place for research-based knowledge in teacher professionalism. Downplays technical know-how and critical reflection.	Emphasises value of technical know-how to effective classroom practice. Empirical education research is considered valuable BUT not necessary or desirable for teachers themselves. Research needs to be translated into protocols for application in the classroom. Looks to educational research to deliver certainty.	Values craft and technician approaches as well as research-informed practice. Teacher exercises own judgement as to how research-based considerations are relevant. Research informs and improves technical knowledge – it provides reference points for critiquing protocol interventions. Draws on body of theory mastered by teachers through years of study and reflection. Engages with research and common sense critically – able to accept uncertainty and complexity.

the complex interactions between a beginning teacher's own positionality, the ethos and experiences gained in their practice context, and the role of other external influences such as the level of engagement they have with the theoretical underpinnings of their discipline and pedagogical frameworks. This is one of the reasons it is important to consider your own starting points, as explored in Task 1.3.

Mentors who recognise a more complex model of teacher development will support their mentee to understand their experiences by guiding them to ask questions of their practice. These questions help the beginning teacher make connections between classroom practice and research, before enabling them to identify targets and engage in further active experimentation. They will engage in a dialogic process that avoids taking a 'judgementoring' stance (Hobson & Malderez, 2013, p. 90). Judgementoring is an approach where mentors reveal their hand far too quickly and remove opportunities for the mentee to engage in reflective practice and develop their own evaluations of their lesson planning and enactment. Instead, effective mentors adopt a spiralling reflection cycle (Kolb, 2014) which supports the beginning teacher to understand the relationship between research and practice through dialogic exchange and experimentation, allowing their mentee to develop increasingly rich models of pupil learning.

Supported reflection and mentoring cycle

Across a training or induction year, a supported reflection and mentoring cycle for a particular aspect of disciplinary thinking may look something like the spiral approach to subject-specific mentoring set out in Table 1.2:

Table 1.2 Example of the spiral approach to subject-specific mentoring developed drawing on the work of Stanford (2019) and Burnham and Crooks (2022)

Focus	Teaching historical thinking in relation to causation			
	Intention for development of mentee's understanding	Mentee is asked to plan and teach	Mentee is asked to read	Mentor and mentee discussion focus
Beginning of teaching practice	To comprehend how pupils develop their understanding of causal factors in the context of a relatively simple causation enquiry, involving one actor but with mounting causal likelihood as events progress.	Mentee is provided with pre-planned lessons to enable them to teach the enquiry: why did the peasants revolt in 1381?	A. Chapman, 2021. 'Camels, diamonds and counterfactuals: a model for teaching causal reasoning', *Teaching History*, 112.	• What aspects of causal reasoning are pupils asked to engage with in this enquiry? • How can a teacher help to structure pupils' thinking around causal factors?
Middle of teaching practice	To understand – through planning and teaching a mainly uni-directional causal enquiry involving one moving part and two interrelated actors – how the sequencing of enquiries enables the curriculum to be the progression model.	Mentee is asked to plan a sequence of lessons for the enquiry: why did the Civil War break out?	M. Stanford, 2019. 'Did the Bretons break? Planning increasingly complex "causal models" at Key Stage 3', *Teaching History*, 175.	• How do students 'get better' at causal reasoning? • Do you agree with Stanford's argument about teaching why William won in Year 7?
Nearing the end of teaching practice	To understand that a multi-directional causation enquiry with interrelated factors also requires planning to equip pupils to express the nuances and complexity of the historical events, and in doing so to support the progression of their causal reasoning.	Mentee plans a causation enquiry with the enquiry question: what were the causes of the First World War?	J. Woodcock, 2011. 'Does the linguistic release the conceptual? Helping Year 10 to improve their causal reasoning', *Teaching History*, 119.	• How do students 'get better' at causal reasoning? Relate back to Stanford's article in *Teaching History* 175. • How does language release conceptual understanding? • How can you provide opportunities for pupils to develop their ability to write increasingly sophisticated causal arguments in your causation enquiry?

Task 1.3 Considering starting points

- Reflect on your own starting points as you entered ITE.
    - What experience did you bring to the course that you wished was recognised?
    - What did you believe 'success' would look like, and what was your attitude to failure?
    - Where did you think you would learn most about becoming a history teacher:
        - from classroom experiences?
        - from your mentor or other colleagues?
        - from research?
    - How would you now explain the process of becoming an effective classroom teacher?

Mentoring as a subject-specific endeavour

Much has been written about mentoring in more general terms (Maynard & Furlong, 1993; McIntyre & Hagger, 1996; Hagger & McIntyre, 2006; Tomlinson, Hobson, & Malderez, 2010), and beginning teachers, and their mentors, are surrounded by a wealth of advice and guidance to help them develop their classroom practice (DfE, 2019a; 2019b). However, very little of this guidance is subject-specific, depending instead upon the application of generic teaching and learning skills and pedagogical approaches. In the English context, there has been a growing acceptance of generic approaches, and at the time of writing there is no Department for Education (DfE) requirement for mentors to be grounded in the same subject discipline as their mentee (DfE, n.d.). Indeed, teachers in England identify lack of subject-specific guidance as a serious shortcoming of the support offered to those tasked with the mentoring role (TeacherTapp, 2022).

Interpreting this generic guidance through a subject-specific lens is really challenging for mentors and their mentees, even where their subject specialism is shared. To be assessed as competent for independent practice, beginning teachers must demonstrate their specialised teacher knowledge within three key areas: professionalism, disciplinary curricular understanding, and classroom enaction. Mentoring in practice, however, often fails to give the subject-specific elements of these areas sufficient attention; frequently, disciplinary and subject-specific pedagogical issues get overtaken by more pragmatic logistical concerns. Lindgren identified that the primary focus of most mentor relationships was on the everyday functional concerns of the classroom, combined with the provision of emotional and personal development support. In fact, educative mentoring, the kind that asks 'teaching questions' connected to an understanding of teaching the discipline, were rarely noted (Lindgren, 2005).

As Shulman described (1986), developing beginning teachers' expert pedagogical content knowledge requires awareness of the discipline's underlying concepts and the steps by which a secure conceptual framework and increasingly powerful knowledge can be built. This is a complex process, intimately tied to subject-specific disciplinary understanding. It cannot be explored and developed by introducing student teachers to theories of generic classroom enaction alone. As Rosenshine asserted of his own generic principles for teaching, 'it would be a mistake to claim that all the teaching procedures which have emerged in this research apply to all subjects, and all learners, all the time' (Rosenshine & Stevens, 1986, p. 377). To hope that generic principles and subject knowledge will combine in some serendipitous way to translate into appropriate subject-specific teaching practices would be similarly misguided. Where the mentoring of teachers involves the augmentation of subject knowledge and pedagogical content knowledge, lack of subject-specialist mentoring limits this development and prevents the full benefits of a mentoring relationship from being realised (Hobson et al., 2015; Hobson et al., 2020). Beginning teachers therefore need to be supported to engage with their subject community and understand the pedagogical traditions of their discipline. Mentors should encourage their mentee to look beyond behaviour and attend to the learning that is happening in their classroom (Brooks, 2017) by supporting them to reflect on the subject-specific approaches which enhance emerging disciplinary understanding. This is learning which cannot be separated from the curricular object.

Task 1.4 will give you the opportunity to consider what being a history teacher and mentor means for you in your context.

Subject-specific mentoring of beginning and early career history teachers

The primary purpose of a history-specific mentor should be to support the mentee to attain a developed understanding of teaching history as a specialist discipline. In doing so, their objective is to help their mentee set down a pattern of thinking about their own ongoing engagement with the subject in its broadest sense.

The very best history mentors are constantly engaged in an act of modelling. Not just modelling their classroom practice – although this is obviously an important component of their role. Rather, they also model the processes that take place behind the curtain, and the thinking and preparation history teachers engage in that may not be instantly visible.

Encouraging engagement with scholarship and subject-specific pedagogy and curricular thinking

Good history mentors make continual subject knowledge enhancement attractive, sharing and enthusing over the latest historical scholarship they've read or their insights gleaned from podcasts and documentaries. They also reveal how this subject-knowledge enhancement stimulates their curriculum design and enquiry planning. In this way, they demonstrate how and why developing subject knowledge (the focus of Chapter 2) should be a career-long priority for the continually improving history teacher.

The nature of historical learning

Upon commencing their ITE programme, few beginning teachers have any explicit awareness of the different forms their historical knowledge takes (explored in Chapter 3). A key role of the history-specific mentor is therefore to make these domains visible to the beginning teacher. Beginning teachers need to be supported at this formative stage to grasp the different aspects of history-specific thinking that teachers scaffold to enable their pupils to engage in historical reasoning and develop their own historical consciousness (Clark & Peck, 2018; Chapman, 2021). This can be very affronting for these burgeoning professionals who, influenced by their own experiences of history education, often enter the endeavour with their own preconceptions of what history should be taught and how they wish to teach it. The history mentor therefore must be prepared to open up and reveal for their mentee the different types of historical knowledge – substantive, disciplinary, procedural, and epistemic, as well as to enable them to employ the necessary skills to manage the process of historical learning and communication (Chapman, 2021).

Thinking about planning for historical understanding

It's not uncommon for beginning history teachers to think the curriculum is comprised of a teacher's personal top ten favourite historical topics. Consequently, they will benefit from mentors explaining the reasons why certain periods or topics in history have been included and sequenced in the curriculum in that school context. Effective mentors will articulate explicitly for the mentee the 'professional wrestling' (Riley & Byrom, 2008) that takes place in the department when a new scheme of work is suggested. They will also encourage their mentee to understand the nature of historical enquiry as a vehicle for disciplinary thinking (Riley, 2000) to support planning (see Chapter 4). Furthermore, they will help them to appreciate that there is a significant and coherent body of history teacher theorising which has established a shared understanding of the most effective approaches for teaching specific aspects of historical thinking (Harris, Burn, & Woolley, 2013). They will also demonstrate why making history accessible and enjoyable for all young people, and across every key stage, should be a key aim of any history teacher (explained in Chapter 5).

Providing history-specific feedback and identifying targets for development

A significant aspect of the role of the mentor is that of creating and facilitating dialogic, history-specific reflective conversations and lesson feedback (ideas expanded upon in Chapter 6). In these post-lesson reflective discussions, the beginning teacher is assisted to develop reflective practices and derive overarching areas for development.

Beginning teachers are inevitably concerned with the behaviour of pupils and their own teaching actions in the classroom. One aspect of a mentor's job is therefore to help isolate and support practise of elements of classroom enaction that enables the mentee to see progress in these areas. However, subject-specific mentors help their mentee to examine their classroom with a different lens – to gradually focus less upon the performative elements of their practice and increasingly focus upon the learning taking place. Skilled mentors help their mentees to avoid the 'observation trap' and think beyond the surface-level 'symptoms' of lessons to both the true 'causes' of those symptoms and the consequent outcomes (Crooks & London, 2022). It is vital in these conversations for the history-specific thinking to be 'rendered visible' to the mentee (Healy, Walshe, & Dunphy, 2020, p. 14).

Understanding the purposes and relevance of the historical discipline

History-specific mentors also need to help their beginning teachers to develop their understanding of the value and purposes of school history, and to appreciate how to communicate these purposes to young people in meaningful ways that maintain the substantive and disciplinary integrity of the historical method (concepts discussed in Chapter 7).

History mentors should seek to show their mentee how they ensure the evolving nature of history, a discipline with contested purposes, is reflected in their curriculum. This might involve revealing the processes by which curricular change enables silences to be addressed, or by explaining how the department has expanded the range of voices heard in the curriculum, without losing its sense of cohesion (Dennis, 2021). The teaching of sensitive and controversial histories (explored in greater depth in Chapter 8) also needs to be addressed, particularly as it is an area of anxiety for so many new teachers.

Additionally, in a post-pandemic world, the role of ICT, and its opportunities for enhancing and challenging engagement with the historical discipline also need to be understood by the beginning teacher. History mentors therefore need to be prepared to support their mentee to develop the skills necessary to deliver remote learning and use ICT judiciously with pupils (see Chapter 9 for more on this).

Inducting into the community of history teachers and educators

Modelling engagement with historical curriculum and pedagogical thinking should be a central aspect of mentor meetings. Knowing about organisations such as the Historical Association (HA) and Schools History Project (SHP), and spending time on the shared-reading of history-specific educational literature, enables the beginning teacher to understand that they are joining a rich tradition of history-specific conversations about effective classroom approaches and assessment. Awareness of this wider community can then act as a springboard into engagement with continuing subject-specific professional development to strengthen their practice for the longer term (see Chapter 10).

> **Task 1.4 Reflecting on what it means to be a history teacher and mentor**
>
> - Reflect on your own beliefs about the value of being a history-specific mentor.
> - What experience have you had personally of subject-specific mentoring (as either mentor or mentee)?
> - How familiar are you with the idea of substantive and disciplinary knowledge in history education?
> - In your own training to become a teacher/career so far, have you engaged with educational research/practitioner theorising that has history and historical pedagogies as its focus? How important do you think this is in the development of beginning teachers?

Preparing mentees for career-long development

In the introduction to this chapter, it was argued that mentoring is the bedrock of effective teacher development. The way this mentoring is realised will vary depending on the structure of the programme being followed. Some programmes may centralise (and therefore genericise) their programmes. In these contexts, creating and seizing opportunities to explore a history-specific understanding of teaching and learning needs to be prioritised and planned for through a structured curriculum and regular reflective discussions.

An effective mentor's role will inevitably change as the mentee grows in confidence and capability in the classroom. The mentor's role will shift from that of experienced expert, possessing the necessary disciplinary, contextual, and professional knowledge required to guide their mentee into the profession, to that of collaborator and co-enquirer – especially if the beginning teacher later becomes a full member of the curriculum team. Mentoring practices will also need to change to reflect the beginning teacher's progression through different phases of development. For example, practices which are often utilised in the early months of training, such as observation of experienced colleagues or joint planning to facilitate their own effective initial teaching experiences, can be returned to in the later stages of a training or induction year, with the focus now being upon pupil learning.

Ultimately the goal is for the beginning teacher to understand that becoming a teacher is a career-long endeavour. The mentor therefore also needs to plan for their mentee to develop good habits of self-reflection, so they are equipped to sustain their own growth, exploration, development, and thinking beyond the end of this initial period. This book will now explore how mentors can structure the experiences of their mentees in a cumulative manner, to help them grasp the complexities involved in developing pupils' historical understanding.

Summary and key points

- Mentoring beginning and early career teachers involves developing their abilities as a teacher of their subject, inducting them into the profession, providing pastoral support and, often, assessing their readiness for independent practice.
- Effective mentoring looks beyond short-term solutions and aims to equip the student for the long term.
- Mentoring requires subject-specific approaches which allow the mentee to develop an understanding of teaching history as a specialist discipline requiring specific pedagogical approaches.
- Mentoring approaches need to change to reflect the beginning teacher's own professional progression.
- The end goal of mentoring is to equip the mentee to be self-sustaining in their reflective approach to their own practice and continued professional development.

Further reading and resources

- **CollectivEd: The Centre for Coaching, Mentoring & Professional Learning: https://www.leedsbeckett.ac.uk/research/collectived/**

CollectivED is a research and practice centre based in the Carnegie School of Education, formed to encourage collaborative conversations around research- and practice-based mentoring and coaching. In particular their working-paper series (https://www.leedsbeckett.ac.uk/research/collectived/working-paper-series/) and 'Manifesto for dialogic mentoring' (https://www.leedsbeckett.ac.uk/blogs/carnegie-education/2022/12/a-manifesto-for-dialogic-mentoring/) are worth a read.

- **Move Me On feature in *Teaching History* https://www.history.org.uk/secondary/categories/td-move-me-on**

    Move Me On is a treasure trove of support for a new history mentor. Presented as a problem page, it takes a specific problem or challenge a mentor may be facing when supporting their mentee and offers two responses to that challenge from experienced mentors and teacher educators.

- **Orchard, J. and Winch, C. (2015). What training do teachers need? Why theory is necessary to good teaching. *Impact* (22), 1-43**

    This pamphlet is an excellent introduction to the different domains of learning beginning teachers need to master in order to develop their professional identity. It is available as an open-access text here: https://onlinelibrary.wiley.com/doi/epdf/10.1111/2048-416X.2015.12002.x

References

Adey, K. (1997). First impressions do count: Mentoring student teachers. *Teacher Development 1(1)*, 123-33.

Brooks, C. (2017). Pedagogy and identity in initial teacher education: developing a professional compass. *Geography, 102(1)*, 44-50.

Burnham, S., & Crooks, V. (2022). Reading with your mentee: guided reading guidance. *University of Nottingham History Mentor Support Materials*. Nottingham, UK: University of Nottingham.

Carter, A. (2015). *Carter review of initial teacher training*. Department for Education. London: DfE. Retrieved 1 August 2022

Chapman, A. (ed.). (2021). *Knowing History in Schools: Powerful Knowledge and the Powers of Knowledge*. London: UCL Press. doi: 10.14324/111.9781787357303

Clark, A., & Peck, C. (eds.) (2018). *Contemplating historical consciousness* (1st ed.). New York: Berghahn Books. doi: 10.2307/j.ctvw04bhk

Clarke, D., & Hollingsworth, H. (2002). Elaborating a model of teacher professional growth. *Teaching and Teacher Education 18(8)*, 947-67. doi: 10.1016/S0742-051X(02)00053-7

CooperGibson Research. (2019). *Schools' Experiences of Hosting Trainees and Employing Newly Qualified Teachers*. London: Department for Education. Retrieved January 20, 2023 from https://assets.publishing.service.gov.uk/government/uploads/system/uploads/attachment_data/file/910287/Schools__Experiences_of_Hosting_Trainees_and_Employing_Newly_Qualified_Teachers_-_Research_Brief.pdf

Cornu, R. L. (2005). Peer mentoring: engaging pre-service teachers in mentoring one another. *Mentoring & Tutoring: Partnership in Learning, 13(3)*, 355-66. doi: 10.1080/13611260500105592

Crooks, V. (2019a). A tale of two mentors: mentoring with perspective. A practice insight paper. *CollectivED (9)*, 10-14. Retrieved from https://www.leedsbeckett.ac.uk/-/media/files/research/collectived/collectived-issue-9-oct-2019-final.pdf

Crooks, V. (2019b). Creation not emulation: Developing teacher persona. Retrieved 2 June 2022 from *Becoming a History Teacher*. https://uonhistoryteachertraining.school.blog/2019/10/07/creation-not-emulation-developing-teacher-persona/

Crooks, V. (2021a). *Education NOT Training: The Uncomfortable Truth about Effective Initial Teacher Education*. Retrieved 13 October 2022 from *Becoming a History Teacher*. https://uonhistoryteachertraining.school.blog/2021/08/11/education-not-training-the-uncomfortable-truth-about-effective-initial-teacher-education/

Crooks, V. (2021b). Turning on the head of a pin: Why developing agency in beginning teachers matters. Retrieved 2 June 2022 from *Becoming a History Teacher* https://uonhistoryteachertraining.school.blog/2021/07/14/turning-on-the-head-of-a-pin-why-developing-agency-in-beginning-teachers-matters/

Crooks, V., & London, L. (2022). Avoiding the observation trap: Interpreting generic mentoring approaches through a subject-specific lens. Retrieved 1 August 2022 from *Becoming a History Teacher*. http://uonhistoryteachertraining.school.blog/2022/05/26/avoiding-the-observation-trap-interpreting-generic-mentoring-approaches-through-a-subject-specific-lens/

Dennis, N. (2021). The stories we tell ourselves: History teaching, powerful knowledge and the importance of context. In A. Chapman (ed.), *Knowing History in Schools: Powerful knowledge and the powers of knowledge* (pp. 217-33). London: UCL Press. doi: 10.14324/111.9781787357303

DfE. (n.d.). Check what each person needs to do in the early career teacher training programme. Department for Education. Retrieved 23 January 2023 from *Manage training for early career teachers*. https://manage-training-for-early-career-teachers.education.gov.uk/pages/what-each-person-does

DfE. (2019a). Early career framework. Department for Education. London: Crown. Retrieved 10 March 2022 from https://www.gov.uk/government/publications/early-career-framework

DfE. (2019b). ITT core content framework. Department for Education. London: Crown. Retrieved 31 May 2022 from https://assets.publishing.service.gov.uk/government/uploads/system/uploads/attachment_data/file/974307/ITT_core_content_framework_.pdf

Feiman-Nemser, S., & Buchman, M. (1985). Pitfalls of experience in teacher preparation. *Teachers College Record 87*, 53-65.

Fordham, M. (2016). Teachers and the academic disciplines. *Journal of Philosophy of Education 50*(3), 419-31.

Hagger, H., & McIntyre, D. (2006). *Learning Teaching from Teachers: Realising the Potential of School-Based Teacher Education*. Maidenhead: Open University Press.

Harris, R., Burn, K., & Woolley, M. (2013). *The Guided Reader to Teaching and Learning History*. Oxford: Taylor & Francis Group.

Healy, G., Walshe, N., & Dunphy, A. (2020). How is geography rendered visible as an object of concern in written lesson observation feedback? *Curriculum Journal 31*(1), 7-26. doi: 10.1002/curj.1

Hobson, A., Ashby, P., Malderez, A., & Tomlinson, P. (2009). Mentoring beginning teachers: What we know and what we don't. *Teaching and Teacher Education 25*(1), 207-16. doi: 10.1016/j.tate.2008.09.001

Hobson, A., & Malderez, A. (2013). Judgementoring and other threats to realizing the potential of school-based mentoring in teacher education. *International Journal of Mentoring and Coaching in Education 2*, 89-108. doi: 10.1108/IJMCE-03-2013-0019

Hobson, A., Maxwell, B., Doyle, K., & Malderez, A. (2015). *Mentoring and Coaching for teachers in the the Further Education and Skills Sector in England: Full Report*. London: Gatsby Charitable Foundation. Retrieved 22 June 2022 from https://www.gatsby.org.uk/uploads/education/reports/pdf/mentoring-full-report.pdf

Hobson, A., Maxwell, B., Káplár-Kodácsy, K., & Hotham, E. (2020). *Nature and Impact of Effective Mentoring Training, Education and Development (MTED)*. University of Brighton and Sheffield Hallam University. Brighton & Sheffield: Education & Training Foundation. Retrieved 22 June 2022 from https://www.et-foundation.co.uk/wp-content/uploads/2020/12/ETF_MTED_Final_Report_Hobson-et-al_2020_Final_AH_30_Nov.pdf

Izadinia, M. (2015). A closer look at the role of mentor teachers in shaping preservice teachers' professional identity. *Teaching and Teacher Education 52*, 1–10. doi: 10.1016/j.tate.2015.08.003

Izadinia, M. (2016). Preservice teachers' professional identity development and the role of mentor teachers. *International Journal of Mentoring and Coaching in Education 5(2)*, 127–43. doi: 10.1108/IJMCE-01-2016-0004

Jones, M. (2001). Mentors' perceptions of their roles in school-based teacher training in England and Germany. *Journal of Education for Teaching 27*(1), 75–94. doi: 10.1080/02607470120042555

Koehler, M., Mishra, P., Kereluik, K., Shin, T., & Graham, C. (2014). The technological pedagogical content knowledge framework. In J. Spector, M. Merrill, J. Elen, & M. J. Bishop (eds.), *Handbook of research on educational communications and technology* (pp. 101–11). New York: Springer. doi: 10.1007/978-1-4614-3185-5

Kolb, D. (2014). *Experiential learning*. Upper Saddle River, NJ: Pearson Education.

Korthagen, F. A. (2017). Inconvenient truths about teacher learning: towards professional development 3.0. *Teachers and Teaching, 23*(4), 387–405. doi: 10.1080/13540602.2016.1211523

Korthagen, F. A., & Kessels, J. (1999). Linking theory and practice: Changing the pedagogy of teacher education. *Educational Researcher 28*, 4–17.

La Velle, L., & Flores, M. A. (2018). Perspectives on evidence-based knowledge for teachers: acquisition, mobilisation and utilisation. *Journal of Education for Teaching, 44(5)*, 524–38. doi: 10.1080/02607476.2018.1516345

Lambert, D. (2018). Teaching as a research-engaged profession: Uncovering a blind spot and revealing new possibilities. *London Review of Education 16(3)*, 357–70.

Lindgren, U. (2005). Experiences of beginning teachers in a school-based mentoring program in Sweden. *Educational Studies 31(3)*, 251–63. doi: 10.1080/03055690500236290

Little, J. W. (1990). The mentor phenomenon and the social organization. *Review of Research in Education 16*, 297–351. doi: 10.2307/1167355

Loughran, J., & Menter, I. (2019). The essence of being a teacher educator and why it matters. *Asia-Pacific Journal of Teacher Education 47*(3), 216–29. doi: 10.1080/1359866X.2019.1575946

Maynard, T., & Furlong, J. (1993). Learning to teach and models of mentoring. In D. McIntyre, H. Hagger, & M. Wilkin (eds.), *Mentoring: Perspectives on School Based Teacher Education*. London: Kogan Page.

McIntyre, D. (1995). Initial teacher education as practical theorising: A response to Paul Hirst. *British Journal of Educational Studies 43(4)*, 365–83. doi: 10.2307/3121806

McIntyre, D., & Hagger, H. (1996). *Mentors in Schools: Developing the Profession of Teaching*. London: David Fulton.

Mitchell, H. J. (1999). Group mentoring: does it work? *Mentoring & Tutoring: Partnership in Learning, 7(2)*, 113–20. doi: 10.1080/1361126990070202

Murtagh, L., Dawes, L., Rushton, E., & Ball-Smith, C. (2022). The 'impractical wisdom' of the Early Career Framework. Retrieved 23 January 2023 from *BERA Blog*. https://www.bera.ac.uk/blog/the-impractical-wisdom-of-the-early-career-framework

Osguthorpe, R. D. (2013). Attending to ethical and moral dispositions in teacher education. *Issues on a Teacher Education 1(22)*, 17–28.

Riley, M. (2000). Into the Key Stage 3 history garden: choosing and planting your enquiry questions. *Teaching History 99*, 8–13.

Riley, M., & Byrom, J. (2008). Professional wrestling in the history department: a case study in planning the teaching of the British Empire at Key Stage 3. *Teaching History 112*, 6-14.

Rosenshine, B., & Stevens, R. (1986). Teaching functions. In M. Wittrock (ed.), *Handbook of research on teaching* (3rd ed., pp. 376-91). The American Educational Research Association. New York/London: Macmillan/Collier Macmillan.

Shulman, L. S. (1986). Those who understand: Knowledge growth in teaching. *Educational Researcher*, 4-14.

Stanford, M. (2019). Did the Bretons break? Planning increasingly complex causal models at Key Stage 3. *Teaching History 175*, 8-14.

TeacherTapp. (2022). *Early Career Teachers: The Story So Far.* Sheffield: Education Intelligence. Retrieved 20 December 2022 from https://teachertapp.co.uk/early-career-teachers-the-story-so-far/

Tomlinson, P., Hobson, A., & Malderez, A. (2010). Mentoring in teacher education. *International Encyclopedia of Education* (3rd ed.), 749-56. doi: 10.1016/B978-0-08-044894-7.00689-8.

Winch, C., Oancea, A., & Orchard, J. (2015). The contribution of education research to teachers' professional learning: philosophical understandings. *Oxford Review of Education 41(2)*, 202-16.

Winch, C., & Orchard, J. (2015). What training do teachers need? Why theory is necessary to good teaching. *Impact No. 22 Philosophical Perspectives on Education Policy*, 1-43. doi: 10.1111/2048-416X.2015.12002.x

Worth, J., & Van Den Brande, J. (2019). *Teacher Labour Market in England Annual Report 2019.* Slough: NFER. Retrieved 29 May 2022 from https://www.nfer.ac.uk/media/3344/teacher_labour_market_in_england_2019.pdf

2 Supporting beginning history teachers to develop their subject knowledge

Terry Haydn

Introduction

One of the things that often strikes me in the early stages of working with beginning teachers in their Initial Teacher Education (ITE) year, is the extent to which a considerable proportion of them underestimate the complexity of the processes which influence the extent to which pupils will learn, understand, and retain the content of what they are trying to teach. Some of them think that if they know the topic well, if it is in 'their own heads', and they explain it clearly to their pupils, then the pupils will come to share their knowledge and understanding of the topic being taught. Some journalists, politicians, and people who have never been teachers share this naïveté and view the process of learning as a fairly unproblematic issue. A *Daily Telegraph* editorial suggested that 'as any good teacher knows, the way to drum something important into a child's head is to repeat it' (*Daily Telegraph*, 7 March 2003). This is in spite of the fact that in nearly all classrooms there is not a one-to-one correlation between what is taught and what is learned. Learning is a hit-and-miss affair, and often what is taught is not fully taken on board and understood, or the learning 'leaks away' over time. As Fullan (1999) noted, 'Even when people are sincerely motivated to learn from you, they have a devil of a job doing so. Transferability of ideas is a complex problem of the highest order' (p. 63). As well as the question of pupil comprehension of what is taught, there are the problems of knowledge retention, knowledge application (in the words of Wineburg (1997), 'the chasm between knowing X and using X to think about Y' (p. 256)), and the problem of learner motivation. What proportion of pupils in history classes are trying their hardest to do well in history? Several surveys over the past 50 years have suggested that there have always been significant numbers of pupils who think that history is not useful or interesting, and that it is not important to do well in the subject (Aldrich, 1987; Haydn & Harris, 2010). It can be salutary to ask your mentee at the start of the school placement what proportion of the history they were taught they actually learned – in the sense of knowing it, understanding it, remembering it, and being able to explain it to someone else. All this is before we get to the question of disciplinary knowledge and understanding.

While mentors will be aware that historical subject knowledge is not *just* an aggregation of historical facts, not all beginning teachers are aware of the complexity and breadth of subject knowledge issues. As Wineburg (1997) explains,

Someone who knows history, as opposed to someone who possesses a great deal of historical information, has an understanding of the strengths and weaknesses of claims, the power and the fallibility of evidence, the nature of imaginative reconstruction from fragmented sources . . . . They know how to construct a historical argument, to evaluate and question sources. To know when analogies to other events are appropriate and when they are misleading is not a generic 'thinking skill' or a disembodied system of 'metaknowledge'. It is content knowledge in its richest form. (p. 260)

Nearly all the factors causing the 'learning deficits' listed above relate to aspects of subject knowledge in its broadest sense. It is understandable that at the start of their preparation to become a history teacher, beginning teachers are not fully aware of all the factors that influence the extent to which pupils learn and make progress in history. An important responsibility for the history mentor is to gradually make the beginning teacher aware of the breadth of the subject-knowledge agenda. Handled adroitly, this can be done in a way which interests and enthuses the mentee and makes them realise that these complexities are part of what makes being a teacher such an intellectually challenging and rewarding experience.

Objectives

At the end of the chapter you should have:

- Ideas for a range of conversations with your mentee about subject-knowledge agendas in history teaching.
- Suggestions for helping beginning teachers to augment their subject knowledge in a time-effective way.
- Suggestions for helping your mentee to keep a usable archive of their developing subject knowledge.
- Tentative suggestions about the timing and sequencing of subject-knowledge conversations and interventions.
- Strategies for developing the mentee's awareness of the part that subject knowledge plays in teacher professionalism.
- Strategies for taking account of differences in mentees' competence and attitudes in relation to subject knowledge issues.
- A number of ideas and suggestions for having conversations with your mentee about subject-knowledge agendas, either in formal mentor meetings or 'in passing'.

Principles for mentoring practices relating to subject knowledge enhancement

Communicating the importance of checking pupils' subject-knowledge starting points

It is important to stress to your mentees that they should not make assumptions about what pupils know and understand about the past; pupils' subject knowledge will not match ours. People who have been immersed in the world of history right through their school career and through higher education sometimes forget that not all young people share the levels of knowledge which we as a community of history graduates have acquired. A good example of this is in Grande's (2023a) observations about a lesson on trench warfare that failed because some of the pupils in the class did not know what a trench was. The abstract nature of many terms that are used in history lessons add to possible sources of confusion in pupils' minds. Hence the importance of reminding mentees to check for understanding as a matter of routine when they are trying to get their subject knowledge across to their pupils.

Modelling subject-knowledge enhancement

Perhaps this is to state the obvious, but it is important that in their interactions with beginning teachers, all members of the department set a good example and model effective and diligent development and use of subject knowledge in their teaching. Nothing is more corrosive of mentees' respect for the teachers they are working with than when they do not 'set a good example' in their practice. This means that even if the teacher has reasonably adequate subject knowledge of the topic the mentee is observing them teaching, they should make a point of getting across to the mentee that they are always trying to refine and improve their lessons by augmenting their subject knowledge, rather than just 'trotting out' the same old thing that they have done in previous years. A one-year teacher education course does not produce 'experts' who have a comprehensive grasp of all issues pertaining to history education, but if you have tried to cultivate the dispositions of intellectual curiosity, high standards of professionalism, and a love of the subject you are both teaching, there is more chance that the mentees will be determined to improve and develop as history teachers, even after the assignments have been returned and the licence to teach awarded, and even when no one is looking.

Learning to prioritise subject-knowledge enhancement to balance competing demands

It can be helpful to your mentee if you can clearly distinguish the urgent, the important, and the desirable. In a sense the short-term agendas (for example, the need to ensure that they have strong subject knowledge of the topics they will imminently be teaching, so that pupils always get a lesson that is at least 'solid') are always the most urgent. Part of the mentor's job is to give beginning teachers a very practical basic emergency package so that their first lessons go as well as possible. But as the training year progresses, you want them to become proactive, to be keen to find out more about effective history teaching rather than just focusing on what they are teaching next week. Having a departmental culture of sharing new ideas and resources can help in this respect, and ideally, once 'settled in', beginning teachers will 'share back' with the department.

As with so many other facets of mentoring, there is a need to keep in mind the appropriate balance of pressure and support for your mentee. Yes, you want them to develop into the best teacher that they can be, but you don't want to push them so hard that they are often stressed, anxious, and not finding their placement to be a positive and fulfilling experience. With some beginning teachers, you are 'knocking at an open door' when you work to

Developing subject knowledge 21

improve their subject knowledge; with others, you have to give explicit directions about the department's standards and expectations and, for many, you can coax them to be conscientious and proactive about subject-knowledge issues, if things are handled in a sensitive and encouraging way. Several former students commented on the skilful way their mentors had, through their warm, friendly, unthreatening manner, exhorted them to try things out, read beyond the demands of the topics they were teaching, and generally 'go the extra mile', because of the rewards and professional satisfaction they would enjoy. In the words of one of them, 'She just had a way of making you want to read or watch whatever it was that they suggested . . . it wasn't hard edged and menacing target setting, but it was very effective.'

There is also a judgement call on the pace at which you move your mentee towards professional autonomy in terms of subject knowledge. It is generally accepted that in the early stages of placement, you will need to give quite a lot of direction and guidance to mentees about what to read and what resources to use in their early solo lessons. Once they have settled in and (hopefully) established good working relations with their classes, there is often a transition to allowing the mentee to decide what subject knowledge and resources to deploy in teaching a topic. This is complicated by the fact that some departments and schools want the beginning teacher to follow schemes of work closely at all times, while others allow for more teacher discretion and initiative. This is just my personal view, and it goes against what is standard practice in some academy chains, but I think it is helpful that the mentee has at least one class (and preferably more than one), where they take on responsibility for making decisions about the teaching of a topic, as long as this is within the parameters of the department's scheme of work. The pace at which there is a transition to degrees of mentee autonomy, in terms of what subject knowledge to bring to a topic, will very according to how well they are doing and how keen they are to move away from 'just' using departmental resources. Sometimes they need to be 'moved on', in spite of their understandable apprehensiveness.

Setting subject knowledge enhancement targets

There are difficult judgement calls to be made about how much reading to suggest to mentees and how many tasks or targets to give them so as to avoid overwhelming them. The majority of my ITE trainees tended to be quite apprehensive about whether their subject knowledge would be good enough to teach their first lessons – especially if they were teaching GCSE or A-level groups. Reassurance can be enormously helpful, especially where it is clear they are being conscientious in their approach to acquiring appropriate subject knowledge. However, there may be occasions when mentees are being a bit blasé about subject-knowledge issues. In these cases, there is of course a need to be firm and clear in pointing this out. If the warning is not heeded, and the casualness continues, it is important to formalise subject-knowledge enhancement as a formal target so the mentee cannot subsequently claim that they were not told about this concern. This sort of task is not the most edifying or fulfilling part of being a mentor, but it is an essential part of being a good one. The infinite variety of ways in which beginning teachers can be either quite promising or 'a concern' are part of what makes mentoring such a challenging (but rewarding) job. You need to have the emotional antennae to work out how much mentees can cope with at particular points in the course. One key pressure point is when they start going for interviews. Writing applications, preparing interview lessons, and travelling to and from interviews can be a time-intensive process. This does not mean that there is any excuse for not being conscientious and professional in terms of teaching classes. I have had student teachers who have had to be gently (in the first instance) reminded that pupils should always have a diligently prepared lesson, even when the beginning teacher is hard-pressed because of other commitments.

Selecting appropriate subject-knowledge-enhancement materials

Another tricky part of the mentor's role in relation to the development of subject knowledge is the choice (as well as the quantity) of what you ask the mentee to read or do. I once made the mistake, early in the course, of giving my trainees a very difficult and quite long piece of reading to do. It was a chapter where I find I have to have a lie-down after every few pages of reading, as it is so dense and taxing. It just put them off reading. This is not to say that you should not give them challenging things to read, but there are timing issues involved. In the early stages of the placement, it can be helpful if you suggest or provide texts or resources that will either help them to teach the topic that they are about to teach, or which are accessible and enjoyable to read or watch. There is sometimes a need to keep a lookout for the beginning teacher who only ever uses the textbook/BBC Bitesize/Horrible Histories for their subject enhancement. All of these have their place but, a little like junk food, they shouldn't be the core of the mentees' subject-knowledge diet.

Developing a range of subject-knowledge enhancement approaches with your mentee

As a mentor, even with the best will in the world, there are only so many hours in the week for you to devote to your mentee, given your many other responsibilities. There are different ways of addressing subject knowledge issues with your mentee, and some ways of broaching things are more time-consuming than others. If you select something for you both to read and then discuss in a mentor meeting, this can be a very rich and rewarding experience, but it requires quite a substantial investment of time. At the other end of the spectrum is for you to just briefly summarise the key points of something you have read – this can take as little as a couple of minutes. You can also just give the mentee something to read (or simply to keep in the subject-knowledge section of their teaching file for 'when they have a minute'). If you adopt a flexible approach, and use a range of approaches, it means you can cover more ground. I don't think you can cover every aspect of history teaching in depth in the time available on an ITE course, but if you handle subject knowledge issues adeptly, there is more chance that the mentee will continue to read after the placement and the course are completed.

The importance of secure substantive knowledge

Be explicit with mentees about the importance of possessing secure substantive knowledge of the topics they will be teaching (you may find it helpful to explore Task 2.1 with your mentee to help them understand why this is so important). It can be helpful to add that investments in developing this knowledge make a big difference to the extent to which they will enjoy the lessons that they teach, the extent to which they can feel relaxed and confident in the classroom, and the effect it will have on their relationship with the classes they will be teaching.

Task 2.1 'Chapter and verse': expert views on the importance of secure substantive subject knowledge

Although some aspects of history education have varied in prominence over the years (for example, the part that 'empathy' might play, the role of new technology in history education, the importance of keeping abreast in developments in cognitive science, the role of constructivist ideas about pupil learning in history), as far as I am aware, there has never been a time when possessing strong subject knowledge of topics to be taught was not thought to be a prerequisite for effective history teaching.

At an early point in the placement, it can be helpful to just remind your mentee of the fundamental importance of that fact. The following testimonies from 'experts' in history education are just some examples which can be used to make this point; you may have others.

> At all stages, the subject expertise of the teacher is the most important factor determining the work of the teacher in the classroom. (Ofsted, 1995)
>
> Research shows that there is a close relationship between teachers' subject knowledge and the quality and range of learning experiences in their classrooms. The message is, if you don't know it, you can't teach it. (Dean, 1995, p. 4)
>
> First and perhaps most importantly, where trainees have high levels of subject knowledge they plan and teach confidently. . . . The contribution of substantial subject knowledge to effective teaching is very apparent when an inspector is able to observe a trainee teach two lessons, one where he or she has a mastery of subject content, and the other where he or she has read up on the topic only recently and briefly. The contrast, in terms of confidence, as well as skill, is usually marked. (Baker, Cohn, & McLaughlin, 2000)
>
> Imagine an English teacher who has no knowledge of a new text, or a history teacher teaching a new course on something they know very little about. Or the biology teacher who needs to pick up some physics. Or the French teacher who decides to learn Spanish to offer a second language . . . This is not to say that building subject knowledge is a sufficient condition for improving teaching, but there are a great many cases where it is necessary. To call the need for improving content knowledge a 'myth' is to suggest to teachers that none of the above is needed. (Fordham, 2023)
>
> If a teacher doesn't know the content that they're teaching well enough, then this will cause a myriad of problems that no amount of instructional coaching will fix . . . The quality of a teacher's explanation of X depends directly on their content knowledge of X. The idea that this is less important than developing 'instructional practices' really highlights the limits and pitfalls of instructional coaching. . . . (Hill, 2023)

What strands of subject knowledge are most important?

There was a time when ITE providers were obliged to grade their students on the quality of their subject knowledge. This raised the question of the extent to which we were assessing our students on the same criteria, and whether some strands or aspects of subject knowledge were more important or 'urgent' than others. Within our ITE partnership it was notable that, while mentors believed a number of issues (such as overall subject knowledge, pedagogical subject knowledge, grasp of the National Curriculum for history, understanding of examination specifications, ability to 'answer pupils' subject-related questions securely', awareness of their potential contribution to pupil literacy, and so on) were considered important, the criterion which was regarded almost unanimously as the most vital was that 'students have the intelligence, initiative and conscientiousness to possess or acquire adequate subject knowledge to teach the classes they are responsible for on placement effectively' (from the minutes of a University of East Anglia partnership mentor meeting).

Mentors also flagged up the importance of beginning teachers having some grasp of the historiography around particular topics. This would apply particularly to knowledge of high-profile historical debates and arguments, especially in relation to historical events where opinions have changed over time, such as the historical reputation of Oliver Cromwell, ideas about responsibility for the outbreak of World War I, the 'lions led by donkeys' debate of World War I, or Chamberlain's policy of appeasement in 1938. This is a point echoed by Fordham (2012):

> Take, for example, an enquiry question which can be found in classrooms across the UK: why was the British slave trade abolished in 1807? Those familiar with the debate will recognise the historiography: the primacy of 'saints' such as Wilberforce and Clarkson, as advanced by Coupland; the centrality of economics, as argued by Williams; the role played by slave rebellions, advanced by Hart; the role played by popular support for abolition in Britain, more recently argued by Drescher. . . . A history teacher clearly has to reflect carefully not just on the substance of what is studied, important as that is, but also on the way in which that question has already been approached within the discipline. (p. 247)

As well as the question of the comparative importance of the various strands of subject knowledge, there is also the question of urgency. You can't do everything at once, and some things can be left to later in the placement, but as soon as the mentee starts picking up and teaching classes, they must have the substantive subject knowledge to teach the lessons they are going to teach. If they are teaching examination classes, they also must be familiar with the exam specifications, whether at GCSE or A level. They also need to know how to teach a historical enquiry over a series of lessons and be initiated into the ways that the department handles issues such as feedback and assessment. Of course, they also need to know that not all history departments operate in the same way, that there are different ideas about subject knowledge, and that schools have different systems and philosophies about how to teach history effectively; but these 'secondary agendas' can wait until they have found their feet and have hopefully become relaxed and comfortable about how subject knowledge 'works' in their placement department.

Helping beginning teachers to deploy their subject knowledge effectively

Although substantive subject knowledge is perhaps the most important dimension of the knowledge required to teach a school subject effectively, it is a necessary but not sufficient condition for effective teaching in history. It is not a question of 'the more you know, the better the learning will be'. As experienced mentors will be aware, there is more to it than that. Perhaps the most crucial and challenging part of the mentor's role is helping the mentee to distil the totality of their subject knowledge into something that will make sense to the classes to be taught, and that addresses as fully and effectively as possible the desired 'knowledge takeaway' for the topic (Dawson, 2021). Some of my former ITE students, who were teaching topics for which they possessed degree-level knowledge, acknowledged they found it difficult to translate this into something that Key Stage 3 pupils could understand. This challenge seemed to be particularly acute with complex and convoluted events such as the Reformation (English and European), the Glorious Revolution of 1688, and the sprawling complexities of the French and Russian Revolutions. 'Pitching it' at the right level and rendering the topic 'coherent' for all pupils in the class is of course a challenging task even for very experienced and accomplished history teachers. There are also the questions of what constitutes 'acceptable simplification', and the extent to which you should 'open the topic up' and make connections and comparisons with contiguous historical events across time as well as addressing the resonance and implications of the topic for those of us living in the present day. Task 2.2 will help you think this through with your mentee.

Task 2.2 Learning how to distil overall subject knowledge into an effective introduction to a topic, and learning to formulate clear learning objectives for the topic to be taught

Being able to transform one's overall knowledge of a topic into something that will fit into a short series of lessons, and to do so in a way which will engage pupils and make sense to them, is a crucial skill for a history teacher to possess. Byrom and Riley's *Teaching History* article, 'Professional wrestling in the history department' is an excellent resource for getting across to beginning teachers that it is impossible to teach *everything* about a topic, and so difficult decisions have to be made about what strands of substantive subject knowledge to include. The article also very helpfully suggests sensible criteria for making those decisions (Byrom & Riley, 2008, p. 8).

- Focus on a topic that your mentee will be teaching and ask them to think about *the crux* of what they want the pupils to know and understand at the end of the series of lessons. It is of course helpful if this exercise can be modelled for them, either with reference to the department's schemes of work, or by a 'think-aloud' protocol where you briefly talk them through your ideas about the essential points (or in Dawson's words, 'the knowledge takeaway') that you want the pupils to learn from the study of the topic.

- Before they start to teach a new topic, get them to write down a few thoughts on how they will introduce the topic to the class, and if they do not feel awkward about it, get them to 'try it out' on you. Explain that the first few minutes of teaching a topic can be crucial in determining the extent to which pupils will be attentive, engaged, and committed to learning about the topic in question. Getting them to think about why this topic is important, why it matters, why it is interesting, and why it is relevant to their lives is sometimes a neglected facet of subject knowledge. (Although it is now more than 40 years ago, I can still remember vividly how awful I felt teaching a class about Henry VII when I had not really given any thought to why they should learn about this monarch and what they might get out of it.)
- There is no guaranteed correlation between strong subject knowledge and effective teaching (important though it is). This is because, as well as 'knowing your stuff' you have to be able to explain it well, at a level your audience can understand. It is difficult to overstate the need to have skills of exposition commensurate with your subject knowledge. Moreover, these are skills required in nearly every lesson the mentees teach, so it is important to stress to them just how important skills of exposition are for the history teacher, and to get them to practice their skills of exposition for those important first lessons which are critical for either gaining or losing pupils' confidence. It can be helpful to get someone in the department to model effective teacher exposition. It is not 'cheating' to pick an example that you or a member of your department feel comfortable about – lots of history teachers have 'scripts' that are fluent and well rehearsed and that they know from experience tend to be well received by pupils. (You can also helpfully make the point that everyone in the department has had to refine and develop their skills of exposition – it is something that takes time to develop.)
- The BBC History feature, 'Explain this...' (https://www.bbc.co.uk/teach/class-clips-video/history-ks3-explain-this/zdcwjhv) – featuring explanations of government, communism, capitalism, revolution, suffrage, migration, Parliament, fascism, empire, and industrialisation – is a useful resource to show beginning history teachers how to go about explaining a historical term or idea in a clear and succinct way. As history graduates, we probably understand all these terms, but there is a difference between understanding things and being able to explain them to someone who doesn't understand them. It can be helpful to use one or more of these clips (typically between two and three minutes long) to model how to craft an explanation of a historical term.

Helping mentees to organise and archive their developing subject knowledge

Several decades of working with beginning teachers made me realise that some are better than others at organising and archiving their teaching files, subject-knowledge reading, and resources for future use and so as to avoid having to replan from scratch. Doing things at the last minute and not being able to find things when you need them are significant causes of stress and anxiety for beginning teachers.

Perhaps it is not quite as glamorous an attribute as being a charismatic storyteller, or being brilliant with PowerPoint presentations, but being well organised (and I might add, being reliable) is actually quite an important attribute for a history teacher to possess. I don't think it matters what system mentees use to organise their teaching file or files; what matters is that they have a system that works, so that they can find whatever they want quickly and easily. Finding things after a few weeks of teaching is not a difficult task, but keeping all subject knowledge resources in order after months or years of teaching is quite challenging. The mentee's teaching file is an important document. It doesn't just provide insight into the quality of mentee's thinking when they prepare lessons, it sheds light on their professional efficiency, how conscientious they are, and how much initiative they show in developing their subject knowledge and preparing appropriate lessons for the classes they will teach.

I have worked with many mentors who believe that there is quite a strong correlation between the quality of a beginning teacher's archiving systems and their ability to function well as a teacher. I think it can be helpful if there is light monitoring of mentee's subject-knowledge repositories, with some guidance as to how best to work on this if they are struggling. If there is an element of discretion in how mentees organise their teaching resources, it can be useful to have a discussion about how best to go about archiving subject-knowledge resources in a way which avoids a significant bureaucratic burden, or a situation where the onus is mainly on them 'proving' that they have read things. Obviously, it is not possible to remember every detail of every book and article that is read; light annotation of key points and a good cataloguing system are all that is required.

Teaching mentees to develop their substantive historical knowledge in a time-effective way

Although we want to cultivate the disposition to read widely about history (something that ought to be a labour of love), given the workload pressures as a placement timetable builds, it is sensible for beginning teachers to prioritise developing the subject knowledge to teach the classes in their care. Even single-subject honours graduates will find they are having to teach at least some topics which they have not covered at A level or at university. Significant numbers of modern history graduates have not done courses which cover the span of the National Curriculum at Key Stage 3. It will be difficult for them to read whole books, but alongside *Teaching History*, and the many high-quality history education websites that are available (see Chapter 9), popular history magazines can be a helpful way of quickly becoming acquainted with recent historical scholarship on a wide range of topics. Good ITE providers may well have subscriptions to the leading magazines in this field, and this provides access to the whole archive of past issues of magazines. The *History Today* archive can be accessed at https://www.historytoday.com/the-archive, and the archive for *BBC History Magazine* can be accessed at https://www.historyextra.com/search/?q=index. The *Teaching History* feature 'What are historians arguing about?' (previously titled 'Polychronicon') also provides a useful overview of historical scholarship on a wide range of historical topics (https://www.history.

org.uk/publications/module/8697/teaching-history-regular-features/9163/what-historians-have-been-arguing-about). The weekend broadsheet newspapers often have reviews of recently published history monographs, and some of these are open access. There is also a wide range of history podcasts, but it is perhaps worth pointing out to mentees that it is generally quicker to read an article than to listen to a podcast. For mentees with long commutes, podcasts can be an effective way to build subject knowledge efficiently.

Developing mentees' disciplinary subject knowledge

In the same way that beginning teachers must not make assumptions about what pupils will know and understand, we must not assume that history graduates will have a comprehensive grasp of the 'nuts and bolts' of history as a discipline. Beginning teachers need to understand that, as with other disciplines, history has its rules, procedures, and conventions for ascertaining the validity of claims to knowledge; this is not the same as understanding the historiography of particular topics, which is not generally problematic for mentees. Nor is it simply a matter of getting to grips with the idea of second-order concepts in history (addressed in Chapter 3).

In my experience, not all those beginning their training are absolutely clear about, for example, the relationship between facts, claims, and accounts (or even what a fact is), or the difference between 'a source' and 'evidence', the difference between 'history' and 'the past', and the nature of historical knowledge (for example, that it does not, like science, have 'covering laws'). They are often not aware of the ideas that pupils are working with in their understanding of the past. In the words of Lee and Ashby (2000), 'Many stories are told, and they may contradict, compete with, or complement one another, but this means that students should be equipped to deal with such relationships, not that any old story will do . . . . Students who understand sources as information are helpless when confronted by contradictory sources' (p. 200). Not all of them will be familiar with the idea of 'historical perspectives' as a way of making sense of the world that they live in, nor will all of them fully grasp the importance of getting across to pupils the idea that historical knowledge is 'differentially secure' (Stenhouse, 1975). It is helpful if they are not only aware of Hexter's (1971) idea of 'the second record', but that they are able to explain the idea of the second record to pupils. Put crudely, the idea is that, as well as interrogating 'the first record' (the remaining sources of evidence of the past), it is helpful to understand 'the second record' (the expertise, experience, interests, motives, and values of the historian who is interpreting the sources). For a fuller explanation of Hexter's work see Hoepper (2007); Heller (2022). This can be helpful in moving pupils from crude ideas about 'bias', to the more helpful idea of 'position'. Other helpful sources for moving pupils forward in this area include Lang, (1993), Le Cocq (2000), and Vella (2020). Another strand of disciplinary understanding which lies outside the realm of second-order concepts is the difference between public and private testimony. Again, beginning teachers need to understand the importance of this, and be able to transmit an understanding of it to their pupils. The recent furore over Fox News' handling of the 2020 Trump election 'steal' claim is a powerful example of this (see Helderman & Dawsey, 2023 for a useful source on this episode).

Developing subject knowledge 29

> A tweet from Sam Wineburg (2023) on the implications for history education of recent developments in AI:
>
> 'The footnote does 3 things; it says how I know, and if you don't believe me, go check. And if you follow my footnotes, you see the formation of the argument I put before you. Chat GPT hides all this by severing the link between information and source. Like Donald Trump, it asks for faith without evidence. Like Donald Trump, it asks for blind adherence. Like Donald Trump, it is a threat to democracy'.

Figure 2.1 The importance of footnotes and references

Another important idea that mentees need to be able to explain to pupils is that of the 'community of professional practice' which debates and makes judgements on claims to historical knowledge and accuracy (Seixas, 1993). Pupils do not arrive in secondary schools understanding the idea that some stories about the past might be more accurate and trustworthy than others; this is something that must be taught explicitly over the course of Key Stage 3 and beyond.

Additionally, beginning teachers need to understand the important role of references and footnotes in historical disciplinary knowledge. History graduates will of course be aware of the contribution that referencing makes to historical knowledge, but they need to be aware that many of the pupils they teach will not share their understanding. This has become more important than ever in an era where young people get such a high proportion of their historical information from unreferenced social media sources rather than from sources mediated by the historian, the history teacher, or the textbook. Wineburg (2023) points out the importance of referencing conventions in ascertaining the reliability of claims to knowledge – see Figure 2.1.

Task 2.3 will allow you to explore some of these ideas, and in particular the nature of historical enquiry, with your mentee.

Task 2.3 Learning to ask historical questions

Sometimes beginning teachers struggle in their early practice because they have not always thought through what sorts of question historians ask of the past. The work that they devise for pupils is sometimes over-reliant on comprehension and recall questions – if the pupils can read, they can get the answer. There are of course, some history textbooks which also do this. It can be helpful to show them some examples of this – beginning teachers can learn from bad practice as well as good.

The following list contains suggestions for guiding beginning teachers of history to ask appropriate historical questions when they devise activities and enquiries for their pupils. It is adapted from a workshop led by Ros Ashby, 'An introduction to school history' (Workshop Institute of Education, University of London, 11 February 1995). It might be helpful to give your mentee this list of questions at an early stage of the placement.

- What are historians trying to do when they investigate the past? Why do they bother?
- What happened? Events, time periods, timelines, story lines, chronology, accounts, sequencing.
- Why did it happen? Explaining things, actions, events, developments, cause, motive, ideas, beliefs.
- What changed? What stayed the same? Patterns in/of the past, looking for similarities and differences, charting change.
- How did what happened and what changed affect things? Consequences and significance for people at the time, for us now.
- How do we find out what we want to know? What problems are there in finding out and being sure? What claims can we make? Looking at sources, asking them questions, deciding whether they can be used as evidence for a particular question or what they can be used as evidence for, sources, evidence, relevant, reliable.
- Why might we get different answers to our questions? Purposes, interests, concerns for reconstructing the past, why was this produced? Problems of available evidence, issues of interpretation.

Teaching mentees to 'open up' historical topics

Perhaps understandably, if you ask your mentee to teach the Black Death or the Peasants' Revolt they will tend to focus on these particular historical episodes, but there is obviously a case for getting beginning teachers to make connections across time in order to develop a more coherent 'big picture' of the past. There is a body of research in history education (see, for example, Howson, 2007; Shemilt & Howson, 2017) to suggest that many pupils see school history as a series of disconnected episodes which 'stand alone', rather than being related to a broader 'map' of the past which helps them to make some sense of how particular things (government, technology, protest, food production, response to epidemics) have evolved over a long period of time. Or, in the words of one pupil, 'My problem Miss, is how the different bits fit together' (quoted in Ward, 2007). Teaching a topic in such a way that pupils have a sound understanding of the events themselves, *and* where they fit into the 'big picture' of the past, is difficult. It is about seeing the wood *and* the trees. It is also helpful if they have a working chronological grasp of how things have changed and developed, as well as an overall sense of systemic change. It is useful to know the order of the kings and queens of England, but pupils also need to understand how the power of the monarchy has changed over time. It is useful if you can model trying to get this balance between 'focus' and 'breadth' right when planning observation lessons for your mentee, there are also helpful readings about how to address this challenge (see, amongst others, Rogers, 2008; Shemilt, 2009; Nuttall, 2013; Ingledew, 2017; Richards, 2018). This issue is also addressed in Chapter 4.

Assessment and progression issues

Precise factual knowledge of historical events is useful – and not just for examinations. But obviously, there is more to getting better at history than simply aggregating more substantive knowledge of the past. Another important dimension of subject knowledge is understanding what it means 'to get better at history', and to be able to explain the criteria for 'getting better' to pupils. As far as I am aware, there is only one history textbook that addresses this issue explicitly (Dawson, 2003).

Although written some time ago, Tim Lomas' *Teaching and Assessing Historical Understanding* (1993) remains one of the most succinct (two pages) resources for explaining ideas about the ways in which pupils can make progress in history. Lomas suggested 12 ways in which pupils might demonstrate progression in their learning. In addition to 'greater historical knowledge', these included greater skill in the selection of relevant information, a greater ability to make connections and comparisons across time, and the ability to explain rather than simply describe. Greater independence of thought, the ability to balance differing viewpoints, and increased awareness and acceptance of uncertainty were also to be encouraged. Taylor (2012) also provides a useful summary of ways in which pupils can get better at history. Although it is challenging to cover all facets of subject knowledge in the time available for mentoring, I think that it is an 'essential' task to ensure that at some point in the placement, you have a discussion with your mentee about what it means to get better at history.

This links to the question of how we assess pupils' progress in history. I think this is a very complex and difficult issue, even for experienced teachers. I don't know many colleagues who are utterly relaxed and confident about assessment issues in history. This means you can't do it 'all in one go', within one or even two mentor meetings. To assuage mentee anxiety, it is helpful if they are inducted into 'the way we do things here' (in the department, in the school) as soon as possible. This includes questions such as what to do with the work that pupils produce, and what recording and feedback approaches are used. If they are working with GCSE and A-level classes, they need to know the criteria for awarding marks to questions. But by the end of the placement, they need to know about how things might work elsewhere and be reasonably up to date with current debates around the assessment of pupil progress in history. Given the breadth of the issues involved with assessment in history, you probably need a combination of discussion at formal mentor meetings and a 'drip-feed' of incidental conversations about assessment over the course of the placement.

There are resources which you can draw on (explored in Task 2.4), to refresh your own understanding of assessment in history, to use as vehicles for discussion with your mentee, and to suggest as reading for your mentee, sometimes as resources which must be read and digested, and sometimes as material for them to archive and read when they have the time.

Task 2.4 Suggested readings on assessment at Key Stage 3

You may have your own tried-and-tested resources in this area. These are just a few materials that I think are useful for a beginning history teacher in the early stages of their placement:

- What's the wisdom on assessment' (Historical Association, 2021).
- All the 'What's the wisdom' pieces in *Teaching History* are an invaluable resource for beginning history teachers. My only caveat is that mentees can sometimes think that it is a great resource, put it in their teaching file, and then never quite get round to using it to follow things up, in spite of their best intentions. It can be helpful to pick out one or two of the articles mentioned and give them to the mentee as directed reading.
- 'Where do marks on KS3 assessments come from?' (Bajkowski, 2023).
- 'The knowledge that flavours a claim: towards building and assessing historical knowledge on three scales' (Hammond, 2014).
- 'Key Stage 3 assessment', Virtually Teachers Podcast (Hibbert et al., 2023).
- 'Assessment after levels' (Brown & Burnham, 2014).

Knowledge and understanding of teaching approaches in history lessons

What sort of things can you do in a history lesson? Experienced history teachers will be aware of a wide range of activities which can be used, but don't assume that mentees will be familiar with the full breadth of possibilities. Much will depend on their own experiences of learning history in school. Many of my former trainees expressed particular concern about how to avoid just 'lecturing' to pupils in A-level lessons (and found Diana Laffin's (2009) work to be helpful).

The issue of teaching methods has been complicated by recent developments which have tended to polarise views on this. There are those who believe that it is helpful to be able to use a wide range of teaching approaches to maximise pupil engagement, warning of the danger of a 'limited diet' of approaches to learning in history 'turning pupils off'. McFahn (2021), for example, argues that 'information gathering sequences . . . should be varied to keep interest: tables, card sorts, graphs, decision making activities, post it challenges, competition'. However, over the past few years, there has been a reaction against the idea that variety of teaching approach *necessarily* improves pupil learning in history. Oak National Academy recently stated that 'to maximise coherence and consistency, which we know benefits teachers and pupils, lesson materials will be developed to standardised templates and lesson flow: a quiz followed by an explanatory video and slides, then a worksheet, then another quiz . . . Lessons across key stages 1–4 will include the above five lesson components, plus teacher guidance information' (quoted in Morgan, 2023). Drawing on other research, Morgan also makes the point that what works in one subject might not work in another.

A further area of polarisation relates to arguments about the comparative merits of 'direct instruction' approaches and 'active learning' approaches, differing teaching strategies that are often caricatured, with the debates conducted in a simplistic and polemical manner. Just about anything in teaching can be done well or badly. The idea that group work is necessarily bad and a waste of time or that direct instruction is necessarily boring for pupils is unhelpful. Often, there is a correlation between the quality of exposition with which the teacher introduces an activity and the degree of enthusiasm with which pupils will engage with that activity. So, how does a mentor handle these developments? I think the first point is that whatever their personal beliefs and preferences, mentees must fit in with the pedagogical 'ethos' of the department and policies of the school; they are not 'free agents', they are apprentices, learning their trade, and they are working as part of a team. The second point is that at some point in their ITE year, they need to learn about approaches to teaching and learning in history that are different to those of the department. They may be applying for jobs in schools which have different ideas about how to teach history; we should be equipping them to work well in any school. I have real concerns about beginning teachers not having some latitude to prepare and teach a series of lessons that they have put together themselves. Some of my former students who worked in highly directive environments were worried about not being allowed to learn how to plan a series of lessons for themselves and being told that 'you have to do it this way; there is no alternative'. Crooks (2023) makes the important point that this creative and intellectually challenging element of the job is part of what keeps teachers in the profession, enjoying their work in spite of the challenges.

A further point is that evidence about which teaching strategies are most effective is often limited and simplistic (Goldacre, 2014; Wrigley, 2016). It is difficult to definitively 'prove' the comparative effectiveness of different teaching approaches because of the number of variables involved, and the difficulties involved in isolating one variable. So, beginning teachers need to learn about the limitations and uncertainties of research findings. Stenhouse's (1975) idea of the function of educational research as being to enable teachers to test ideas against their own experience is a helpful precept to offer to beginning teachers, so that they are (hopefully) willing to try things out, in an open-minded way, and see how it works for them. I was not a great fan of roleplay and practical demonstration until I came across the work of Ian Luff and Ian Dawson. I also learned that these activities worked best when they were accompanied by high-order subject knowledge (for some examples, see https://terryhaydn.co.uk/pgce-history-at-uea/drama-and-role-play/).

There are some sources which are particularly useful for giving beginning teachers ideas about what they can do in their lessons. I have found the section of the *Facing History and Ourselves* website to be an excellent (and under-used) resource in this respect (https://www.facinghistory.org/how-it-works/teaching-resources/teaching-strategies). Many of my former trainees found Russel Tarr's ideas for teaching activities very helpful (Tarr, 2016; 2018; 2022 and www.activehistory.co.uk), and I have found Ian Dawson's *Thinking History* website to be inspirational (https://thinkinghistory.co.uk/), not just for the ideas for teaching history that it contains, but also the depth and breadth of subject knowledge therein. A fuller list of useful sites can be found in Chapter 9.

Fordham (2017a) and Riddle (2023) both make the important point that given the limited amount of time that history gets on the school curriculum, all history teachers need to use that time to best effect. Riddle provides three helpful suggestions for ascertaining and providing knowledge of a topic quicky and efficiently; Fordham suggests some principles or considerations for deciding on the most helpful and appropriate teaching approaches.

Knowledge about how pupils learn in history

The past few years have seen an increase in interest in and use of cognitive psychology in teaching. Much of the literature on cognitive psychology is generic, in that it talks to ideas about learning in general, as opposed to learning in particular school subjects. Concerns have been expressed about whether this shift fails to take account of the differences in academic disciplines and school subjects (see for example, amongst many others Counsell, 2016; Fordham, 2017b; Grande, 2023a). A good example of this which might be helpful to use with mentees is Grande's (2023b) post about how to make things memorable to pupils in history, and the difference between this and 'retrieval practice'. This is not to suggest that beginning teachers should disregard insights from cognitive science. It is not an 'either-or' thing. It's just that it is generally good practice to start with the learning issue in history classrooms. Sometimes there will be insights from cognitive science that shed light on a learning issue or problem in the history classroom. A much-cited and useful example is Willingham's (2009) dictum that 'Memory is the residue of thought'. Some insights from cognitive science might have resonance across school subjects. Adam Boxer's (2022) post about how long you should spend questioning one pupil ('Keeping the one, losing the many') is about questioning in science, but it struck me as something that would apply in a similar way to questioning in history lessons, and it had a big impact on my thinking about questioning.

Resources which are particularly focused on learning issues *in history* include Counsell, Burn and Chapman (2016) and part one of Donovan and Brailsford (2005). Banham and Dawson's work (n.d.) on raising attainment in history is also a valuable resource, but perhaps the most important thing is that your mentee is aware of the importance of reading *Teaching History*. It is the equivalent of the *British Medical Journal* for doctors. If they are going to be history teachers, they should read it.

Of course, in the longer term, if we are to maximise beginning teachers' 'professional and decisional capital' (Hargreaves & Fullan, 2012), we want them to become knowledgeable about education in general, as well as teaching and learning in history, but given the exigencies of the time available, understanding how pupils learn in history needs to be a priority.

Summary and key points

- It is important to convey to mentees that it is essential for them to have secure substantive historical knowledge for every lesson they teach. Whether you are a head or a beginning teacher, it is a basic professional responsibility.
- As the chapter indicates, it is not *just* about the volume of subject knowledge that the beginning teacher possesses. They need to know how to select from, deploy, and explain that subject knowledge in a way that will make sense to the pupils they teach.

- To assuage initial mentee anxieties, they need to be inducted into the way that the department 'does things' in relation to subject knowledge and providing feedback to pupils as quickly as possible, but without overloading them with 'too much stuff' in the first few days of placement. There are difficult judgement calls to be made here.
- 'Passing' the mentee gives them a licence to teach in any school. It is therefore important that by the end of the course, they are aware of how things might be done in other history departments. It is important that they realise that teachers have to 'fit in' with departmental and school policies and approaches, and act as part of a team, whatever their personal preferences. This is part of teacher professionalism. You can also make the point that some schools give individual teachers more autonomy than others in terms of how they teach history, and that they vary in the extent to which teachers must follow departmental schemes of work.
- There are also longer-term objectives in terms of trying to cultivate the highest standards of professionalism and the dispositions which will enable the mentee to develop further as a history teacher once the ITE year is completed. We want the beginning teacher to be knowledgeable about teaching and learning in history, open-minded to new ideas and developments, and we want them to be the sort of teacher who will make full contributions to their department and be a good departmental colleague and team player. We want them to be the sort of teacher who will continue to assiduously develop their subject knowledge after the course is completed, after their reference is written, and when no one is looking.
- Beginning teachers need to be made aware of the necessity to keep up to date with new developments in history teaching. It is part of being professional.

Further reading and resources

- **Chapman, A. (2021). 'Introduction: historical knowing and the "knowledge turn"', in A. Chapman (ed.),** *Knowing History in Schools: Powerful Knowledge and the Powers of Knowledge* **(pp. 1–31). London, UCL Press**

  Chapman's introductory chapter is an excellent summary of the powerful knowledge debate as it pertains to history. I think all the chapters are very interesting and useful, and the book is a free download from UCL Press.
- **Harris, R. (2021). 'Where are we and where are we going?'** *Teaching History* **185, 60–8**
- **Historical Association index of subject knowledge resources**

  https://onebighistorydepartment.com/2019/02/08/lists-and-indices-of-sources-of-knowledge/. Retrieved 17 March 2023. https://onebighistorydepartment.com/2020/02/26/new-reading-list-with-reviews/. Retrieved 17 March 2023.
- *History Education Research Journal* **https://uclpress.scienceopen.com/collection/UCL_HERJ**

  One of the leading journals for history education. Particularly helpful for those mentees who are intent on gaining a master's-level qualification and may be thinking of going on to do a PhD.
- ***History Today* and *BBC History Magazine***

Of course, it is essential to keep up to date with *Teaching History*, but given that there is not time for them to read every new history book that comes out during the course of the ITE year, these magazines provide a respectable 'short-cut' for keeping up to date with historical scholarship.

- **Maddison, M. (2020). '10 things to remember when teaching history . . .', *Practical Histories*, https://practicalhistories.com/2020/11/when-teaching-history-remember-to/. Retrieved 17 March 2023**
- **Practical Histories, https://practicalhistories.com/**

    Another very time-effective way of keeping up to date with developments in history education.

References

Aldrich, R. (1987). Interesting and useful. *Teaching History 47*, 11–14.

Bajkowski, M. (2023). Where do the marks on KS3 assessments come from? Retrieved 23 March 2023, from *One Big History Department*. https://onebighistorydepartment.com/2023/01/17/where-do-marks-on-ks3-assessments-come-from/

Baker, C., Cohn, T., & McLaughlin, M. (2000). Inspecting subject knowledge. In J. Arthur & R. Phillips (eds.), *Issues in History Teaching* (pp. 211–19). London: Routledge.

Banham, D., & Dawson, I. (n.d.). *Raising Attainment through Visible Learning*. Retrieved 12 January 2023, from *Thinking History*, http://www.thinkinghistory.co.uk/Issues/attainment/index.htm

Boxer, A. (2022). Keeping the one, losing the many. Retrieved 23 March 2023 from *A Chemical Orthodoxy* (Blog): https://achemicalorthodoxy.wordpress.com/2022/05/25/keeping-the-one-losing-the-many/

Brown, G., & Burnham, S. (2014). Assessment after levels. *Teaching History 157*, 8–17.

Byrom, J., & Riley, M. (2008). Professional wrestling in the history department: a case study in planning the teaching of the British Empire. *Teaching History 112*, 6–14.

Chapman, A. (2021). Introduction: historical knowing and the 'knowledge turn'. In A. Chapman (ed.), *Knowing History in Schools: Powerful Knowledge and the Powers of Knowledge* (pp. 1–31). London: UCL Press. Retrieved 23 March 2023 from https://discovery.ucl.ac.uk/id/eprint/10118305/1/Knowing-History-in-Schools.pdf

Counsell, C. (2016). *Genericism's children*. Retrieved 18 November 2022, from *The Dignity of the Thing* (Blog): https://thedignityofthethingblog.wordpress.com/2016/01/11/genericisms-children/comment-page-1/#comment-953

Counsell, C., Burn, K., & Chapman, A. (2016). *MasterClass in History Education: Transforming Teaching and Learning*. London: Bloomsbury.

Crooks, V. (2023). Unintentional teachers: looking beyond vocation to attract people into the teaching profession. Retrieved 17 March 2023, from *Becoming a History Teacher* (Blog), https://uonhistoryteachertraining.school.blog/2023/02/28/unintentional-teachers-looking-beyond-vocation-to-attract-people-into-the-teaching-profession/

Dawson, I. (2003). *What Is History? A Starter Unit for Year 7*. London: Hodder.

Dawson, I. (2021). *Takeaways and Their Central Role in Planning KS3 Courses*. Retrieved 13 October 2022, from *Thinking History* website, www.thinkinghistory.co.uk

Dean, J. (1995). *Teaching History at Key Stage 2*. Cambridge: Chris Kingston Publishing.

Donovan, M., & Brailsford, D. (2005). *How Students Learn History, Maths and Science*. Washington, DC: National Research Council.

Fordham, M. (2012). Disciplinary History and the Situation of History Teachers. *Educational Sciences 2*, 242–53.

Fordham, M. (2017a). Should teaching methods be prescribed? Retrieved 13 March 2023, from *Clio et cetera* (Blog), https://clioetcetera.com/2017/02/19/should-teaching-methods-be-prescribed/comment-page-1/

Fordham, M. (2017b). Thinking makes it so: cognitive psychology and history teaching. *Teaching History 166*, 37–42.

Fordham, M. [@mfordhamhistory]. (2023, 16 February). I don't think this can be a myth . . . (Tweet). Retrieved 23 March 2023 from Twitter: https://twitter.com/mfordhamhistory/status/1626329584034521091

Fullan, M. (1999). *Change Forces: The Sequel.* London: Falmer.

Goldacre, B. (2014). *I Think You'll Find It's More Complicated Than That.* London: Fourth Estate.

Grande, J. (2023a). This week in history . . . I'm trying to improve my coaching. Retrieved 21 November 2022 from *Curricular Pasts: Reflections from a History Classroom* (Blog), https://curricularpasts.wordpress.com/2022/06/05/10-this-week-in-history-im-trying-to-improve-my-coaching/

Grande, J. (2023b). This week, in history . . . you can't 'action step' your way to effective teaching. Retrieved 12 March 2023 from *Curricular Pasts: Reflections from a History Classroom* (Blog), https://curricularpasts.wordpress.com/2023/03/05/12-this-week-in-history-you-cant-action-step-your-way-to-effective-teaching/

Hammond, K. (2014). The knowledge that flavours a claim: towards building and assessing historical knowledge on three scales. *Teaching History 157*, 18–24.

Hargreaves, A., & Fullan, M. (2012). *Professional Capital.* London: Routledge.

Harris, R. (2021). Where are we and where are we going? *Teaching History 185*, 60–8.

Haydn, T., & Harris, R. (2010). Pupil perspectives on the purposes and benefits of studying history in high school: a view from the UK. *Journal of Curriculum Studies 42*(2), 241–61.

Helderman, R., & Dawsey, J. (2023). A Trump veteran at Fox struggled to balance lies with the network's interests. Retrieved 12 March 2023 from *Washington Post*, https://www.msn.com/en-us/news/politics/a-trump-veteran-at-fox-struggled-to-balance-election-lies-with-the-network-s-interests/ar-AA18w4my

Heller, M. (2022). Hexter on the historians' personal second record. *Social Science Files #25.* Retrieved 12 March 2023 from https://michaelgheller.substack.com/p/25-hexter-on-the-historians-personal

Hexter, J. (1971). *The History Primer.* New York: Basic Books.

Hibbert, D., Lewin, R., Bateman, C., Davies, S., & Hill, M. (2023). KS3 assessment (Audio podcast episode). *Virtually Teachers.* Virtually Podcasts, https://podcasts.apple.com/gb/podcast/virtually-teachers/id1509813344

Hill, M. [@michaeldoron]. (2023, February 4). If a teacher doesn't know enough . . . (Tweet). Retrieved 27 July 2023 from Twitter, https://twitter.com/michaeldoron/status/1626504876124504065?s=12&t=c5b_m66-tapqvrAp3HPUZA

Historical Association. (2021). What's the wisdom on . . . assessment? *Teaching History 185*, 56–59.

Hoepper, B. (2007). Historical literacy. *QHistory Queensland History Teachers Association* (1), 1–11. Retrieved 6 March 2023 from https://www.academia.edu/31617435/Historical_Literacy

Howson, J. (2007). 'Is it the Tuarts and then the Studors or the other way round?' The importance of developing a usable big picture of the past. *Teaching History 127*, 40–47.

Ingledew, D. (2017). Move me on. *Teaching History, 167*, 56–9.

Laffin, D. (2009). *Better Lessons in A Level History.* London: Hodder.

Lang, S. (1993). What is bias? *Teaching History* (October), 9–13.

Le Cocq, H. (2000). Beyond bias: making source evaluation meaningful to year 7. *Teaching History 99*, 50–5.

Lee, P., & Ashby, R. (2000). Progression in historical understanding among students ages 7-14. In P. Sternes, P. Seixas, & S. Wineburg (eds.), *Knowing, Teaching and Learning History* (pp. 199-222). New York: New York University Press.

Lomas, T. (1993). *Teaching and Assessing Historical Understanding.* London: Historical Association.

Maddison, M. (2020). *10 things to remember when teaching history.* Retrieved 23 March 2023 from *Practical Histories,* https://practicalhistories.com/2020/11/when-teaching-history-remember-to/

McFahn, R. (2021). Principles. Retrieved 3 March 2023 from *History Resource Cupboard,* https://www.historyresourcecupboard.co.uk/enquiry-principles/

Morgan, J. (2023, February 15). Should teachers be told how to structure their lessons? Retrieved 27 July 2023 from *Times Educational Supplement,* https://www.tes.com/magazine/teaching-learning/general/should-teachers-be-told-how-to-structure-lessons

Nuttall, D. (2013). Possible futures: using frameworks of knowledge to help Year 9 connect past, present and future. *Teaching History 151,* 33-44.

Ofsted. (1995). *The Annual Report of Her Majesty's Chief Inspector of Schools 1993 to 1994.* London: Ofsted.

Richards, H. (2018). The devil is the detail: are we teaching history the wrong way around? *Teaching History 172,* 52-60.

Riddle, H. (2023, 11 March). Three ways to determine baseline knowledge in the history classroom. *What Went Well.* Retrieved 13 March 2023 from https://whatwentwell.org/2023/03/11/three-ways-to-test-baseline-knowledge-in-the-history-classroom/

Rogers, R. (2008). Raising the bar: Developing meaningful historical consciousness at Key Stage 3. *Teaching History 133,* 24-30.

Seixas, P. (1993). The Community of inquiry as a basis for knowledge and learning: the case of history. *American Educational Research Journal 30*(2), 255-75.

Shemilt, D. (2009). Drinking an ocean and pissing a cupful: how adolescents make sense of history. In L. Symcox & A. Wilschut (eds.), *National History Standards: the Problem of the Canon and the Future of Teaching History* (pp. 141-210). Charlotte, NC: IAP.

Shemilt, D., & Howson, J. (2017). Frameworks of knowledge: dilemmas and debates. In I. Davies (ed.), *Debates in History Teaching* (2nd edition) (pp. 66-79). London: Routledge.

Stenhouse, L. (1975). *An Introduction to Curriculum Research and Development.* London: Heinemann.

Tarr, R. (2016). *A History Teaching Toolbox.* London: Active Books.

Tarr, R. (2018). *A History Teaching Toolbox Volume 2.* London: Active Books.

Tarr, R. (2022). *A History Teaching Toolbox: Omnibus Edition. Practical Classroom Strategies 3.* London: Active Books.

Taylor, T. (2012). Teaching historical literacy. Retrieved 12 February, 2021, from The *National Literacy Project,* https://www.civicsandcitizenship.edu.au/cce/expert_views/teaching_historical_literacy_the_national_history,9323.html

Vella, Y. (2020). Teaching bias in history lessons: An example using Maltese history. *History Education Research Journal 17*(1), 99-114.

Ward, R. (2007, February 13). Creating a curriculum that will help all young people in Britain understand the world in which they live. *Why history matters: Conference of the Institute of Historical Research.* (12-13 February 2007). Institute of Historical Research.

Willingham, D. (2009). *Why don't students like school?* San Francisco: Jossey-Bass.

Wineburg, S. (1997). Beyond 'breadth and depth': subject matter knowlede and assessment. *Theory into Practice, 36*(4), 255-61.

Wineburg, S. [@samwineburg] (2023). The footnote does 3 things . . . (Tweet). Retrieved 12 March 2023 from Twitter, https://twitter.com/samwineburg/status/16336840721731174 40

Wrigley, T. (2016). Not so simple: the problem with evidence based practice and the EEF toolkit. *Forum 58*(2), 237-52.

3 Supporting beginning teachers to understand and utilise substantive and disciplinary historical concepts

Victoria Crooks

Introduction

For many history undergraduates the conceptual underpinnings of the historical discipline are a bit of a mystery. History is not often articulated in terms of isolated conceptual understandings. Instead, the beauty of successful historical writing is found in the holistic way substantive and disciplinary knowledge blend to create coherent and convincing historical arguments. Historians very rarely present their ideas with the kinds of 'signpost sentences' pupils are often taught to include in their own historical writing, sentence starters such as: 'Another cause of x was y . . .'. Rather, the disciplinary lens through which historians interpret a period and apply abstract concepts is integrated into their argument in more subtle, perhaps even implicit, ways. For example, when McDonough (2012) makes a qualified claim about one of the reasons for the Nazi Party's rise to power, the causal nature of that claim is evident but not explicitly stated:

> One of the most remarkable aspects of the Nazi breakthrough in September 1930 was that nearly a quarter of those who voted in 1930 had never voted in any previous Weimar election. (p. 89)

Consequently, when beginning teachers start their training, they often assume that history teaching is all about the transference of substantive knowledge, and that the disciplinary aspects of historical learning just fall into place naturally. When asked to consider where their understanding of substantive concepts, such as democracy, have developed from, they are rarely able to identify being explicitly taught these concepts - they just 'know' (Ashby & Lee, 2000, p. 203). The idea that teachers plan to include both first- and second-order conceptual knowledge in their teaching, to teach pupils ways of thinking historically about this substantive knowledge, is quite an alien notion for most beginning teachers. While they may come to understand the distinction between the two types of historical conceptual knowledge and be able to identify them, understanding how to make them accessible and part of their pupils' practice can often become a key challenge of the early years of a history teachers' career.

DOI: 10.4324/9781003223504-3

Objectives

At the end of the chapter, you should be able to:

- Understand the role of substantive (first-order) and disciplinary (second-order) concepts in history education.
- Reflect on why beginning teachers find articulating the purposes and development of conceptual knowledge so challenging.
- Consider how the assumptions made about a beginning and early career teacher's understanding of the role of conceptual knowledge can create misconceptions.
- Understand how beginning teachers can be supported to plan for the development of conceptual knowledge and therefore improve pupils' understanding of history as a discipline.

What do we mean by conceptual understanding in history education?

Chapman (2021) suggests that 'disciplinary education seeks to move students on' from their '"everyday" ideas about historical knowledge' – ideas and preconceptions based on their life experience and prior learning (p. 11). Conceptual understanding, at the level of first-order (substantive) and second-order (disciplinary or procedural ideas about history) provides pupils with a mechanism for making sense of history. The substantive concepts show pupils that phenomena recur and evolve in meaning as they encounter them in different contexts in the past (Fordham, 2016), while the disciplinary concepts equip them to access the procedural aspects of the subject, to understand how history works and is created.

Substantive conceptual knowledge

As explored in Chapter 2 of this book, developing secure substantive knowledge is an important element of any teacher's development. Understanding the distinction between their own subject knowledge and the subject knowledge required for teaching is of even greater importance. Accordingly, beginning and early career teachers need to peel back each layer of their own historical understanding so that they can plan explicitly for their pupils' learning of these more tacitly acquired aspects of the curriculum (ideas for exploring this with your beginning teacher are included in Task 3.1).

As illustrated in Figure 3.1, substantive knowledge includes both propositional knowledge and an understanding of substantive-concepts knowledge. Propositional knowledge includes 'factual' content knowledge about individual events such as the dates and actors involved in specific battles, and colligatory knowledge, where a series of events are grouped together around a theme which is tied to a specific time or place in history, for example the 'Fall of the Roman Empire' or 'the Renaissance' (van Boxtel & van Rijn, 2006, p. 1). General (for example 'assassination') and historical concepts (for example 'archduke'), on the other hand, are the ideas which help us to frame and describe the substance of history by providing terms to describe abstract historical ideas (Chapman, 2021, p. 13).

Utilising historical concepts 41

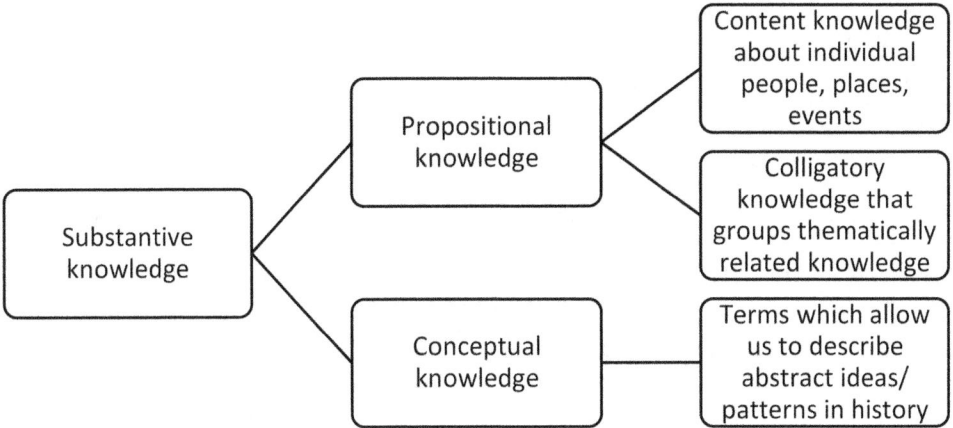

Figure 3.1 The different forms of historical substantive knowledge

---

Task 3.1 Conceptual expositions

- Select a substantive concept (such as empire, monarchy, the church, feudalism, democracy) and ask your mentee to plot how the meaning of this concept changes over time.
- Ask them to prepare an exposition for a class based around this concept. What understanding of the concept would the pupils need at this point in the curriculum? How would the beginning teacher illustrate the concept and make the abstract ideas it encompasses understandable?
- Ask them to experiment with using narrative vignettes, images, role play and relating the concept to modern experience in their explanation.
- Explore afterwards what they found difficult about the task and how they tried to anticipate possible misconceptions pupils might have about the concept.

One way of helping beginning history teachers to understand the distinctions between different conceptual bases of the discipline is to help them think about the different categories of substantive conceptual knowledge pupils will encounter in their historical studies. Haenen and Schrijnemakers (2000, p. 24) provide one such taxonomy for understanding by distinguishing between three types of historical concepts (Table 3.1).

Exploring these categories with beginning teachers, through examining classroom-based resources, can provide some interesting insights into the assumptions they make about pupil understanding of concepts (Task 3.2). The everyday concepts are those most likely to be overlooked in preparation for lessons as pupil familiarity is often assumed, while the unique historical concepts are more commonly planned for and explicitly taught due to their connection to substantive content knowledge. Few beginning teachers grasp immediately,

Table 3.1 Table derived from Haenen and Schrijnemakers' (2000) taxonomy for substantive concepts (p. 24)

Concept type	Definition	Examples
Everyday concepts	frequently used in historical contexts but not specifically historical	universal, heritage, style
Unique historical concepts	terms which apply to singular moments and people in history	D-Day, Napoleon, the Peace of Westphalia
Inclusive historical concepts	terms which apply more generally to bring together a classification of distinct events	castle, king, parliament, church, revolution

however, that effective planning for introducing inclusive historical concepts requires strategic encounters with the concept beyond one lesson or even one sequence of lessons. Instead, many assume the development of conceptual understanding is akin to the process observed in osmosis.

Task 3.2 Identifying substantive concepts

Identify a section of guided reading that pupils undertake as part of a lesson in the department. Ask your mentee to:

- Highlight the everyday concepts, unique historical concepts, and inclusive historical concepts in the text.
- Identify which conceptual terms they anticipate pupils will need support to understand.
- Consider possible misconceptions pupils might have developed about these terms through their 'everyday' or non-historical encounters with them.
- Suggest ways pupils could be supported to understand these concepts.
  - Which terms can be presented through a simple word bank of definitions?
  - Which terms could be best supported with visual stimulus?
  - Which terms need to be explored in the context of pupils' past encounters with the word?
  - Which terms need to be explicitly planned to be re-encountered (previously or subsequently) in the sequence/wider scheme of work/programme of study?

Mental models

As pupils develop their understanding of substantive concepts they build mental models (schemata) - internal representations of specific or interrelated concepts. Introducing different aspects of a concept, through carefully sequenced concrete substantive examples, supports the development of these schemata. However, 'concepts do not occur without reference to other concepts' (Rosch, 1983, p. 77), and the schemata pupils develop for understanding historical concepts does not come about as a result of their history education alone. Pupils' mental models for understanding are developed through their interaction with their environment (Gentner & Stevens, 1983, p. 14), their pre-existing beliefs, everyday experiences, and the subject knowledge they acquire from their other subject studies in school. Pupils are inherently 'cross-curricular' in the way they view the world and acquire knowledge – they take their understanding of 'monarchy' in history into their reading of *Macbeth* in English and vice versa. This means that while a concept may be taught explicitly through the curriculum, the understanding that each pupil has of that concept will be different.

For example, the unique substantive concept of a 'castle' may conjure the imposing image of the 13th-century Clifford's Tower for a pupil from York, while a second pupil from Nottingham may instead think of a 17th-century mansion house, and a third pupil from Great Yarmouth may instantly be transported in their mind to a sandy beach and their bucket and spade. Some pupils may have a more nuanced understanding of the concept due to their experiences of all three categories of 'castle' while on holiday, through their studies in geography and art, or even through playing chess. Other pupils may have no reference point beyond the immediate teaching context. Each pupil accesses conceptual understanding with their own personal pre-existing mental model. These mental models may be highly sophisticated, but it is also possible that they may be incomplete or have unanticipated structures (Chi, 2008).

Recognising that pupils' conceptual understanding is developed via these mental models is important. It helps explain to the beginning teacher why, despite their diligent planning, the pupils still aren't quite grasping the lesson content as intended – Task 3.3 will help you to explore these ideas with your mentee. It demonstrates why lessons need to include diagnostic tasks which establish prior knowledge, experience, and understanding of concepts, such as Kühberger's (2022) 'concept cartoons' in *Teaching History 186*. It also shows why knowledge of the wider curriculum, which helps to understand how subject content intersects across that curriculum, can be so beneficial. Appreciating how pupils' conceptual models may be influenced by simultaneously studying a humanities curriculum including units about Japan in geography, Shintoism and Buddhism in religious studies and World War II and the atomic bomb in history creates real opportunities for deepening pupil understanding (Crooks, 2021).

Task 3.3 Key substantive concepts

- With your mentee make a list of all the substantive concepts that you believe pupils will encounter through your school history curriculum.
- How does your list of substantive concepts compare with the collaboratively designed list of concepts hosted on Michael Fordham's blog site *Clio et cetera*, which the contributing history teachers thought pupils should learn in Key Stages 2 and 3? https://clioetcetera.com/2017/11/09/substantive-concepts-at-ks2-ks3/

- Discuss how we decide which concepts are 'key' and should be explored in a curriculum. What influences our choices?

    It may be worth exploring, for example, why the *Clio et cetera* list of substantive concepts for Key Stage 3 contains the concept of 'racism' but not 'race', and why neither appear in the Key Stage 2 list. Similarly, there are very few concepts from non-European cultures contained within the list.

    - What does the list suggest about the priorities and perspectives of those contributing and collating such a list in the UK in 2017?
    - Why and how might the list look different if it had been collated in a different context (e.g. following the George Floyd protests/the tearing down of the Colston statue in 2020)?
    - How far is it really possible for us to design a definitive list of concepts?
    - What role is played by pupils' pre-existing understandings of these concepts?

- Organise for your mentee to undertake an observation in another subject such as geography, religious studies, or English, where pupils are likely to encounter 'historical' concepts in a different context. Ask your mentee to record the substantive concepts introduced in the lesson and reflect on whether this has any implications for how the concepts are addressed in history. What are the possible misconceptions that might arise?

Planning for substantive conceptual understanding

Planning for the development of historical conceptual understanding requires beginning teachers to have subject knowledge beyond the lesson they are teaching in that moment. Awareness of the interconnected nature of these terms and how they are encountered in the history curriculum is important for planning meaningful encounters with these ideas. Such an awareness is not always immediately evident to beginning teachers, particularly when operating outside of their own period specialisms.

'The Reformation', for example, is a very specific historical concept, situated in a particular temporal context. Teachers will often look to provide simple definitions of such terms to provide an access point into the concept, but even these 'simple' definitions require significant understanding of everyday, unique, and inclusive historical concepts (see Figure 3.2).

'Mapping' concepts (see Figure 3.3) to show the relationship between other unique and inclusive historical concepts is a useful tool for exploring how and when a well-planned curriculum allows pupils to encounter the substantive knowledge, with concrete examples, necessary for abstract concepts to develop meaning. A map like this helps to reveal the multiplicity of ways pupils may have encountered the concept previously. It also supports the beginning teacher to consider what may need to be emphasised in relation to this concept to equip pupils for more nuanced understandings later in their history education.

Utilising historical concepts 45

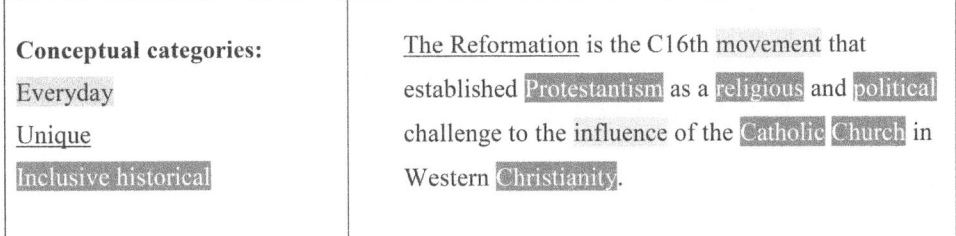

Figure 3.2 Concept categories covered in a simple definition of the Reformation

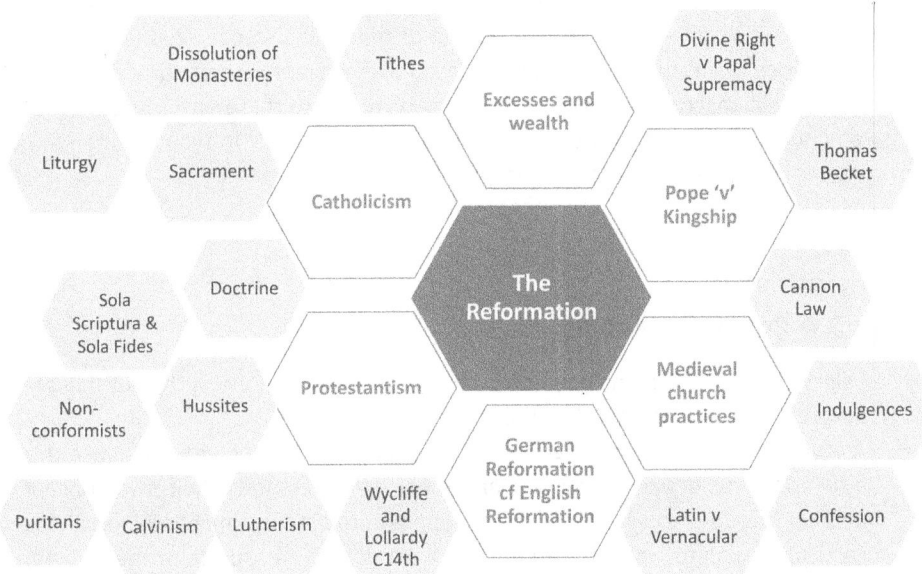

Figure 3.3 Concept map for the Reformation

Evolving concepts

Where more generalised historical concepts are concerned, the changing nature of their meaning, over time and in different contexts, is another key idea that beginning teachers and pupils need to grasp. Pupils may be familiar with a concept in the present but 'it can also refer to different phenomena', and it is also the case that historians sometimes disagree in their conceptual definitions (van Drie & van Boxtel, 2003, p. 27). Consequently, pupils need to be supported to understand that a single abstract concept can have multi-layered meaning.

The concept of 'revolution' cannot, for example, simply be reduced to a definition such as 'a period of great change'. The 18th and early 19th centuries are a period that has often been referred to as 'The Age of Revolution' (Hobsbawm, 1973), for this period witnessed revolutions in the economic, social, cultural, intellectual, technological, and political spheres of life; revolutionary uprisings that led to war; and revolution through the transformation of agriculture, transport, and industry. The fluidity of the concept in this period is striking, but notions of 'revolution' are not unique to that era. Indeed, revolution as a concept was well established by the 1688 Glorious Revolution, and more recently has been used in the context of events as contrasting as the Iranian Revolution of 1979 and the 20th- and 21st-century Digital Revolution. An appreciation of these competing and yet associated meanings is important if pupils are to understand their use in historical accounts or consider how people involved in such events perceived their roles (Lee, 2005). In their article in *Teaching History 115*, Burnham and Brown (2004) assert that 'our job [as history teachers] is to get pupils to carry on reflecting upon [a concept], to allow its meaning to change throughout their time learning history in school and beyond, not to learn a single fixed definition and have done' (pp. 8-9). This takes systematic planning, as illustrated in their approach for tracking the concepts of 'imperialism' and 'empire' at the end of the article. Pupils need to be provided with opportunities to encounter certain key substantive concepts in a multitude of contexts across the curriculum, so they can develop their ability to use these terms with increasing fluency and nuance. Task 3.4 provides some reading and activities for your mentee to help them consider the evolving nature of substantive concepts.

Task 3.4 Concept mapping

- Select an example of a unique or historical concept and model with your mentee how to map the concept across the curriculum.
- Ask your mentee to identify a concept they feel less familiar with and make this a focus for subject-knowledge enhancement before creating their own concept map for you to discuss in a mentor meeting. In the mentor meeting look at the curriculum plan for the department and consider which aspects of the concept map could be explicitly encountered in the curriculum. What planning might need to happen to make these encounters more likely?
- Read van Drie & van Boxtel (2003) in *Teaching History 110* together. Select a lesson where the pupils will be introduced/reintroduced to a historical concept. Plan a dialogic concept-mapping task for pupils to complete which will help to reveal how their understanding of the concept is developing.
- Look at Figure 5 from Burnham and Brown (2004) in *Teaching History 115*: 'Ideas for assessing pupils' thinking about the terms "empire" and "imperialism", using a range of methods that arise naturally across the Key Stage'. Ask your mentee to define 'empire' or 'imperialism' in the different enquiries presented in the article (they are likely to find this challenging if the enquiries lie outside their own subject-knowledge expertise, so this may also provide an opportunity for focused subject-knowledge enhancement). Discuss how these different ways of conceptualising 'empire'/'imperialism' might change a pupil's understanding of the concept. Why is it important for discussion around abstract concepts to take place in the context of propositional knowledge?

The importance of substantive concepts

Developing pupils' understanding of substantive concepts is important if they are to progress in their abilities to think historically and articulate that understanding through the creation of cogent historical arguments. Hammond (2014) explored the different 'forms' of substantive knowledge pupils draw on to create convincing historical analysis, while Palek (2015) asserted that pupils who have a secure understanding of relevant substantive concepts are able to develop more convincing and sophisticated causal arguments by making connections with other topics in the curriculum. Indeed, Palek (2015) contends that some substantive concepts, 'such as slavery', are so fundamental to pupils' historical understanding they need to be prioritised in the curriculum (p. 24). Allowing beginning teachers access to these insights at the very start of their career enables them to understand why they need to think beyond individual lessons and plan for substantive understanding beyond the simple recall of factual knowledge.

Disciplinary concepts

Defining historical disciplinary conceptual knowledge

The work of the Schools Council History Project (SCHP) in the 1970s advocated disciplinary, second-order, conceptual knowledge as a way to understand and involve pupils in the methods of history making in classrooms (Schools History Project, 1976). Consequently, disciplinary knowledge has become 'embedded in GCSE examination specifications, which were introduced in 1986, and in the various iterations of the National Curriculum for history in England since 1991' (Harris, 2021, p. 99). The English National Curriculum for Key Stage 3 currently defines six main facets of historical disciplinary knowledge (conceptual and procedural):

> Historical concepts such as continuity and change, cause and consequence, similarity, difference and significance . . . understand[ing] the methods of historical enquiry . . . and discern[ing] how and why contrasting arguments and interpretations of the past have been constructed. (DfE, 2013, p. 1)

The role of historical disciplinary knowledge

In his book *Thinking Historically*, Lévesque (2008) asserts that disciplinary conceptual knowledge, often referred to as procedural knowledge, is so vital in historical study that 'without these concepts, it would be impossible to make sense of the substance of the past, as "they shape the way we go about doing history"' (p. 30). The disciplinary or second-order concepts therefore help us to organise the process of studying history, providing a lens through which we explore questions about the past and make meaning. When used in the context of a meaningful historical enquiry, 'metahistorical' knowledge equips pupils with the procedural awareness they need to make sense of the past (Lee, 2005, p. 32). The second-order concepts provide pupils with an introduction to the 'rules of the game', allowing them to 'develop more sophisticated ideas' about the nature of history (Lévesque, 2010, p. 45). 'They are not what history is "about", but they shape the way we go about doing history' (Ashby & Lee, 2000, p. 199).

However, as explained in the introduction to this chapter, it is not uncommon even for history graduates to be largely unaware of their existence. Indeed, as Lévesque (2008) goes on to explain, 'because these concepts are rarely apparent in use, they are often left hidden in historians' investigations and even more so in school textbooks, thus leading to the naive assumption that they do not influence historical inquiry and are unworthy of study' (p. 30).

Making visible the implicit historical processes, which beginning teachers have used in their undergraduate or postgraduate historical study, almost as a matter of subconscious automatism, is a big challenge for a mentor. While second-order knowledge and understanding (disciplinary/ second-order concepts) of causation (and consequence), change (and continuity), similarity and difference, historical evidence, historical significance, and historical interpretations may have become part of your common framework of understanding as an experienced teacher, for the novice they can feel both baffling and overwhelming in their scope and complexity. Indeed, it is not uncommon, almost at the very end of the training programme, to find a beginning teacher proclaiming they still don't really understand the disciplinary concepts or how they inform the formulation of an enquiry question. Grasping what disciplinary concepts are, as well as how to break them down for pupils and how to structure enquiries within a programme of study that enable pupils to have incrementally more complex engagements with conceptual thinking, is really tricky. It can be further complicated by the approach schools themselves take to integrating (or not integrating) disciplinary knowledge into their curriculum. Some beginning teachers may find themselves in departments where disciplinary knowledge (both conceptual and procedural) is explicitly taught and clearly augments the substantive foci of the curriculum. Others may be placed in departments where substantive knowledge acquisition is regarded as the primary goal, and disciplinary knowledge is seen as extraneous (Harris, 2021, p. 114). There is also a chance that some beginning teachers may find themselves in departments where the curriculum has become divorced from the true discipline of history because historical learning is being seen purely as a set of critical thinking 'skills' with little reference to the substantive elements of the history curriculum (Byrom, 2013).

A second-order conceptual 'canon'?

The six concepts defined in the National Curriculum (DfE, 2013) do not, however, represent an unquestioned 'canon'. Indeed, variation has been seen in the way historical disciplinary knowledge is expressed in different national contexts and across time. The concept identified by the current English National Curriculum Order as 'similarity and difference' has, for example, also been referred to as 'social, cultural, religious and ethnic diversity' (DfE, 2000; DCSF, 2007) and grouped in with the notion of empathy (Lee & Shemilt, 2011), and in at least one international context, this disciplinary idea has been articulated as historical perspective (Seixas & Morton, 2013).

Seixas and Morton (2013), writing in the Canadian context, established the 'Big Six' concepts that comprise historical thinking. In a significant departure from the National Curriculum in England, the 'the ethical dimension' is included as the sixth concept. This involves teaching pupils to understand the actions of past individuals in context without imposing our own ethical standards of today, while navigating the extent of our responsibility for historical crimes

Utilising historical concepts 49

and drawing on the past to inform responses to current ethical dilemmas (see Chapter 7 for more discussion on this point). Meanwhile in the Netherlands, van Boxtel and van Drie's (2018) conceptualisation of historical disciplinary knowledge departs from the clear-cut articulation of second-order concepts that can be found in the English National Curriculum. Instead, they identify 'three types and six components of historical reasoning', defining disciplinary historical reasoning as being about knowing 'how to analyse and interpret historical phenomena and sources and how to construct evidence-based arguments' to enable historical reasoning 'about: continuity and change, causes and consequences, similarities and differences' (van Boxtel & van Drie, 2018, pp. 151-2). In this context, second-order conceptual understanding is part of a complex model of historical reasoning involving interconnected processes and conceptual thinking. Furthermore, the German history education literature draws on the didactic tradition and the work of Rüsen and, in contrast to the English National Curriculum, emphasises the ideas of narrative competence and historical consciousness as critical elements in historical disciplinary understanding (Körber, 2021).

It is important, therefore, to help beginning teachers appreciate that historical disciplinary understanding encompasses a broader range of forms than those articulated purely within their own national context, and that these differences are manifested in historical scholarship and sometimes even in examination specifications which place subtly different emphasis upon the application of conceptual and procedural knowledge to meet their assessment objectives. Task 3.5 will help you explore your own understanding of the disciplinary content of your curriculum.

Task 3.5 Articulating the disciplinary content of your own curriculum

Read Harris' (2021) chapter 'Disciplinary knowledge denied?' in A. Chapman (ed.), *Knowing History in Schools: Powerful Knowledge and the Powers of Knowledge* (pp. 97-128). Knowledge and the Curriculum. London: UCL Press. This is an open-access text and can be accessed at: https://discovery.ucl.ac.uk/id/eprint/10118305/1/Knowing-History-in-Schools.pdf

- Examine your own curriculum. Are you able to articulate the relationship between substantive and disciplinary knowledge in the curriculum plan?
    - Do you balance substantive and disciplinary knowledge in your curriculum plan, or do you privilege one over the other?
    - Are disciplinary concepts used to frame a substantive curricular object, or do they sit in isolation from each other?
- When and how do you revisit or spiral back to each second-order concept within and across key stages? Which disciplinary concepts do pupils find more difficult to grasp? How does your curriculum provide opportunities for pupils to encounter the second-order concepts in different ways and therefore overcome these barriers?

- Could you explain all this to a beginning teacher? Are there aspects of your own understanding of disciplinary thinking that need to be sharpened before you can articulate the role and value of disciplinary knowledge – both in terms of conceptual and procedural understanding?

The interconnectedness of historical knowledge

One aspect of second-order conceptual understanding that beginning teachers struggle to grasp is that the second-order concepts neither sit in isolation from substantive content knowledge, nor from one another. Just as second-order concepts provide lenses through which the past might be explored and understood in historical investigations, so too the substantive knowledge taught in schools needs to be understood in relation to its second-order lenses. The challenge for beginning teachers is knowing which disciplinary lens will best help pupils engage with the desired substantive knowledge. Working out which lens to cover at any given point is a challenge and relies on the teacher (and pupils) being able to navigate different disciplinary focuses with some fluidity. For example, it is rare that a 'Medicine Through Time' change-and-continuity enquiry would not also stray into questions relating to causation, consequence, or significance at points, although a well-crafted enquiry question would maintain the primary focus upon change and continuity. Beginning teachers require support to see that pupils therefore need to encounter and have opportunities to apply their understanding of disciplinary concepts through a variety of substantive contexts. Through sequenced enquiries, which revisit disciplinary concepts and show the ways that disciplinary concepts are related and dependent upon one another, pupils are able to develop their mastery of these concepts. Task 3.6 will help your mentee consider this relationship between historical enquiries and their disciplinary focus.

Task 3.6 Understanding the relationship between enquiry questions and their disciplinary focus

At the beginning of their Initial Teacher Education (ITE) year, new teachers may find it difficult to identify the disciplinary focus of an enquiry.

- In discussion with your mentee unpick the disciplinary focus for each of these enquiry questions:

    - 'How did the First Crusaders make it all the way into Jerusalem?' (Foster & Goudie, 2017, pp. 16-19)
    - 'Did Benin's Oba rule like Mali's Mansa?' (Another History Is Possible, n.d., https://anotherhistoryispossible.com/enquiries-schemes-of-work/did-benins-oba-rule-like-malis-mansa/)
    - Why was there a witch-craze in East Anglia in 1645-7?
    - Why is George Africanus remembered by the people of Nottingham?
    - 'What's worth knowing about the First World War?' (Worth, 2014, pp. 42-4)

As your mentee progresses, they will start to devise and plan their own enquiries. At this point your mentee will need to start thinking more independently about the relationship between the substantive and the disciplinary.

- Ask your mentee to complete the following table (the first example is completed for them) before a mentor meeting and then discuss this together in the meeting.

Substantive topic	Rationale (Links to curriculum? Relationship to scholarship? etc.)	Possible disciplinary focus	How might this 'look' as an enquiry question?
The Norman Conquest	Conquest, control, assimilation. Political, economic and cultural changes. Schama's 'truckload of trouble' interpretation.	Teachers have tended to move away from a focus on causation and conflict to focus on significance, change and continuity, or historical interpretations.	Why have people told different stories about the Norman Conquest? (Historical interpretations) Did the Normans bring a 'truckload of trouble' to England after 1066? (Change and continuity)
King John			
The Black Death			
The campaign for women's suffrage			
British America			

Teaching History's 'Cunning Plan' feature provides a whole range of planned enquiries that could be used to support this activity.

- Select one of the following to discuss with your mentee to consider how historical scholarship can help reveal the kinds of questions historians are asking about a period/event in history and therefore illuminate helpful disciplinary conceptual foci. Read and discuss one of the following:

  - The history book your mentee is currently reading for their subject-knowledge enhancement.
  - An article from a history publication (like *The Historian* or *BBC History Magazine*) which summarises some recent historical scholarship.
  - A 'Polychronicon' or 'What Have Historians Been Arguing About' article from *Teaching History* to explore some of the academic and scholarly thinking on your chosen topic.

- Ask your mentee to identify which second-order concept sits at the heart of the interpretation being offered in the scholarship (refer to the end of Chapter 3 for a summary of each disciplinary concept).

> - Generate some possible enquiry questions (with a clear disciplinary focus) based on the scholarship text. Experiment with changing the disciplinary focus. What does this do to the historical rigour of the question? See Riley's (2000) *Teaching History 99* article, 'Into the Key Stage 3 history garden: choosing and planting your enquiry questions' for examples of how different second-order concepts can be applied to the same topic.

How can you support beginning teachers to understand and teach the disciplinary concepts?

If beginning teachers are to plan and teach history lessons which lead to a meaningful understanding of the past, they must be aware of how substantive and disciplinary knowledge combine in their enquiry questions. This means they need to secure their own understanding of the second-order concepts. It is often assumed that beginning teachers will pick up how the 'theory' of conceptual understanding is introduced and framed for pupils through their observation of lesson activities. However, most beginning teachers need this to be made explicit for them. Mentor meetings provide fertile grounds for discussions which draw theory and practice together, for example by reading and discussing the practical theorising and exemplar enquiries of classroom teachers writing in *Teaching History*. Mentoring activities involving rehearsal of elements of classroom practice outside of the lesson are becoming increasingly popular as instructional coaching is adopted in schools. However, the curricular object at the heart of these practices is often overlooked. It is well worth using time in a mentor meeting to rehearse with your mentee how those tried-and-tested pedagogical approaches which problematise conceptual understanding (for example card sorts, road maps, and living graphs) are articulated to pupils and implemented in the classroom to promote historical thinking (Grande, 2022).

A great deal has been written about each of the disciplinary concepts, and it would be impossible to capture this wealth of practical theorising here. The approach taken in this book is to focus on how you can support beginning teachers to understand each disciplinary concept, identify activities to teach that concept, and avoid common misconceptions. Each section also includes a selection of suggested readings. Task 3.7 provides some suggestions for how you might structure introducing and developing your mentee's understanding of the second-order concepts.

Concept: cause and consequence

What does this involve?

The second-order concepts of historical cause and consequence involves understanding the reasons for, and the results of, historical events and the changes that occur within and across historical periods. The curriculum should look to support pupils to understand the relationship between cause and consequence and help pupils to see that not all consequences were intended, nor were they inevitable. To achieve this, pupils need opportunities to analyse cause and consequence in terms of interrelated factors to demonstrate an understanding of the historical context and the agency of groups and individuals (actors) involved.

What are we aiming for pupils to understand when applying this concept by Key Stage 5?

Pupils who have developed a secure understanding of cause and consequence over the course of their studies will be able to identify and evaluate the relative importance of different factors and agents in a multi-directional enquiry with interrelated factors. They can develop explanatory links between causes and their effects upon the outcome of historical events. They can communicate the nuances and complexity of historical events by using precise language to articulate the nature of these factors in terms of their temporal, spatial, and agentic influence.

Structuring beginning teachers' understanding of this concept

Beginning teachers need to be supported to understand that 'explaining why' something happened is not the same as explaining in more detail what something is; rather, it is about giving a reason for how something came to happen or occur, and involves selection of evidence, categorising ideas into themes and factors, drawing causal links between factors, deciding a hierarchy of causes, sustaining an argument, and addressing alternative interpretations (Woodcock, 2010).

One way you can support your mentee's understanding of this concept is by exploring different typologies of causation, for example:

Evans (1997)	Chapman (2003, p. 47)
• Necessary.	• Content (economic, ideological, cultural, political).
• Sufficient.	• Time (short term, medium term, long term).
• Hierarchy.	• Role (underlying, catalysts).
• Absolute.	• Weight (relative importance).
• Relative.	

Introducing your mentee to *The Terrible Tale of Alphonse the Camel* will prove a helpful basis from which to begin discussions about their own understanding of causation, and how they might use historical narratives to make complex historical ideas tangible for pupils. A short film can be accessed at: https://thecamelsback.org/.

Classroom activities that make this concept visible to pupils

- Concrete analogies (e.g. Alphonse the camel).
- Diamond 9.

- Questioning.
- Narratives and role plays.
- Card sorts.
- Causation webs.
- Zone of influence.
- Applying the vocabulary of cause and consequence.

Enquiry questions to explore with your mentee

- Did the end of slavery make people free? (Husbands & Kitson, 2002)
- How did World War I lead to World War II? (Rodker, 2019)
- Why did allies turn to enemies by 1958? (Canning, 2020)

Common misconceptions beginning teachers often communicate to pupils around this concept

- Causation should be privileged over consequence in history curricula because it is more complex. (Consequences are more self-evident.)
- Events in history are inevitable.
- There are only one or two ways of understanding factors: by categorising them in terms of their temporal role (short term, long term), or the 'conditions' they represent (political, social, economic, cultural).
- All factors are equal and it's just a 'matter of opinion'.
- Privileging causes generated by the actions of individuals are more significant than causes generated by context/events, e.g. taking the approach that the really bad things happen because of evil individuals.
- Ill-informed counterfactual thinking which leads to tangential possibility-thinking and unhelpful 'rabbit holes'.

Recommended reading to develop the beginning teacher's understanding

Essential starting point
Historical Association. (2019). What's the wisdom on causation? *Teaching History 175*.
Historical Association. (2021). What's the wisdom on consequence? *Teaching History 182*.

Further Reading
Carroll, J. (2022). Terms and conditions: using metaphor to highlight causal processes with Year 13. *Teaching History 187*.
Chapman, A. (2003). Camels, diamonds and counterfactuals: a model for teaching causal reasoning. *Teaching History 112*.
Navey, M. (2018). Dealing with the consequences: What do we want students to do with consequence in history? *Teaching History 172*.
Stanford, M. (2019). Did the Bretons break? Planning increasingly complex 'causal models' at Key Stage 3. *Teaching History 175*.
Woodcock, J. (2011). Does the linguistic release the conceptual? Helping Year 10 to improve their causal reasoning. *Teaching History 119*.

Concept: change and continuity

What does this involve?

Change and continuity is one of the fundamental organising concepts of history. It involves understanding how historians draw on their knowledge of chronological turning points and trends over time to frame the past. It requires problematising the nature, pace, extent, and process of change, while simultaneously appreciating that the concurrent continuity of the period provides the context in which changes are made possible. It is this interplay between change and continuity that makes this disciplinary concept particularly challenging, largely because it requires a secure substantive understanding of the wider period and chronological frameworks.

What are we aiming for pupils to understand when applying this concept by Key Stage 5?

By the time they reach A level, pupils who have a secure understanding of change and continuity should be able to identify, analyse, and evaluate change and continuity within a defined period of time. They can identify trends, turning points, and the baseline continuities that create the chronological frameworks for periodisation. They also understand the role of interpretation in the defining of historical periods, are able to consider diversity of experience, and are able to draw on their conceptual thinking to write historical narratives. They will be able to use analytical vocabulary to construct an argument in response to a real historical debate.

Structuring beginning teachers' understanding of this concept

Beginning teachers need to understand that change and continuity can be problematised beyond turning points. This involves getting pupils to ask questions about the patterns they can observe within and across periods of time, for example by asking:

- What kind of change was occurring?
- How widespread was the change? Was it experienced in all places by all people?
- How fast or slow was the change?
- What stayed the same during this period of change? Why was this unaffected?
- Was the change progressive or regressive?

Foster's (2008) use of a road map as a metaphor for historical change and continuity is an excellent way to begin exploring the complexity of historical change and continuity with your mentee. Taking some time in a mentor meeting to 'model' its use by getting your mentee to create their own road map for the topic will force them to mobilise their substantive knowledge to consider the interplay of factors such as the speed, rate, nature, and direction of historical change. As you discuss the road map, make a note of the kinds of questions you are asking about the change/continuity you are observing. This will help the beginning teacher to identify and understand the difference between questions which promote knowledge retrieval and questions that promote historical reasoning.

Classroom activities that make this concept visible to pupils

- Road maps.
- Living graphs.
- Turning points timelines.
- Washing lines.
- Card sorts.
- The use of metaphors, drawing shapes to represent changes.
- Applying the vocabulary of change and continuity.

Enquiry questions to explore with your mentee

- Did the Normans bring a 'truck load of trouble' to England? (Historical Association, 2021)
- How far did trade and migration change England in the sixteenth century? (Laffin, 2019)
- Was there more continuity than change in British-Jamaican relations between 1760 and 1870? (Another History Is Possible, n.d.a)

Common misconceptions beginning teachers often communicate to pupils around this concept

- Change is only ever a progressive experience.
- Continuity means *everything* staying the same.
- Only change requires effort (in fact, maintaining the status quo can require as much, if not more, effort on the part of the people involved).

Recommended reading to develop the beginning teacher's understanding

Essential starting point
Historical Association. (2020). What's the wisdom on change and continuity? *Teaching History 179*.

Further Reading
Banham, D. (2000). The return of King John: Using depth to strengthen overview in the teaching of political change. *Teaching History 92*.
Counsell, C. (2011). What do we want students to *do* with historical change and continuity? In I. Davies (ed.), *Debates in History Teaching* (London: Routledge).
Foster, R. (2013). The more things change, the more they stay the same: developing students' thinking about change and continuity. *Teaching History 151*.

Concept: similarity and difference

What does this involve?

This concept has appeared in many different guises in the various iterations of the English National Curriculum and has been described variously as historical perspective and diversity as well as similarity and difference. It explores how people experienced the world in the past. It recognises that not all people in a particular place and period experienced events and institutions in the same way, nor did they perceive these experiences through the same lens or worldview. Importantly, it is the disciplinary concept that ensures present-day values and perspectives are not read into the motivations of people in the past; instead, our understanding of people in history is based on historical evidence.

What are we aiming for pupils to understand when applying this concept by Key Stage 5?

Pupils who have a well-developed understanding of similarity and difference will recognise that the past embodies a multiplicity of experience. They are able to understand that we don't hear all these many 'voices' from history fairly represented because of the way the source record has been compiled and is drawn upon to form evidence. They understand the link between the second-order concept of similarity and difference and the development of different narratives about the past that come to influence interpretations of that event. They are able to avoid presentism and don't fall into the empathy trap of imposing their own thoughts and feelings, devoid of evidential basis, upon historical actors. Critically they can make valid generalisations that reveal they have a firm grasp of the complexity of the past.

Structuring beginning teachers' understanding of this concept

Beginning teachers need to understand that providing pupils with one-dimensional encounters with a particular period leads to narrow, unrepresentative thinking about the past; it is akin to going on holiday to Paris, claiming the whole of France has the same form and features as the cultural metropolis, and that the French all possess the same outlook as the one Parisian you spoke to at the railway station. Beginning teachers need to be shown how planning a curriculum, which exposes pupils to carefully curated enquiries that allow them to 'world build' (Hill, 2020), can develop nuance in the way pupils perceive both the ordinariness and exceptionality of people in the past and therefore think in more historical ways about their motivations and actions. They also need to be supported to understand the role of generalisation in expressing similarity and difference, while still conveying the complexity of the past and the multiplicity of people's experience.

Beginning teachers also need to understand how empathy has often been employed as a means for exploring some of the affective elements of similarity and difference. However, pupils' own lack of knowledge about the wider context of a period, combined with their tendency to approach the past with presentist perspectives, mean the use of empathetic tasks in the classroom is ridden with risk. Through the CHATA project, Lee and Shemilt (2011) outlined the different degrees to which pupils can think empathetically about the past, but where empathy work is attempted it is vital that beginning teachers approach it with care and that they do so having thought through the implications of what they are asking of their pupils (Low-Beer, 1989). Considering how 'cultural history' of this nature might be better served by 'recasting the concept of empathy as historical perspective' (Benger, 2020) is just one way to explore the common pitfalls of this kind of school history with your mentee.

Classroom activities that make this concept visible to pupils

- Historical fiction and storytelling.
- Role play/character cards/society lines.
- Analysis of different images from one period.
- Dodgy generalisations game (Counsell, 2009).
- Field trips, redesigning a museum to reflect a wider range of voices.

Enquiry questions to explore with your mentee

- Who were the gladiators? (Flynn, 2012)
- When and for whom has 1688 been 'Glorious'? (Chapman, 2013)
- What mattered to people in Britain in the period 1625-1714? (Snelson, 2021)

Common misconceptions beginning teachers often communicate to pupils around this concept

- Similarity and difference are just like change and continuity and involve exploring people's attitudes and experience across periods of history rather than within the same contemporaneous moment.
- It is possible to make generalisations about the distant past that attribute the same worldview, characteristic, attribute, or preference to all the people in a particular time or place.

Recommended reading to develop the beginning teacher's understanding

Essential starting point
Historical Association. (2020). What's the wisdom on similarity and difference? *Teaching History 180*.

Further Reading
Benger, A. (2020). Teaching Year 9 to argue like cultural historians: recasting the concept of empathy as historical perspective. *Teaching History 179*.

Boyd, S. (2019). From 'Great Women' to an inclusive curriculum: how should women's history be included at Key Stage 3? *Teaching History 175*.

Dennis, N. (2021). The stories we tell ourselves: History teaching, powerful knowledge and the importance of context in A. Chapman (ed.), *Knowing History in Schools: Powerful Knowledge and the Powers of Knowledge*. Knowledge and the Curriculum. London: UCL Press.

Lewis, C. (2018). Teaching black Tudors as a window into Tudor England. *Teaching History 173*.

Olivey, J. (2022). What did it mean to them? Creating a progression model for teaching historical perspectives in Key Stage 3. *Teaching History 186*.

Concept: historical evidence

What does this involve?

Evidential enquiry in schools involves revealing the historical process, thereby unveiling the evolving nature of the discipline, and quashing any notions of history as a static body of received knowledge. It reveals how historians define a line of enquiry and then question sources (remnants of the past), depending on what they want to find out, to provide them with evidence. The historian will then weigh that evidence, alongside their knowledge of the provenance of these sources, to form their own interpretations of those events. In school this involves developing enquiry questions which ask specifically about the nature of that evidential basis and reveal something of how historical source material is understood and used (Ashby, 2011).

What are we aiming for pupils to understand when applying this concept by Key Stage 5?

By the time they reach A level, pupils should understand that history is constructed from a variety of evidence/sources. They will be able to draw on their understanding of the wider period and to establish the meaning of sources and the provenance of a source to make judgements about its reliability and utility for a given purpose. They will have an evidential language toolkit which they will draw on to reflect the varying degrees of certainty with which they leverage sources to act as evidence to support their claims about the past. Students will be able to cross-reference sources, comment on utility, and recognise how historians identify sources that are useful to their own enquiries, and handle the uncertainties inherent in constructing plausible arguments from the evidence available at that point in time.

Structuring beginning teachers' understanding of this concept

It is easy to assume that beginning history teachers should have a secure grasp of the role of sources and evidence. However, in some contexts, archival work is not a compulsory element of undergraduate study, and consequently beginning teachers come to this concept with a range of starting points. Your mentee may therefore need support to understand how lines of enquiry are formed in response to source material and the range of sources that can be used in the development of an evidential enquiry.

Begin by exploring with your mentee an evidential enquiry within your department curriculum. Explore your mentee's understanding of the differences between historical sources, historical interpretations, and evidence; it is vital that they have a secure grasp of the differences before they begin to devise their own evidential enquiries. Consider how the enquiry question sets the parameters for which sources can/should be used in combination to generate evidence in response to the enquiry. Explore some of the dangers of decontextualising sources when using 'gobbets' with pupils. Look at some pupil work responding to an evidential enquiry question. Track through the way pupils, who have demonstrated a secure understanding of the task, marshal their substantive knowledge of the period to interrogate the source material and form lines of argument based in evidential understanding.

Classroom activities that make this concept visible to pupils

- Using sources to develop evidence to answer a meaningful enquiry question.
- Supermarket evidential sweep (Foster & Gadd, 2013).
- Providing the source in its original format (for example by drawing on the National Archives Education resources).
- Using material culture as well as written sources.
- Gradual-reveal activity – students are given a momentary glimpse of a source, identifying what they can see to encourage focus on different 'layers' within the source.
- Layers of inference diagram (Riley, 1999).
- Creating a mini archive/ oral history project.

Enquiry questions to explore with your mentee

- Who is buried in the box? (Arkinstal, 2013).
- Who can tell us the most about the Silk Road? (Exploring historians' use of material culture as evidence) (Trapani, 2019).
- Why is it so difficult to tell whether there was a Blitz spirit? (Historical Association, 2019, p. 25).

Common misconceptions beginning teachers often communicate to pupils around this concept

- Evidence and sources are the same thing.
- Evidential enquiry involves looking at an exhausting number of sources to fill in the gaps and discover the 'truth' of historical events.

- Gobbets are sufficient for giving pupils an insight into the whole source.
- Judging a source to be biased is an adequate reason to dismiss it as evidence.
- Source reliability and source utility are measures of the same aspect of a source's application.

Recommended reading to develop the beginning teacher's understanding

Essential starting point
Historical Association. (2019). What's the wisdom on evidence and sources? *Teaching History 176.*

Further Reading
Aitken, A. (2017). Building the habit of evidential thinking. Teaching History 168.
Card, J. (2004). Picturing place: What you get may be more than what you see. *Teaching History 116.*
Counsell, C. (2000). 'Didn't we do that in Y7?' Planning for progression in evidential understanding. *Teaching History 99.*
LeCoq, H. (2000). Beyond bias: making source evaluation meaning to Year 7. *Teaching History 99.*

Concept: historical interpretations

What does this involve?

The formation of historical interpretations is the bedrock of the historical discipline. The second-order concept of interpretation allows pupils to view the past as more than a received, unchanging repository of facts to be learnt. Instead, by examining how and why historians (and others) construct different views of past events, they are supported to understand that history is an evolving dialogue between historians who may have formed very different understandings of past events based on their own beliefs, the evidential basis, and historical process. It also equips pupils to understand that history is subject to 'change' as further evidence comes to light, or as historians adopt different lenses through which they can view the past.

What are we aiming for pupils to understand when applying this concept by Key Stage 5?

Pupils who have a developed understanding of historical interpretation have grasped that historians reach conclusions about the past based on the way they compile and privilege the evidence. They understand why valid interpretations of the same event exist (e.g. due to the positionality of the historian, the concerns of the historical moment in which the historian is writing) and are able to draw on their understanding of the period to compare interpretations and give reasons for their differences.

Structuring beginning teachers' understanding of this concept

Most beginning teachers will be aware of the concept of historical interpretations through their work on historiography at undergraduate level. However, it is important they understand that, for National Curriculum purposes, historical interpretations are subsequent and purposeful reflections and therefore different to sources.

They need to understand the importance of bringing historical scholarship into the classroom so that pupils can see interpretations in context. They need to understand for themselves how interpretations change over time and how this connects to the way the historical record is formed (at the level of what is recorded, makes it into the archives, and is selected by historians for investigation). For particular topics, they will need to have the various schools of thought introduced to them (for example the Orthodox, Revisionist and Post-Revisionist interpretations of the Cold War), so they can develop the 'double-vision' of thinking about the period itself and the understand the influences of the period of the interpreter (Card, 2004).

Beginning teachers need to understand that asking pupils to make judgements about the accuracy and truthfulness of interpretations leads to oversimplification, and reinforces the misconception that there is a narrative truth which can be attained. Instead, beginning teachers need to be supported to see how constructive analytical approaches to interpretations can be achieved.

Classroom activities that make this concept visible to pupils

- Exploring interpretations behind popular/political collective memory, paintings, museums, monuments.
- Guided reading of historical scholarship to identify the interpretation being presented.
- Using a variety of interpretations:
  - Academic scholarship
  - Education resources (museums/ textbooks)
  - Non-fiction media (documentaries, podcasts, blogs)
  - Fiction (novels, films, TV drama)

Enquiry questions to explore with your mentee

- Why has there been so much interest in Mary I? (Stephen, 2007)
- Why have interpretations of the Battle of Rorke's Drift in 1879 changed over time? (Fullard, Wheeley, & Fordham, 2011)
- Why can historians not agree as to whether Thatcher 'rolled back the State' or not? (Head, 2020)

Common misconceptions beginning teachers often communicate to pupils around this concept

- Historical interpretations are about pupils reaching their own, reasoned judgements.

- Using source evidence to answer questions about the past is the same as dealing with interpretations.

Recommended reading to develop the beginning teacher's understanding

Essential starting point
Historical Association. (2019). What's the wisdom on interpretations of the past? *Teaching History* 177

Further Reading
Ashby, R. (2005). Students' approaches to validating historical claims. In R. Ashby, P. Gordon, and P. Lee (eds) (2005). *International Review of History Education, Volume 4. Understanding History: recent research in history education.* (London: Routledge).
Card, J. (2004). Seeing double: how one period visualises another. *Teaching History 117.*
Keates, D. (2020). Unpicking the threads of interpretations: tangling up Year 9 in the messy world of views on Oliver Cromwell. *Teaching History 179.*

Concept: historical significance

What does this involve?

Historical significance is how we confer meaning to past events by considering their influence, impact, and legacy. It explores how, as the social processes that underpin this 'meaning-making' shift, the criteria used to decide if an historical event, person, or group should be deemed significant enough to be remembered or remarked upon also shifts. Understanding why some events are considered more significant than others requires an understanding of how certain factors work to elevate or silence aspects of the past. Historical significance fundamentally underpins the process of historical enquiry – we ask questions of the past because we think there is something significant to find. It is a meta-concept in that it both incorporates and underpins all the other concepts.

What are we aiming for pupils to understand when applying this concept by Key Stage 5?

Pupils who have grasped this complex meta-concept will be able to consider why certain historical events and actors have been attributed significance and why these judgements may change over time. They are able to apply and derive their own criteria to make their own judgements of significance, and recognise that statements about significance are interpretations in their own right and may therefore be contested.

Structuring beginning teachers' understanding of this concept

Beginning teachers often find this concept the hardest to grasp, and regularly reduce significance to consequences or causal factors. They need to understand that significance is multi-faceted and open-ended and can change, both in terms of the period over which we are trying to ascertain significance and, of course, the provenance of the claim of significance.

Pupils cannot be taught to understand significance simply by being given a list of criteria which they apply to test whether events can be deemed significant or not. Instead, beginning teachers need to be helped to reveal to pupils how judgements of significance are reached and how the application of different criteria might change these judgements. They need support to see that overwhelming pupils with too many different criteria within one lesson or a short sequence can cause significant misconceptions to emerge.

They also need to understand that the way significance is used in Key Stage 4 GCSE specifications is *not the same* as the way historical significance is understood by the history-teaching community.

Models of significance which are helpful to introduce beginning teachers to include:

Partington* (1980)	Phillips (G.R.E.A.T - WW1) (2002)	Counsell's Five R's (2005)
• **Important** (to people in the past) • **Profundity** (how deeply lives were affected) • **Quantity** (how many lives affected) • **Durability** (for how long were lives affected) • **Relevance** (to the present). * N.B. Partington's criteria were derived from considering how teachers select curricula	• **Ground-breaking** • **Remembered by all** • **Events that were far-reaching** • **Affected the future** • **Terrifying**	• **Remarkable** (remarked upon by people at the time and/or since) • **Remembered** (important at some point in history in the collective memory of a group(s)) • **Resonant** (it is possible to connect with experiences, beliefs, or situations across time and space) • **Resulted in change** (had consequences for the future) • **Revealing** (of some other aspect of the past)

Ultimately one of the most challenging aspects of teaching historical significance is that it is almost impossible to explore in isolation from the other second-order concepts. As a meta-concept, this needs to be embraced, while also ensuring the distinctive aspects of significance are given an opportunity to be considered.

Classroom activities that make this concept visible to pupils

- Identifying criteria/selecting criteria to use/creating own criteria.
- Local history studies.
- Balloon/boxing match debate.
- 'We didn't start the fire' song activity (Allsop, 2009).

Examples of significance enquiry questions

- Why was the First World War called the Great War? (Phillips, 2002)

- Why do Australians still care about Ned Kelly? (Brown & Woodcock, 2009)
- What does studying Josephine Butler reveal about Britain in the 19th century? (Counsell, 2005)

Common misconceptions beginning teachers often communicate to pupils around this concept

- Conflating significance with importance.
- Thinking about significance purely in terms of consequences.
- Believing providing pupils with lists of criteria allows them to 'do' significance.

Recommended reading to develop the beginning teacher's understanding

Essential starting point
Historical Association. (2020). What's the wisdom on historical significance? T*eaching History 181.*

Further Reading
Brown, G., and Woodcock J. (2009). Relevant, rigorous and revisited: using local history to make meaning of historical significance. *Teaching History 134*.
Counsell, C. (2004). Looking through a Josephine-Butler shaped window: focusing pupils' thinking on historical significance. *Teaching History 114*.
Hunt, M. (2000). Teaching historical significance. In J. Arthur and R. Phillips (eds.), *Issues in History Teaching.* London: Routledge.
Phillips, R. (2002). Historical significance – the forgotten 'Key Element'? *Teaching History 106.*
Worth, P. (2023). Falling forward: Three strategies to support pupils' study of historical significance. *Teaching History 190.*

Task 3.7 Exploring the disciplinary concepts

It is important that your mentee has a strong working knowledge of the second-order concepts and understands how they can be introduced to pupils and used as a lens through which substantive knowledge can be made meaningful. Just as with the pupils they teach, beginning teachers will develop increasingly complex models of understanding as their careers progress. A range of supporting mentoring activities will help them to do this in a systematic way which better facilitates more active noticing and reflection upon their part. Providing them with a scaffold, such as a table, where they can develop their own 'repository of understanding', can also be very helpful.

- Ask your mentee to read the Historical Association's 'What's the Wisdom On' articles/ watch the 'What's the Wisdom on' films on the HA, website and make a record of their 'key takeaways' of the principles of historical thinking involved in

each second-order concept in their disciplinary concepts table (you may wish to use a format similar to that modelled for each second-order concept above).
- Across a series of mentor meetings, explore each second-order concept by identifying a relevant *Teaching History* article to read and discuss in a mentor meeting alongside looking at an enquiry taught in the department which focuses on that concept. Identify the pedagogical approaches used in the enquiry that help to introduce the conceptual thinking to pupils in more concrete ways. Get them to record these approaches to create a 'toolkit' for planning.
- Use a mentor meeting to rehearse with your mentee the exposition/instruction-giving/questioning that enables pedagogical approaches such as the change and continuity roadmap to be effective in enabling pupils to grasp the historical ideas required for disciplinary thinking.
- Ask your mentee to generate enquiry questions for a particular substantive topic, reflecting different disciplinary foci. Discuss the strength of these enquiry questions. Look at some examples of successful enquiries ('Cunning Plans' and 'Triumphs Show' in *Teaching History* are a good place to start). Joint-plan an enquiry sequence around one of these enquiry questions and task your mentee with planning and teaching one of the lessons from the sequence the following week. When you observe this lesson, focus your observation and the subsequent post-lesson discussion on how successfully the lesson supported pupil understanding of the disciplinary dimension of historical thinking, rather than, for example, behaviour.

Progression in disciplinary understanding

It is important that your mentee has a clear idea of how pupils can 'get better' in their disciplinary understanding, but also that they recognise progression in history is complex and very unlikely to happen in a linear way; Task 3.8 will help you explore this with your mentee. One way of articulating this progression can be seen in the 'signposts' developed by Ford (2014) for each of the second-order concepts of the English National Curriculum. These were developed from Seixas and Morton's 'guideposts' for historical conceptual thinking. These 'signposts' are not intended as a prescriptive or exhaustive list of pupils' expected progress. Indeed, as Ford asserts, 'there is . . . no necessity for students to tackle each "signpost" in turn . . . students may master more difficult aspects of the concept while still struggling with more straightforward elements' (Ford, 2014, p. 35). There is no ladder of incrementally harder skills to work through and, as Cook (2018) rather beautifully describes it, pupils' understanding is 'more like a web that grows increasingly intricate as time goes on' (p. 65).

Task 3.8 Progression in disciplinary understanding

Can you explain what you would expect a pupil to be able to do to demonstrate understanding of each second-order concept at each stage of their history education?

For example, what would you expect to be different about the way a Year 7 pupil conceptualises causation compared with an A-level student?

- Track with your mentee how your departmental curriculum seeks to develop pupils' conceptual understanding of each second-order concept across Key Stage 3. How does each enquiry incrementally introduce pupils to different 'guideposts' (Seixas & Morton, 2013) or 'signposts' (Ford, 2014) required to demonstrate a broad and deep grasp of the concept? How do the enquiries posed through the curriculum provide opportunities for pupils to select and apply these guideposts to answering different historical questions?
- Look at some examples of pupil outcome tasks from different enquiries which focus on the same second-order concept across your departmental curriculum (for example, assessment pieces which focus on causation from Key Stage 3, GCSE, and A-level pupils). Identify which aspects of the disciplinary concept are introduced at each level and how pupils express their understanding with increasing degrees of nuance and sophistication.
- Discuss the danger of 'flight paths' for conceptual understanding (Burnham & Brown, 2004; Ford, 2014). Look at some examples of A-level/ GCSE/Key Stage 3 mark schemes and talk with your beginning teacher about how to avoid generalised mark schemes which suggest the guideposts/signposts of conceptual understanding can and should be encountered in a discrete and linear fashion.

Summary and key points

- Beginning teachers need to have the conceptual basis of history made evident to them and be supported to view history education as comprising of more than memorisation of substantive (propositional) knowledge.
- Substantive (first-order) conceptual understanding involves being able to identify and describe how certain phenomena can be observed in different historical contexts, and how previous understandings of these concepts adapt as they are applied across time.
- Beginning teachers need to understand the connection between their own wider substantive knowledge and their ability to identify and articulate the contexts that give meaning to substantive concepts.
- Disciplinary (second-order) conceptual understanding reveals how history works and is created. The second-order concepts provide a lens through which to view the substantive object and substantive conceptual understanding of the past. Teachers use second-order concepts to frame enquiries which engage pupils in the procedural aspects of historical thinking.
- Beginning teachers find identifying and understanding substantive and disciplinary concepts hard because it involves deconstructing the processes of history making which have become largely subconscious during their undergraduate studies of the subject.

- Beginning teachers need clarity around what is involved in disciplinary conceptual understanding and how to support pupils to achieve this in the classroom. Mentors should create opportunities for their mentees to engage with, discuss, and implement the ideas presented in the practitioner research on disciplinary concepts. Exploring real-life examples of disciplinary thinking from within their own departmental curriculum, as well as being provided with opportunities to plan and rehearse pedagogical approaches intended to deepen pupils' disciplinary understanding, will help to refine their practice.

Further resources

- **Harris, R., Burn, K., & Woolley, M. (eds.). (2013).** *The Guided Reader to Teaching and Learning History* **(1st ed.). London: Routledge.**

    This excellent book provides history teachers with key extracts from influential history education thinkers, including academic researchers and classroom teachers. Section 2 provides an accessible route into the main thinking around historical disciplinary understanding.

- **Thomas, E. (2017).** *100 Ideas for Secondary Teachers: Outstanding History Lessons.* **London: Bloomsbury.**

    Part 1 and 2 of this classroom-practice-orientated book collate a range of practical strategies and activities which can be used in the classroom to develop pupils' conceptual understanding. It may prove a useful reference book for beginning teachers who have got stuck on a pedagogical treadmill and are finding it hard to expand their repertoire of suitable activities.

- **'What's the wisdom on . . .' articles and films from the Historical Association's website, available here: https://www.history.org.uk/publications/categories/903/module/8697/teaching-history-regular-features/9356/whats-the-wisdom-on and https://www.history.org.uk/secondary/categories/wtwo-films**

    Both the articles and films provide a short guide to the 'story so far' for new history teachers, including a synthesis of key articles and blogs, around different aspects of professional thinking, in particular in relation to disciplinary knowledge.

References

Allsop, S. (2009). 'We didn't start the fire': using 1980s popular music to explore historical significance by stealth. *Teaching History 137,* 52-9.

Another History Is Possible. (n.d.a). *A Level Coursework Enquiry.* Retrieved 2 April 2023 from Another History Is Possible: https://anotherhistoryispossible.com/a-level-enquiry/

Another History Is Possible. (n.d.b). *Enquiries.* Retrieved 28 March 2023 from Another History Is Possible: https://anotherhistoryispossible.com/enquiries-schemes-of-work/did-benins-oba-rule-like-malis-mansa/

Arkinstal, P. (2013). Cunning Plan 154: who is buried in the box? *Teaching History 152,* 28-9.

Ashby, R. (2011). Understanding historical evidence: teaching and learning challenges. In I. Davies (ed.), *Debates in History Teaching* (pp. 137-47). London: Routledge.

Ashby, R., & Lee, P. (2000). Progression in historical understanding among students aged 7-14. In P. N. Stearns, P. Seixas, & S. Wineburg (eds.), *Knowing, Teaching and Learning History: National and International Perspectives* (pp. 199-222). New York: New York University Press.

Benger, A. (2020). Teaching Year 9 to argue like cultural historians: recasting the concept of empathy as historical perspective. *Teaching History 179*, 24-35.

Brown, G., & Woodcock, J. (2009). Relevant, rigorous and revisited: using local history to make meaning of historical significance. *Teaching History 134*, 4-11.

Burnham, S., & Brown, G. (2004). Assessment without level descriptions. *Teaching History 115*, 5-15.

Byrom, J. (2013). Alive . . . and kicking? Some personal reflections on the revised National Curriculum (2014) and what we might do with it. *Historical Association Teaching History Curriculum Supplement, Iss. 153*, 6-14.

Canning, P. (2020). Cunning Plan 179: using TV producers' techniques to make the most effective use of retrieval practice. *Teaching History 179*, 66-9.

Card, J. (2004) Seeing double: how one period visualises another. *Teaching History 117*, 6-11.

Chapman, A. (2003). Camels, diamonds and counterfactuals: a model for teaching causal reasoning. *Teaching History 112*, 46-53.

Chapman, A. (2013). Cunning Plan 151: When and for whom has 1688 been 'Glorious'? *Teaching History 151*, 20.

Chapman, A. (2021). Introduction: historical knowing and the 'knowledge turn'. In A. Chapman, *Knowing History in Schools: Powerful Knowledge and the Powers of Knowledge* (pp. 1-31). London: UCL Press.

Chi, M.T. (2008). Three types of conceptual change: Belief revision, mental model transformation, and categorical shift. In S. Vosniadou (ed.), *Handbook of Research on Conceptual Change* (61-82). Hillsdale, NJ: Erlbaum. doi:10.1111/j.1756-8765.2008.01005.x; https://education.asu.edu/lcl/publications/chi-m-t-h-2008-three-types-conceptual-change-belief-revision-mental-model, accessed 21 December 2022.

Cook, R. (2018). From flight paths to spiders' webs: developing a model of prgression for KS3. *Teaching History, 172*, 64-70.

Counsell, C. (2005). Looking through a Josephine-Butler shaped window: focusing pupils' thinking on historical significance. *Teaching History 114*, 30-6.

Counsell, C. (2009). Cunning Plan 135: challenging generalisations. *Teaching History 135*, 13-15.

Crooks, V. (2021). What a wonderful world: teaching humanities. Retrieved 20 June 2022 from *Becoming a History Teacher*. https://uonhistoryteachertraining.school.blog/2021/05/11/what-a-wonderful-world-teaching-humanities/

DCSF. (2007). *National Curriculum: History – Programme of Study for Key Stage 3 and Attainment Target*. London: Department for Children Schools and Families.

DfE. (2000). *The National Curriculum for England: History*. London: Department for Education.

DfE. (2013). *National Curriculum History Programmes of Study: Key Stage 3*. London: Department for Education.

Evans, R. J. (1997). *In Defence of History*. London: Granta.

Flynn, N. (2012). Cunning Plan 149.1: a Year 7 lesson on gladiators. *Teaching History 149*, 26-7.

Ford, A. (2014). Setting us free? Building meaningful models of progression for a 'post-levels' world. *Teaching History 157*, 18-25.

Fordham, M. (2016). Knowledge and language: Being historical with substantive concepts. In C. Counsell, K. Burn, & A. Chapman, *MasterClass in History Education: Transforming Teaching and Learning* (pp. 43-58). London: Bloomsbury Academic.

Foster, R. (2008). Speed cameras, dead ends, drivers and diversions: Year 9 use a 'road map' to problematise change and continuity. *Teaching History 131*, 4-8.

Foster, R., & Gadd, S. (2013). Let's play Supermarket 'Evidential' Sweep: developing students' awareness of the need to select evidence. *Teaching History 152*, 25-9.

Foster, R., & Goudie, K. (2017). Cunning Plan . . . for developing an enquiry on the First Crusade. *Teaching History 166*, 16-19.

Fullard, G., Wheeley, T., & Fordham, M. (2011). Cunning plan 142: Why do historical interpretations change over time? *Teaching History 143*, 48-9.

Gentner, D., & Stevens, A. L. (1983). *Mental Models*. New York: Taylor & Francis Group.

Grande, J. (2022). Generic mentoring: challenges (and potential opportunities) of generic mentoring in ECT and ITT programmes. HTEN Conference. Online. https://sites.google.com/view/hten/home.

Haenen, J., & Schrijnemakers, H. (2000). Suffrage, feudal, democracy, treaty . . . history's building blocks: learning to teach historical concepts. *Teaching History 98*, 22-9.

Hammond, K. (2014). The knowledge that 'flavours' a claim. *Teaching History 157*, 18-24.

Harris, R. (2021). Disciplinary knowledge denied? In A. Chapman (ed.), *Knowing History in Schools* (pp. 97-128). London: UCL Press. doi: 10.14324/111.9781787357303

Head, S. (2020). 'That's just the tip of the iceberg': building Key Stage 5 students' analysis of interpretations in the short, medium and long term. *Teaching History 180*, 59-63.

Hill, M. (2020). Curating the imagined past: world building in the history curriculum. *Teaching History 1980*, 10-20.

Historical Association. (2019). What's the wisdom on evidence and sources? *Teaching History 176*, 21-5.

Historical Association. (2020). What's the wisdom on change and continuity? *Teaching History 179*, 50-3.

Historical Association. (2021). *Lesson sequence: The Normans – taster lesson*. Retrieved 4 March 2023 from The Historical Association: https://www.history.org.uk/secondary/resource/10044/lesson-sequence-the-normans-taster-lesson

Hobsbawm, E. J. (1973). *The Age of Revolution: Europe 1789-1848*. London: Cardinal.

Husbands, C., & Kitson, A. (2002). Cunning Plan for 'Black Peoples of America'. *Teaching History 107*, 65.

Körber, A. (2021). Historical consciousness, knowledge, and competencies of historical thinking: an integrated model of historical thinking and curricular implications. *Historical Encounters, 8(1)*, 97-119.

Kühberger, C. (2022). Historical learning using concept cartoons: engaging with pupils' prior conceptions. *Teaching History 186*, 62-73.

Laffin, D. (2019). Cunning plan 175: using the England's Immigrants database. *Teaching History 175*, 64-5.

Lee, P. (2005). Putting principles into practice: Understanding history. In S. Donovan & J. Bransford (eds.), *How Students Learn: History, Mathematics, and Science in the Classroom* (pp. 31-78). Washington, DC: National Academies Press.

Lee, P., & Shemilt, D. (2011). The concept that dares not speak its name: should empathy come out of the closet? *Teaching History 143*, 39-49.

Lévesque, S. (2008). *Thinking Historically: Educating Students for the Twenty-First Century*. Toronto: University of Toronto Press.

Lévesque, S. (2010). On historical literacy: Learning to think like historians. *Canadian Issues* (Winter 2010), 42-6. https://www.proquest.com/scholarly-journals/on-historical-literacy-learning-think-like/docview/1008913862/se-2

Low-Beer, A. (1989). Empathy and history. *Teaching History 55*, 8-12.

McDonough, F. (2012). *Hitler and the Rise of the Nazi Party*. London: Taylor & Francis Group.

Palek, D. (2015). 'What exactly is parliament?' Finding the place of substantive knowledge in history. *Teaching History 158*, 18-25.

Partington, G. (1980). *The Idea of an Historical Education*. Windsor: National Foundation for Education Research in England and Wales.

Phillips, R. (2002). Historical significance – the forgotten 'Key Element'? *Teaching History 106*, 14-19.

Riley, C. (1999). Evidential understanding, period knowledge and the development of literacy: a practical approach to 'layers of inference' for Key Stage 3. *Teaching History 97*, 6-12.

Riley, M. (2000). Into the Key Stage 3 history garden: choosing and planting your enquiry questions. *Teaching History 99*, 8-13.

Rodker, A. (2019). Cunning plan 174: creating a narrative of the interwar years. *Teaching History 174*, 16-17.

Rosch, E. (1983). Prototype classification and logical classification: the two systems. In E. K. Scholnick (ed.), *New Trends in Conceptual Representation: Challenges to Piaget's Theory* (pp. 73-86). Hillsdale, NJ: Lawrence Erlbaum Associates.

Schools History Project. (1976). *A New Look at History: Schools History 13-16 Project*. Retrieved 20 December 2022 from Schools History Project: http://www.schoolshistoryproject.co.uk/wp-content/uploads/2015/12/NewLookAtHistory.pdf

Seixas, P., & Morton, T. (2013). *The Big Six Historical Thinking Concepts*. Toronto: Nelson Education.

Snelson, H. (2021). Cunning Plan 183: Teaching a broader Britain, 1625-1714. *Teaching History 183*, 58-60.

Stephen, A. (2007). Cunning Plan 129: Why has there been so much interest in Mary I? *Teaching History 129*, 48-9.

Trapani, B. (2019). Who can tell us the most about the Silk Road? Historical scholarship, archaeology and evidence in Year 7. *Teaching History 177*, 58-67.

van Boxtel, C., & van Drie, J. (2018). Chapter 6 historical reasoning: conceptualizations and educational applications. In S. Metzger & L. Harris (eds.), *The Wiley International Handbook of History Teaching and Learning* (pp. 149-76). Hoboken, NJ: Wiley-Blackwell.

van Boxtel, C., & van Rijn, M. (2006). *Picturing Colligatory Concepts In History: Effects of Student-Generated Versus Presented Drawings*. Utrecht: Research Centre Learning in Interaction, Utrecht University, the Netherlands. Retrieved 21 December 2022 from https://citeseerx.ist.psu.edu/document?repid=rep1&type=pdf&doi=efd74c2f27c48e26a923daa84f434c08480c3e44

van Drie, J., & van Boxtel, C. (2003). Developing conceptual understanding through talk mapping. *Teaching History 110*, 27-31.

Woodcock, J. (2010). Chapter 10: causal explanation. In I. Davies (ed.), *Debates in History Teaching* (pp. 124-36). London: Routledge.

Worth, P. (2014). Cunning Plan: different interpretations of the First World War. *Teaching History 155*, 42-4.

4 Helping beginning history teachers to plan, deliver, and evaluate lessons

Victoria Crooks and Laura London

Introduction

Learning to plan and deliver effective history lessons is the core responsibility of a beginning history teacher. However, many beginning teachers enter their training with little understanding of the levels of preparation, or the scholarly engagement, required for this aspect of teaching. Much of the lesson-planning process happens 'behind the curtain' and to a casual observer, or even a pupil, it is an unseen part of a teacher's role.

It is vital that beginning teachers are supported to think carefully about the construction of their lessons and move past the idea of a lesson as a series of activities to be worked through. This chapter will address how mentors can help beginning teachers to plan purposeful history lessons. It will explore the importance of developing an understanding of curriculum coherence early on with beginning teachers. One way for beginning teachers to plan purposeful, coherent, and rigorous lesson sequences is by using enquiry questions to structure their planning. The chapter will therefore provide practical approaches for helping beginning teachers to look beyond lessons as discrete episodes and to plan coherent and intellectually intriguing historical enquiries.

Objectives

At the end of the chapter, you should be able to:

- Appreciate how a history teacher's understanding of the purposes of school history influences their approach to planning.
- Reflect on the role of historical enquiry and how it can be used by history teachers to reveal the historical process for pupils.
- Support beginning teachers to plan purposeful and coherent lesson sequences using historical enquiry questions.
- Identify approaches for supporting beginning teachers to plan for historical understanding.
- Understand the common misconceptions that arise around effective planning, especially as managing workload becomes an issue for beginning teachers.

- Support beginning teachers to assess pupils' historical learning.
- Assist beginning teachers to engage in reflection and evaluation that focusses on their pupils' learning, rather than their own actions in the classroom.

Purposes of school history

In the prologue to *What Is History, Now?* Helen Carr describes her 'way into history' via a childhood full of trips to historical sites and being gripped by historical films. She finishes this description by stating:

> This type of history excited me far more than the history that was offered at school, which I found strangely disappointing. School history didn't fit with my version of history. My history was more than facts and dates; it was the *feeling* of the past, the myth, the magic, the stuff we didn't know. (Carr & Lipscomb, 2021, p. 4)

In the early weeks of a teacher education programme, it is a fascinating exercise to ask beginning history teachers what they think the purposes of school history are and how they think they will achieve these purposes as a history teacher. It is even more fascinating to ask them this same question at the end of their programme as they reflect on how their views have changed. All beginning teachers come to their programme with preconceptions about teaching history, often influenced by their own experiences of education. However, many have never interrogated the varying purposes of *school* history before, nor have they thought about the implications of these different purposes for the way a curriculum is selected, constructed, and taught to pupils. These differing purposes may include viewing history as:

- A way of understanding who we are as a modern society.
- An opportunity to understand the best of what civilisation has thought and recorded for the sake of cultural transmission.
- A mechanism for forming a sense of national identity.
- A medium for understanding 'self' and our own personal historical origins.
- A vehicle for developing criticality and argumentation.
- A disciplinary framework for asking questions about the past.
- A body of substantive knowledge which should be valued for its own attributes.

(Haydn et al., 2014, pp. 18-19)

Grappling with why we are teaching history in schools and why we privilege certain aspects of history over others in our curriculum is essential for becoming a history teacher. Beginning teachers who do not consider the purposes of school history will struggle to understand the rationale for the history they are teaching and find it hard to identify what exactly pupils should be learning and understanding as an outcome of the curriculum. If beginning teachers do not consider what is valuable about the history that they are teaching, lessons can become little more than the 'facts and dates' of Carr's school history experience (Carr & Lipscomb, 2021).

Revealing the principles of planning

Understanding the historical purpose of a lesson is key to the planning process. Rachel Foster (2020) captures this idea in her analogy comparing the crafting of lessons to that of writing a book. For an author, having a strong sense of the overall plot and characterisation of a book is vital. Before they begin to write each chapter, they need to know which characters and plot threads have already been introduced, how and when they will reappear, and which new figures and storylines the reader is yet to encounter (Foster, 2020).

For beginning teachers planning their first lessons, this notion of the bigger picture can seem like an unnecessary distraction. In those early stages of lesson planning, beginning teachers tend to focus more upon their own teaching performance than the pupils' learning. Consequently, lesson planning is often reduced to simply designing enough tasks to occupy pupils for the coming hour. But planning for pupils' learning requires an understanding of the overarching rationale of the lesson sequence. As with the writing of a book, then, history teachers need to have a sense of the endgame. They need to understand how this element of a pupil's history education will contribute to the whole. They need to be able to identify, with clarity and precision, *what* the pupils need to know and *why*, not just in that moment, but in the longer term.

The process by which experienced teachers make decisions about what and why to teach certain aspects of historical knowledge, privileging them over others, can feel confusing and mysterious to beginning teachers. It is therefore no wonder that they tend to concentrate on the *how*, which is most visible in the classroom, when they observe more experienced colleagues. Counsell (2000) refers to the 'tacit criteria' behind the 'professional reasoning [that] gives a clearer rationale for choice and order of content components, micro and macro and short and long-term time-scales' (p. 66). Mentors therefore need to create opportunities to make these 'tacit criteria' explicit to beginning teachers. Task 4.1 outlines practical opportunities for mentors and their mentees to explore the relationship between historical rationale and planning.

Task 4.1 Practical approaches to support beginning teachers to understand the interplay between historical rationale and planning

Help your mentee to develop their understanding of planning by doing the following:

Joint planning with experienced colleagues

Beginning teachers will benefit from mentors who can model for them the careful thought processes and 'professional wrestling' (Riley & Byrom, 2008) required to plan historical enquiries. It is also helpful for beginning teachers to observe and collaborate to practically realise an enquiry's rationale through individual lessons (Crooks, 2020).

Joint planning a short sequence in its entirety provides a helpful opportunity for mentors to make explicit their decisions about what substantive knowledge to include or the choice of disciplinary concepts.

Whispered observation

A whispered observation, where the mentor sits alongside their mentee while observing another colleague and narrates what is happening, is a helpful technique for giving beginning teachers an insight into the bigger picture around a lesson.

- **Prior to the lesson** it is important that the beginning teacher has familiarised themselves with the objectives of the lesson sequence or scheme of work.
- **During the lesson** the mentor deliberately identifies and 'unpacks' the decision-making behind the lesson sequence or scheme of work. For example, they help the beginning teacher to see where certain subject knowledge is introduced for the sake of wider objectives that go beyond this specific lesson.
- **After the lesson,** return to the scheme of work to reflect on how the rationale for both the specific lesson and the bigger picture was achieved.

Beginning teachers can often see the planning process as a time-consuming diversion from the real business of teaching pupils in classrooms. This is not helped by the fact that so much of the planning undertaken by experienced teachers inevitably happens off stage. Joint planning and whispered observations help to reveal the value, and ultimately the joy, of the planning process. Beginning teachers need help to grasp that planning, even if an increasingly internalised process for experienced teachers, is something all teachers must engage with. Critically at the start of their teaching career, beginning teachers need to understand that externalising their patterns of thinking, via detailed written plans, allows them to identify and plan for the key components of an effective history lesson. It also supports them to identify the patterns of thinking implicit in the lesson planning of experienced colleagues whom they observe (Bourdillon & Storey, 2002, p. 89).

Supporting beginning teachers to plan using enquiry questions

Why do history teachers plan using enquiry questions?

Asking meaningful and important questions about historical evidence is a foundational practice of the academic historian. Popularised as an approach to structuring sequences of lessons by the Schools History Project (SHP) textbook series in the 1990s (Harris, Burn, & Woolley, 2013), the purpose and careful design of historical enquiry questions was explored by Michael Riley (2000) in a seminal article published in *Teaching History*. While an enquiry question is a pedagogical tool that is used by a history teacher, rather than a historian, Riley illustrated how enquiry questions can be used to develop coherent historical understanding across Key Stage 3 (11-14 years). Riley also showed how a good enquiry question can provide a means for driving the assessment of historical learning across a sequence of lessons.

In Riley's conceptualisation, good historical enquiry questions should have three key features when utilised in the classroom. He asks teachers to consider the following.

> 'Does each of your enquiry questions:
> - capture the interest and imagination of your pupils?
> - place an aspect of historical thinking, concept or process at the forefront of the pupils' minds?
> - result in a tangible, lively, substantial, enjoyable 'outcome activity' (i.e., at the end of the lesson sequence) through which pupils can genuinely answer the enquiry question?'
>
> (Riley, 2000, p. 8)

Thinking at the level of sequences of learning can, in some cases, be a step too far in the very earliest stages of a beginning teacher's development. However, introducing the idea of planning via enquiry questions at the start of a beginning teacher's education helps them to avoid seeing history lessons purely as a vehicle for memorising historical facts. Instead, early awareness of historical enquiry allows the beginning teacher to see how teachers 'deconstruct' the historical process. It helps to reveal the ways teachers make aspects of the historical thinking undertaken by historians accessible for pupils. In this way, beginning teachers start to see how lesson sequences can be structured to be knowledge (rather than information) rich. This also supports beginning teachers to notice how this careful, systematic, and cumulative building of knowledge is achieved in practice during their observations of experienced colleagues (see Chapter 6).

How do teachers design good enquiry questions?

Beginning teachers should understand that good historical enquiry questions:

- Help to reveal something of the historical process to pupils.
- Make it clear that the substantive knowledge presented in a historian's work is always understood through a disciplinary lens.
- Show that historical understanding is contested and continuously evolving, as new evidence comes to light or new ways of thinking emerge.
- Help to prevent the ahistorical presentation of history as a received and immutable 'story of the past'.
- Are a useful, and disciplinary relevant, tool for history teacher seeking to shape historical learning in the classroom.

One of the most difficult aspects of forming an enquiry question is the challenge of ensuring it is a good enquiry question. Beginning teachers need to be taught to 'sniff out' weak or even ahistorical enquiry questions. They need support to understand that a question like 'What was life like in the [medieval] town?' is just not as historically interesting or rigorous as a question such as 'How much did towns matter in the Middle Ages?' (Riley, 2000, pp. 8-10). They also need to understand that different questions serve different historical purposes and that some substantive foci lend themselves more readily to certain types of question than others.

What are the challenges of enquiry questions for beginning teachers?

1. **Early stage beginning teachers are not always ready to plan a sequence of lessons.**
   Beginning teachers initially find enquiry questions challenging to formulate and apply to their own planning. This means that the process of designing enquiry questions needs to be built deliberately, incrementally, and progressively throughout the mentoring period. If planning in sequences is initially beyond your mentee, then planning individual lesson enquiries can be an entry point into using enquiry questions to support planning.

2. **Beginning teachers might see planning using enquiry questions as another 'thing' to do.**
   Helping beginning teachers to recognise the value of planning enquiry sequences is also key to reducing their workload in the longer term; for example, resources created for a sequence can be used across lessons as the enquiry evolves. However, importantly, enquiry questions will need to be frequently revisited to ensure they are being used to ask relevant historical questions that capture the most recent academic scholarship or reflect our changing context. For an example of how this can be achieved, read Hibbert and Patel's brilliant *Teaching History* article 'Modelling the discipline: how can Yasmin Khan's use of evidence enable us to teach a more global World War II?' (Hibbert & Patel, 2019).

3. **Beginning teachers can view enquiry questions solely as an opportunity to convey substantive knowledge.**
   A way to avoid enquiry questions being little more than a vehicle for comprehension of substantive knowledge (a commonly seen example of this is 'What happened in 1066?'), is to ensure that beginning teachers understand that conceptual thinking is at the heart of enquiry question design. This could take the form of a first-order substantive concept driving the enquiry question, for example 'How revolutionary was the 18th century?', or a second-order disciplinary concept, such as 'How did the Tudors change England after 1485?' (change and continuity).

4. **Beginning teachers can find identifying and applying a conceptual focus to enquiry questions incredibly difficult.**
   The disciplinary concepts, which help to reveal how historians problematise and employ substantive knowledge to answer historical questions, will have underpinned their own academic historical work but will potentially have remained largely implicit during their undergraduate study. This means that the form and function of questions involving second-order disciplinary concepts needs to be explored. This could involve assessing several different options for enquiry questions to consider what historical thinking is involved for pupils and how this might be assessed. Task 4.2 provides some ideas for how to do this with your mentee.

Task 4.2 Identifying and generating effective enquiry questions

Use a mentor meeting to explore the power of different enquiry questions.

- Look at the enquiry question from the department scheme of work and explain the evolution of that question, sharing how changing particular words shifted the emphasis of the enquiry. For example, the following questions all have the same substantive topic focus but the difference in wording results in different emphases:

Enquiry question	Historical conceptual focus
What were the consequences of the Norman Conquest?	Consequence
Did the Normans transform England? (Brown & Burnham, 2014, p. 11)	Change and continuity (and consequence)
Why have different people told different stories about the Norman Conquest?	Interpretation and evidential thinking (and consequence)

- Select a substantive focus and, with the beginning teacher, generate possible enquiry questions. Ask them to analyse and rank these questions to identify the most effective enquiry question that would meet Riley's three criteria: creating intrigue, and asking a question which is historically meaningful and leads to a tangible outcome (2000, p. 8).

For example:

Enquiry question	Historical conceptual focus	Tangible outcome	Intrigue, historically meaningful, tangible?
Who was George Africanus?	?	Narrative description of George Africanus' life.	Although there is a clear answer to this question, it is purely based around the acquisition of substantive knowledge and doesn't require pupils to engage in historical thinking.
How typical was George Africanus in C18th Britain?	Similarity and difference.	Comparison of experiences of different groups in C18th society leading to reasoned judgement, supported with evidence.	Meaningful question, but the outcome task is very challenging in most contexts because of the breadth of understanding about C18th Britain and enslavement in this period that would be required to answer it.

Enquiry question	Historical conceptual focus	Tangible outcome	Intrigue, historically meaningful, tangible?
What can George Africanus reveal about C18th Nottingham?	Evidential enquiry, historical significance.	Reasoned judgement, supported with evidence.	A question which generates intrigue by providing a local perspective. Involves evidential enquiry and develops disciplinary thinking in relation to forming a substantiated judgement to answer the question.
Why is George Africanus remembered by the people of Nottingham?	Historical consciousness, historical significance.	Creation of a new green plaque, with an evidential rationale, based on development of a criteria for historical significance.	This question engages pupils by asking them to create a meaningful, tangible object and asks students to interact with public history.

Riley's (2000) article contains a list of questions on p. 11, designed by Counsell, to illustrate some the pitfalls around generating enquiries about the Treaty of Versailles, which may help you to explore this idea. Additionally, the Historical Association's *One Big History Department* has a crowd-sourced blog ('Ringing the changes: the power of enquiry questions that both chime and resonate') which shares a range of enquiry questions and may also provide stimulus for this activity (Richards, 2019).

Supporting beginning teachers to plan lessons that develop pupils' historical knowledge

Takeaways as the bedrock of planning

Ian Dawson developed the notion of 'takeaways' as a device for identifying the residue knowledge we intend pupils to remember long after the specific substantive knowledge of the lesson has been lost (Dawson, 2008). Beginning teachers most frequently approach planning challenges with a chronological mindset, which can result in pupils feeling that history lessons are simply just one thing after another with little purpose or meaning. Instead, Dawson (2021) asserts that 'takeaways are the bedrock of planning' and should be utilised to 'plan backwards' to reflect what you want to remain with pupils long after the specific details have faded; Dawson (2018) has clearly exemplified this in a list of possible takeaways for a Key Stage 3 medieval-period study.

The relationship between the takeaway – and 'fingertip' and 'residue' knowledge – and the development of a 'hinterland'

Takeaways are the 'understandings we want students to remember – to take away from their study of a topic, an enquiry, a period or from KS3 as a whole so they can be used again in later lessons during KS3 or at GCSE or on other occasions' (Dawson, 2021, p. 2). But what does this mean for the specific historical knowledge we want children to learn and remember? A key aspect of learning to plan is understanding the relationship between what Counsell refers to as 'fingertip' knowledge and 'residue' knowledge:

> The first might be called 'fingertip' knowledge. It is the kind of detail that one needs in ready memory and that is acquired through familiarity after extensive enquiry. It does not matter if much of the detail then falls away. The second type can be likened to the residue in a sieve ... It is also that loose, amorphous objective of 'a sense of period' – the retention of all manner of mental furniture, gleaned from a rich visual and active experience of period stories and scenes. (Counsell, 2000, p. 66)

Grande (2022b) has further explored this idea in his own classroom context by considering how these takeaways, this residue, can only be built through specific propositional knowledge to create a rich hinterland of historical knowledge which is vital for pupils' emerging historical understanding. Indeed, Smith (2014) concluded that the resulting sense of period is 'a precondition for historical analysis and explanation and is difficult to assess in isolation from other forms of historical knowledge and thinking' (p. 15). As Hammond (2014) clearly demonstrated, pupils who write confident, effective historical arguments typically look to 'period knowledge and to wider historical knowledge in order to create a context before focusing in on topic knowledge' (pp. 22-3). Beginning teachers need to understand how to plan and construct this hinterland or sense of period for their pupils. One way for them to develop this is by studying their department's wider curriculum. Their own subject knowledge is also vitally important. Beginning teachers need to develop their own historical subject knowledge to equip them 'to anticipate and decide which elements of the world to construct, refine, and expand at particular points in the curriculum' to build pupils' hinterland understanding of the 'secondary world' of the past' (Hill, 2020, p. 14).

Developing these more amorphous understandings of the past also poses yet another challenge. If developing this hinterland/ residue/ sense of period is so crucial, then how is it achieved? As Dawson (2009) wryly observed, 'I have never been taught to develop a sense of period. It seemingly happened while I wasn't looking' (p. 50). Frustratingly for beginning teachers, the answer is not simple. This kind of meaningful understanding of the bigger picture of the past is built through the sharing of stories and illustrations, rich and often seemingly tangential knowledge which adds depth and breadth to pupils' understanding. It involves exploring horizons wider than those indicated by the specification. The 'meanwhile, elsewhere' project (Bailey-Watson & Kennet, 2019) is one example of an approach history teachers can draw on to develop pupils' global and contextual understanding of specific topics. Engagement with narratives from historical scholarship and historical fiction also provides a source for immersive contextualisation that builds a rich sense of period for pupils, enabling them to exercise empathetic reasoning to make sense of specific substantive knowledge (Smith, 2014). However, while these elements contribute to developing pupils' hinterland knowledge, it is the careful planning of sequenced enquiries that, through the interplay of thematic and depth studies, enable pupils to develop a sense of distinctive periods, places, and people of the past (Dawson, 2009).

Task 4.3 allows beginning teachers to consider how takeaways can support their lesson planning.

Task 4.3 The takeaways test

Beginning teachers can find 'takeaways' difficult to conceptualise. One way to help them break through this barrier is to ask your mentee to apply the following tests to their lesson planning. This can help them identify their 'takeaways' from an individual lesson, sequence, or scheme of work.

The dinner table test

If a pupil is asked by a friend or carer over dinner what they learnt in history today, what would you (the beginning teacher) want them to say?
What is the essential knowledge or disciplinary process you would like them to identify?
Ask your mentee to complete these sentences to reflect this learning:

We've learnt about . . .
We've been learning how to . . .

The school holiday test

If during the school holidays a friend or relative asked a pupil what they had learnt in history that term, what would you (the beginning teacher) want them to say?
What bigger-picture connections would you hope that they could make?
Next year, what do you need pupils to know about X to be able to learn about Y? For example, what do you need the pupils to know and remember about monasteries in the Middle Ages before you teach them about the Reformation?

Reflection

Spend some time in a mentor meeting reflecting with the beginning teacher on how the dinner table and school holiday tests help to inform planning, providing the focus or 'purpose' for lessons or lesson sequences.

82 Victoria Crooks and Laura London

Structuring the planning process for your mentee

The role of subject knowledge in the planning process

At the very beginning of their training, beginning teachers are most concerned about the development of their subject knowledge. For history teachers this can feel like an especially daunting challenge due to the potential breadth and scope of the curriculum, the lack of a common core of substantive knowledge and the super-specialisation that is becoming much more typical at undergraduate level. If possible, providing beginning teachers with opportunities to capitalise on their subject-knowledge expertise in the early stages of their teaching experiences can be incredibly valuable. Teaching within their specialism helps to build a beginning teacher's confidence in their own practice by allowing them to place greater focus on running a room, resourcing, and enaction. It can also build their confidence in their relationships with the rest of the department.

Drawing on the expertise of a beginning teacher to enhance colleagues' understanding of recent scholarship to build a reading list, refresh resources, read together, or create a department library, will benefit the whole department. It also helps to demonstrate that subject-knowledge enhancement is a core aspect of continuing professional development. Early experiences of teaching within their subject-knowledge expertise can help to expose the limitations of taking a task-driven approach to lesson planning. It is key for

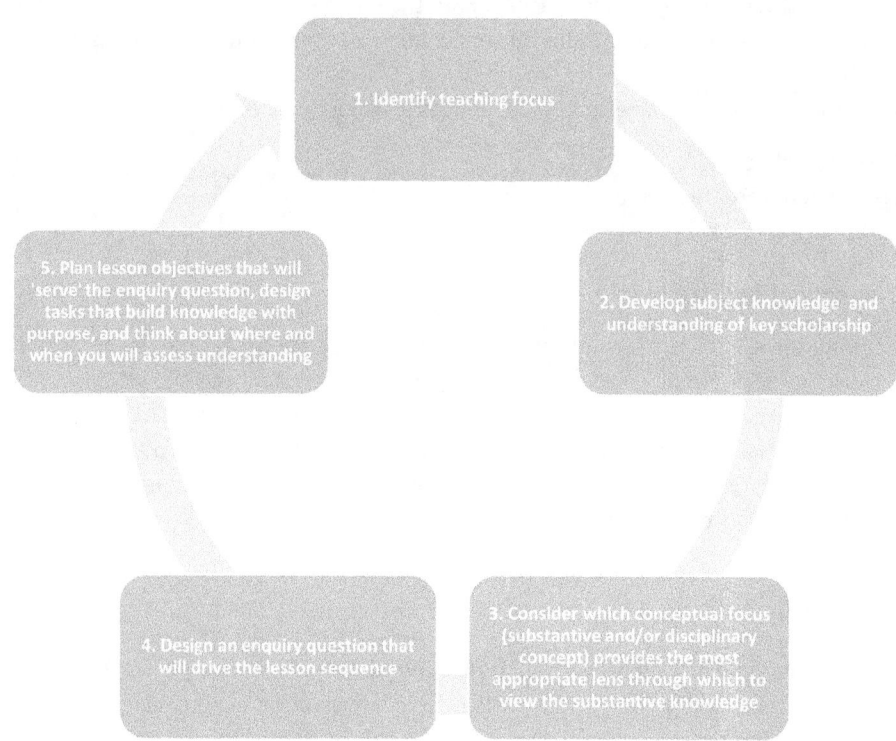

Figure 4.1 Staged process for planning shown as a continuing sequence of stages in a circular flow

beginning teachers to understand that, while the textbook might help us gain rapid entry-level understanding of topics, our aim should always be deeper engagement with the subject knowledge we require for teaching. Mentors can support their mentees to understand this interplay between secure subject knowledge and the increased effectiveness (and often efficiency) of lesson planning by modelling and encouraging them to adopt a staged process for planning lessons (Figure 4.1).

Planning individual lessons

Beginning teachers often feel frustrated by the need to complete lesson-planning documents – seeing them as a barrier to just getting on with the job of resourcing and delivering their lesson. However, the guided explicit articulation of the planning process, through the completion of a lesson-planning proforma, is a critical stage of the beginning teacher's development. Indeed, established teachers' instinctive, almost reflexive, approaches to planning, which fill beginning teachers with a degree of awe, have usually only been made possible because they were supported as early career teachers to lay down a pattern of thinking about their planning. An experienced teacher's brief notes or lesson outline are reflective of the 'accumulated professional knowledge and understanding that has gone into the preparation of that lesson' (Mutton, Hagger, and Burn, 2011, p. 412).

There are many different lesson-planning templates or proformas to help beginning teachers to structure their lessons. Ultimately, the selection of an appropriate planning method will be a matter of personal preference. However, what these planning proformas should have in common is a focus on what pupils need to learn and why they need to learn it. The rationale for the lesson(s), the sense of how this lesson or sequence fits into the bigger picture, the ways conceptual and disciplinary understanding will be built, and the desired takeaways from the learning all need to be central to the planning process. Only once these aspects have been identified and articulated should the how of the lesson be determined.

Task 4.4 Supporting beginning teachers to see their lesson plan as a 'working document'

Review a selection of lesson-planning proformas with your mentee. Evaluate the strengths and limitations of these proformas using the following questions. Does the proforma:

- include an opportunity to show how historical knowledge will be built in the lesson?
- provide an opportunity to demonstrate a clear historical rationale for the lesson?
- show where this lesson fits within the 'bigger picture' and allow for links with previous and future teaching?
- provide an opportunity to show how misconceptions can be addressed and how the lesson can be adapted for the needs of a specific class in advance?
- allow for any flexibility over timings and adaptations that need to be made within the lesson?

One way of supporting beginning teachers to plan sequences of lessons is to encourage them to view planning as a circular rather than linear process (see Figure 4.2). This conveys the need for enquiries to provide pupils with both a sense of direction, and the necessary coherence to understand the relationship between lessons within a sequence of learning. It places the enquiry question firmly at the centre of the planning and requires the beginning teacher to consider its relationship to the enquiry outcome, an outcome which should be tangible and purposeful. It then asks them to 'work outwards' from the enquiry question to identify the lesson takeaways and outcomes. Only once these elements have been determined should the beginning teacher move onto selecting the most appropriate teaching methods and tasks to achieve these objectives.

A worked example of the planning process: Why is George Africanus remembered? (significance enquiry)

This enquiry (shown in Figure 4.2) asks pupils to consider the life of George Africanus, an eighteenth-century enslaved person who became Nottingham's first black entrepreneur, establishing an employment agency: Africanus' Register of Servants. It draws on resources developed by the University of Nottingham in collaboration with Nottingham City Council and hosted by Nottingham City Museums: https://nottinghammuseums.org.uk/leaders-in-the-community-george-africanus/

The enquiry asks pupils to interact with public history, considering how this person of great local, and arguably national, significance has been remembered. It can be assumed that pupils have already completed significance enquiries. They now develop their understanding

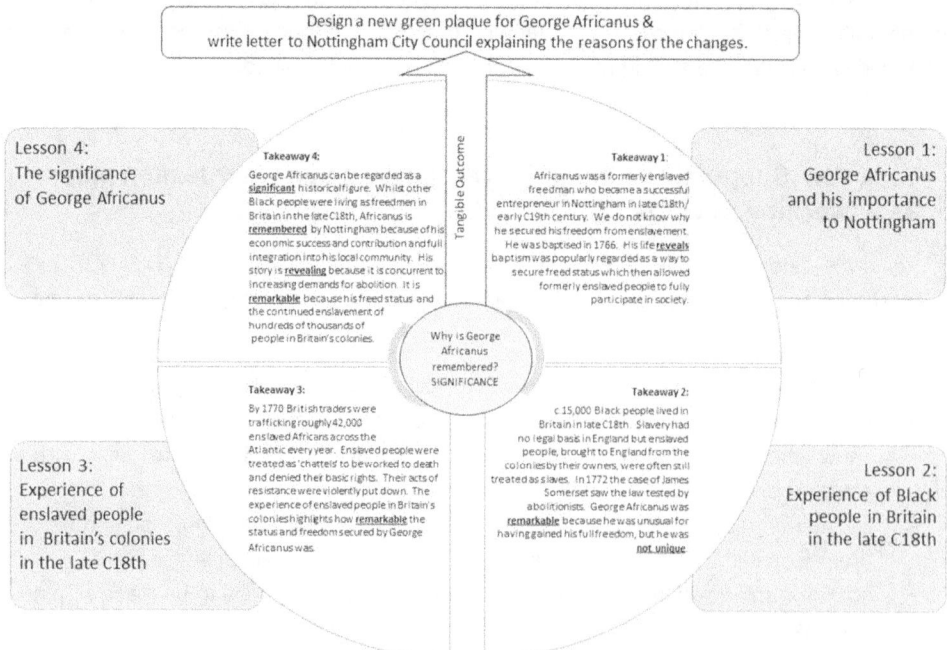

Figure 4.2 A worked example of circular planning for the George Africanus enquiry

of additional criteria for historical significance through setting Africanus' life in the context of the period by considering the experiences of other black people, both freed and enslaved, at the time. Pupils then use this understanding of Africanus' historical significance to create a new green plaque for Nottingham City Council and justify the need for the change to the current green plaque.

This example uses one enquiry question which drives the learning across all four lessons within the enquiry. In some school contexts, enquiries are also created with an overarching question comprised of lessons which have their own individual lesson sub-questions. Where individual lesson enquiry questions are used, it is important they serve the overarching enquiry question and guide the learners to form an answer to the overall enquiry; 'pupils need to be able to explain how tackling any particular lesson question will contribute to the final outcome on which the sequence is focussed' (Historical Association, 2020). In her *Teaching History* article 'Here ends the lesson: shaping lesson conclusions as an iterative process in improving historical enquiries', Worth (2018) explores how lesson endings can do just this, by providing opportunities for pupils to assess how their new learning from the lesson can be used to help answer the enquiry question.

However, it is important to recognise that departments plan differently, with many departments using historical questions to shape whole units of study and/or planning using individual lesson questions. Your mentee will need to adapt to their department's approach and can still benefit from devising individual lesson questions, as this process will allow them to engage and interest their pupils, while also homing in on an aspect (or aspects) of historical learning in the lesson.

Selecting the appropriate pedagogy

Beginning teachers tend to fall into tried-and-tested patterns in their choice of pedagogical approach; once they discover a toolkit of tasks that seem to work (for example, reading comprehension questions, labelling a source, completing a table with information from the textbook), they often stick with them. They can also struggle to distinguish between high-value and low-value tasks. Word searches or copying from the board could be considered lower value activities (Haydn & Stephen, 2022). Experienced teachers can of course fall into similar traps; however, experienced colleagues also possess a much larger toolkit of potential approaches and a much firmer grasp of the conditions in which different tools might be appropriately deployed. They also understand that a varied approach can stimulate pupils' motivation for learning (Hall, 2021). Grasping the relationship between the selection of appropriate pedagogies and intended outcomes is therefore an important part of a beginning teacher's development (Haydn & Stephen, 2022). Having a firm grasp of the rationale for the enquiry and the takeaways also makes the selection of these pedagogical approaches much easier and more effective.

For example, 'Do Now' retrieval practice tasks have become common place in classrooms with the popularisation of Rosenshine's 'Principles of Instruction' (Sherrington, 2019; Lemov, 2021). There are many obvious benefits to having children retrieve their substantive subject knowledge regularly. However, some schools' interpretation of this approach overlooks the needs of specific subjects. In history this can mean beginning teachers employing retrieval practice activities involving the recall of information that are divorced from a meaningful context and done with no real sense of historical purpose (Whitburn, 2022). This kind of approach can result in pupils viewing history as simply furnishing them with knowledge for 'quizzes and game-shows' (Haydn & Harris, 2010, p. 249). It also necessitates supporting beginning teachers to understand how retrieval practice can help achieve the lesson purpose. For example, in history it might be that more meaningful retrieval can be achieved through approaches such as the use of initial stimulus material (Phillips, 2001), and that this could also help beginning teachers to simultaneously cultivate intrigue and create the vital 'hook' into the lesson (Riley, 2000). Likewise, blank timelines could be annotated at the beginning of a lesson to retrieve and secure the chronological understanding needed for pupils to access the rest of the lesson.

Card-sorting methods are sometimes derided as time-consuming, with little impact upon pupil learning. This can certainly be the case if the task simply involves knowledge acquisition or the one-time categorisation of factors – in this situation other methods, such as simple colour-coding, are often more appropriate. However, card sorts can be highly effective when used to allow pupils to wrestle with a problem and to visually arrange (and rearrange) this knowledge to reveal their evolving thinking as their ideas are challenged (Counsell, 2004). Consequently, if the lesson rationale requires pupils to wrestle with the marshalling of knowledge and the construction of argument and counterargument in response to an enquiry question, or if the intention is to reveal the 'agency [pupils], and historians, have in constructing a causal argument' (Grande, 2022a), the need to select a card sort becomes evident. When beginning teachers understand this relationship between pedagogical choice and learning intention, they can make more efficient and effective planning choices. One way to support beginning teachers to do this is to provide them with opportunities for observation of, and post-lesson discussions with, experienced colleagues; these sessions should be focused on pedagogical decisions and take place throughout the training programme and in their first and second year of teaching.

Planning using existing resources

Mentors often seek to reduce the workload burden of beginning teachers by asking them to teach from established lessons, departmental resources, and schemes of work (DfE, 2018). Most mentors take the decision to share department resources with their mentees. This seems the most sensible (and kind) option; however, as a note of caution, many departments' shared resource drives have been created over several years, by many busy teachers, with different levels of experience. Therefore, your shared drive may not be an exemplar of carefully curated best practice (whose is?). Beginning teachers sometimes find it hard to distinguish between resources of varying quality and, if this is the case for your mentee, some time with them navigating shared resources would be well spent.

Mentors can sometimes find themselves confused as to why the beginning teacher is struggling with their lesson planning and why it is taking them so long to plan lessons for which they have already had resources provided. In fact, planning from an established resource is still a complex process for a beginning teacher. While beginning teachers should never be made to 'reinvent the wheel' purely for the sake of it, 'off-the-shelf' lessons present a different kind of challenge for the novice, especially if the thinking or rationale is not articulated in a plan and is simply manifested as a PowerPoint presentation or resource. If

Planning, delivering, and evaluating lessons 87

Task 4.5 Modelling planning from an existing departmental plan or resource

Supporting a beginning teacher to plan from existing departmental materials is an important stage in their planning development. It requires a mentor to make their own planning process visible for the beginning teacher and to help them understand what is required when planning for teaching and learning in this context. Mentors can therefore support their mentee by engaging in a reflective planning approach such as this:

> Select an existing departmental plan and resource for a lesson both you and your mentee will teach the following week.

⬇

> Model for your mentee the process of understanding the plan and resource and identifying the subject knowledge required to teach the lesson. Then consider how to best apply this for your own class context – use this opportunity to also explore how class data and information about SEND needs, for example, informs your thinking.

⬇

> With your mentee complete the lesson plan pro-forma from their training provider for your class, demonstrating how you use the department resources as a springboard into your own lesson planning process. Be explicit about identifying the rationale/learning objectives and planning for the needs of your class.

⬇

> Get your mentee to observe you teaching that class, noting where you put the emphasis on the subject knowledge, the kinds of questions you ask to develop and check for understanding, how you adapted and diverged from the departmental resource due to your class context.

⬇

> Ask your mentee to now plan the same lesson, using the same resource for their own class. Observe them teaching the group and/or film them teaching.

⬇

> Engage in a post-lesson reflective discussion which explore what they have learned about taking these 'off the shelf' resources and putting them into action with a group.

not mediated by the mentor, these resources can result in the beginning teacher viewing the lesson as a series of tasks to be completed, rather than as a carefully crafted sequence of activities with the intention of promoting specific aspects of historical thinking. Beginning teachers do not always understand the role of class context in the creation of such a lesson and therefore do not sufficiently consider the needs and context of their own teaching groups. Moreover, when they have scant idea of the purpose of the lesson within the sequence or enquiry, or of the pupils for whom the lesson was designed in the first place, beginning teachers are often more reluctant to make changes or adaptations to their lessons despite the formative feedback they receive from pupils in the lesson itself.

Equally, because the ways that established teachers plan to use these kinds of resources is often an internalised thought process and undertaken beyond the gaze of the mentee, it is easy to understand why beginning teachers sometimes think you can simply open the PowerPoint and teach. Helping beginning teachers to navigate these poor proxies for planning is therefore just as important as teaching them to plan from scratch. Task 4.5 helps you to explore with your mentee planning from existing departmental plans or resources.

Planning for assessment

Beginning teachers often find the distinction between formative assessment and summative assessment confusing. Indeed, the relationship between the two is a bit messy. At its best, assessment helps to provide a necessary sense of direction and purpose within a lesson or sequence of lessons. At its worst, when summative assessment becomes too dominant a feature, lessons can simply become an exercise in teaching to the test. One benefit of the circular planning method is that it clarifies both the stage-posts that need to be reached on the way to answering the enquiry question and the purpose of the outcome task as an opportunity to provide a tangible answer to the coherent enquiry (Riley, 2000; Brown & Burnham, 2014).

Formative assessment

Establishing at the start of the process what the key takeaways are that pupils need to secure at each stage of the enquiry makes it easier to design and implement effective formative assessment. That is not to say that this is a simple process. It is important to remember that these takeaways will vary depending on the pupils' pre-existing schema and interpretation of what has been taught (Fordham, 2017). Regular and informal checking for what pupils know and understand (Grande, 2022c) can help the teacher diagnose and address misconceptions and inform their adaptive teaching decisions. It also reveals to pupils the aspects of their knowledge and understanding that need development. Beginning teachers need to observe and try out a wide variety of approaches for checking understanding. This helps them to avoid the tendency to find the one approach they feel comfortable with and stick with it regardless. There are many ways of checking for understanding at a whole-class level, but examples of some methods include:

- Whole-class targeted questioning to sample the attainment range.
- Posing hinge questions which help both the teacher and pupils to identify if they are ready to move on in the learning.
- Mini-whiteboards to reveal the thinking and understanding of all pupils.
- True/false or multiple-choice questions.
- Analysis of a written or visual source which requires pupils to draw on a summary of their learning in the lesson.
- Analysis of a model written response to a question and adding supporting examples or knowledge to develop it further.

- Judgement lines completed individually in books, as a whole class creating a physical line, or placing Post-it notes on a line relative to their judgement.
- Think, pair, share feedback and questioning.
- Whole-class voting.
- Exit tickets between lessons in a sequence.

Summative assessment

Summative assessments are often used to assess what has been learnt by the end of a scheme of work incorporating several enquiries. The data created by a summative assessment often fulfils competing purposes. Unlike formative assessment, the information resulting from summative assessment often has a wider audience than the teacher and the pupil themselves. Summative judgements usually produce data which can be of interest to senior leadership, parents, recipients of pupils' next-steps applications and the government. These considerations lead to the pressure for summative assessments to produce quantitative and trackable data, and in many schools have resulted in a greater focus on exam-style questions (including at Key Stage 3) rather than on supporting pupils to reveal their mastery of historical understanding and expression (Counsell, 2021). Planning for summative assessment should be rooted in principles for assessing pupils' historical learning, rather than assessment designed simply to serve whole school assessment and reporting policies. Pupils' progress in history is not straightforward, and data that tracks pupils' attainment through assessments, which are focused on different aspects of historical thinking, is very unlikely to capture this complexity. It is important that your mentee understands these tensions and recognises that they might not always wholeheartedly agree with their school or department assessment policy. Ultimately, at this stage of their career your mentee is unlikely to be able to do anything about this. However, recognising these tensions and asking questions about assessment in the safety of a mentor meeting will support them to make future decisions about summative assessment as their career progresses.

Summative assessment tasks can include:

- Oral outcomes – for example, engaging in a debate, giving a presentation or recording a podcast.
- Written outcomes – for example, a review of a piece of scholarship, a blog, a piece of historical fiction, a letter to an historian, responses to examination questions.
- Visual/experiential outcomes – for example, a documentary film, a computer game, or a museum of material culture (Riley, 2019).

Effective assessment also requires planning for the mark scheme that will be applied to any summative task. Brown and Burnham (2014) have written convincingly about the need for task-specific mark schemes which act as 'professional tools' for teachers to 'judge progress and to inform the feedback' (p. 14), rather than being atomised into components shared with pupils and to be ticked off as success criteria are met.

It is not unusual for beginning teachers to have little grasp of the role of summative assessment beyond preparation for examinations, especially in contexts where they are required to fit their planning around the summative assessment framework that already exists in a department. Consequently, mentors need to make opportunities to explicitly unpack the decision-making around assessment design and the creation of mark schemes, just as much as they provide opportunities to engage in marking and moderation of these summative outcomes. It is important that beginning teachers understand that such summative assessments also have formative uses. For example, when pupils receive and act on summative feedback, or assessments are used by the teacher to inform adaptations to their planning for the next time they teach this enquiry or lesson sequence, summative assessment acquires a formative purpose. Task 4.6 explores how mentors can support beginning teachers to develop their understanding of assessment.

Task 4.6 Supporting beginning teachers with assessment

Select an example of a Key Stage 3 assessment task and identify a sample of pupil responses which can be compared with Key Stage 4 and Key Stage 5 assessment pieces.

- Discuss what 'mastery' in history looks like. What is the end goal for pupils' historical understanding by the time they get to Key Stage 5? Work back and consider what desired outcomes might look like by the end of each key stage.
- Look at the assessment sample. How do the tasks differ? What is similar? Can you identify how opportunities are created for pupils to demonstrate progression in their historical understanding? Consider how disciplinary conceptual understanding is interpreted in the examination assessment framework. What implications, if any, does this have for Key Stage 3 teaching in your context?
- Explore the mark scheme and consider how generic marking criteria can make assessment complicated and how task-specific mark schemes are created and used.
- Undertake some reading around assessment in history specifically. 'What's the wisdom on ... history assessment' in *Teaching History* 185 (Historical Association, 2021) is a good place to begin exploring the literature.

Evaluating lessons

In the initial stages of learning to teach, beginning teachers are most concerned with their own performance as teachers. Gradually, as they become more confident in the planning and delivery of lessons, beginning teachers become more attuned to what pupils have learnt and understood from the lesson. Helping beginning teachers to evaluate their lessons effectively should reflect this development, so that lesson evaluations are useful, prevented from becoming formulaic, and support beginning teachers to improve the quality of both teaching *and* learning.

During their teacher-training programme, beginning teachers should therefore be encouraged to undertake evaluations of different types and lengths (Table 4.1) to achieve these different purposes.

Table 4.1 Approaches to lesson evaluations

Evaluation type	Purpose of the evaluation	Approach to the evaluation	Potential benefits/pitfalls
Immediate post-lesson evaluation.	To identify the strengths of the lesson and obvious development points.	Quick two-column table on the bottom of the lesson plan where immediate reflections are recorded.	Increases ease and therefore regularity of reflection, but often results in a focus only on the performative teaching aspects of the lesson.
Lesson plan annotation.	To evaluate the effectiveness of the lesson tasks, pupil engagement, and 'flow'.	Marking up different sections/ elements of the lesson plan with annotations (in a different colour) to note adaptations which evaluation suggests would have enabled the lesson to be more effective.	Increases ease and therefore regularity of reflection; especially helpful if the plan is to be retaught to a parallel group, but can skew the focus onto the 'logistics' of the lesson – instruction giving, pace, etc.
Detailed self-evaluation.	Selecting one lesson in a sequence, or one lesson each week to probe the planning, enaction, and pupil outcomes from that lesson.	Targeted evaluation of the lesson through reflection upon a series of more focused and precise questions such as: • How did the plan translate into the enaction of the lesson? • How effective was the enquiry question? Did the pupils develop new understanding from this lesson which supported them to answer the enquiry question? • How did the lesson add to pupils' understanding of the second-order conceptual focus? • What were pupils' key takeaways from the lesson? How was pupil understanding checked and acted upon in the lesson? • Were there any misconceptions arising in the lesson or in pupil work? • Did all pupils make progress in their understanding? Were pupils supported or hindered by the lesson structure? Was scaffolding provided for pupils in the right places in the lesson? For those pupils who grasped the key takeaways quickly, was sufficient challenge provided in the lesson? How can that be improved? • Was the classroom managed effectively? • Were pupils invested in their learning? • How should this reflection affect the planning for next lesson?	Increases focus upon pupil learning and the effectiveness of the lesson for developing pupils' historical understanding – especially if there is a keen focus on the curricular object. However, beginning teachers often need to be persuaded of the value of these deep evaluations as they take time and do not appear to yield immediate tangible benefits. Selecting a particular focus for the evaluation can also be beneficial, but requires confidence and insight to select the most helpful foci.

(continued)

Table 4.1 Cont.

Evaluation type	Purpose of the evaluation	Approach to the evaluation	Potential benefits/pitfalls
Work scrutiny.	Pupil work from the lesson or sequence is scrutinised to evaluate whether the intended learning has translated into pupil understanding.	Taking a sample of pupil work from across the attainment range – both the focused outcome tasks and the preparation work leading to those outcomes – to analyse how pupils have approached the tasks, the rate of completion in each task, and the quality of the tangible outcomes to consider how far the lesson or enquiry rationale has been achieved.	Moves the focus of the reflection onto the pupils and their outcomes. Allows for the learning of all to be considered and provides formative feedback for re-teaching and future planning. However, this type of evaluation can lead to focus on written outcomes rather than the historical thinking that was taking place in the lesson.
Self-observation.	Identifying critical episodes from the lesson which impacted upon pupil learning.	Filming the lesson and watching it back while completing a 'self-observation' before identifying three or four critical moments in the lesson which seemed to change the course of the lesson for better or worse. This might include clarity of teacher explanations, modelling, pupil engagement, or the construction of historical thinking and reasoning (Gestsdóttir, van Boxtel, & van Drie, 2018; Crooks, 2022).	An incredibly revealing activity if used strategically. Enables the beginning teacher to reflect with greater objectivity. However, this approach is time-consuming and viewing oneself on film can be a distraction.

Summary and key points

- Exploring the purposes of school history with your mentee will support them to plan meaningful and rigorous lessons focused on pupils' historical learning.
- Allowing mentees to teach within their historical specialism can help to build their confidence and support them to recognise the importance of continual subject-knowledge enhancement.
- Beginning teachers need to understand the rationale of lesson sequences to appreciate how pupils' historical understanding develops in the longer term. It is important that beginning teachers understand where lessons 'fit' in the bigger picture.
- Discussing and designing enquiry questions with your mentee can support them to understand how pupils' historical knowledge and understanding is built.
- Mentors can support their mentees to plan effectively by modelling lesson-planning decision-making. If this is not made explicit to beginning teachers, it can be difficult for them to understand the complexity of lesson planning.
- Taking a staged approach to planning, with a focus on knowledge takeaways, can help beginning teachers to plan effectively.
- Beginning teachers will need support to integrate formative and summative assessment into their planning.
- Beginning teachers will need guidance from their mentors to meaningfully evaluate their lessons and focus on pupils' learning rather than their teaching performance.

Further reading and resources

- **Section 2.3 Classroom Practice** from the Historical Association's website section for Beginning Teachers, available here: www.history.org.uk/secondary/module/8763/teaching-for-beginners/10251/23-history-classroom-practice

  This section of the Historical Association's Beginning Teacher resources is a very useful starting point for mentors looking for further advice and resources to support beginning teachers' lesson planning.
- **Thinking History** available at: https://thinkinghistory.co.uk

  This website provides history teachers with detailed descriptions and activities for a wide range of historical topics. It affords an excellent opportunity for mentees to reflect on their pedagogical decisions and broaden their repertoire of activities.

References

Bailey-Watson, W., & Kennet, R. (2019). 'meanwhile, elsewhere...': Harnessing the power of community to expand students' historical horizons. *Teaching History 176*, 36–43.

Bourdillon, H., & Storey, A. (2002). *Aspects of Teaching and Learning in Secondary Schools: Perspectives on Practice.* London: Routledge.

Brown, G., & Burnham, S. (2014). Assessment after levels. *Teaching History 157*, 8–17.

Carr, H., & Lipscomb, S. (2021). *What Is History, Now?* London: Weidenfeld & Nicolson.

Counsell, C. (2000). Historical knowledge and historical skills: A distracting dichotomy. In J. Arthur & R. Phillips (eds.), *Issues in History Teaching* (pp. 54–71). London: Taylor & Francis Group.

Counsell, C. (2004). *History and Literacy in Year 7, History in Practice.* London: Hodder Murray. Retrieved 12 October 2022 from https://www.hoddereducation.co.uk/media/Documents/History%20Community/History%20and%20Literacy%20in%20Y7/history_literacy_y7.pdf

Counsell, C. (2021). History. In A. S. Cuthbert & A. Standish (eds.), *What Should Schools Teach?* (pp. 154-73). London: UCL Press.

Crooks, V. (2020). The many faces of lesson planning Part 2 of 2. Retrieved from *Becoming a History Teacher*, https://uonhistoryteachertraining.school.blog/2020/02/09/the-many-faces-of-lesson-planning-part-2-of-2/

Crooks, V. (2022). What am I meant to be looking for? Supporting beginning teachers to undertake effective observations of other teachers. Retrieved from *Becoming a History Teacher*, http://uonhistoryteachertraining.school.blog/2022/10/11/what-am-i-meant-to-be-looking-for-supporting-beginning-teachers-to-undertake-effective-observations-of-other-teachers/

Dawson, I. (2008). Thinking across time: planning and teaching the story of power and democracy at Key Stage 3. *Teaching History, 130,* 14-22.

Dawson, I. (2009). What time does the tune start: From thinking about a 'sense of period' to modelling history at Key Stage 3. *Teaching History 135,* 50-7.

Dawson, I. (2018). *Exploring and Teaching Medieval History in Schools.* Retrieved 13 October 2022 from *Historical Association*, https://www.history.org.uk/secondary/resource/9290/exploring-and-teaching-medieval-history-in-schools

Dawson, I. (2021). Takeaways and their central role in planning KS3 courses. Retrieved 13 October 2022 from *Thinking History*, https://thinkinghistory.co.uk: https://thinkinghistory.co.uk/Issues/downloads/Takeaways.pdf

DfE. (2018). *Addressing Teacher Workload in Initial Teacher Education (ITE): Advice for ITE providers.* Department for Education. London: Crown copyright. Retrieved 31 October 2022 from https://assets.publishing.service.gov.uk/government/uploads/system/uploads/attachment_data/file/915985/Addressing_Workload_in_ITE.pdf

Fordham, M. (2017). Thinking makes it so: cognitive psychology and history teaching. *Teaching History 166,* 37-42.

Foster, R. (2020). An introduction to . . . lesson planning: part 1 (webinar). *Historical Association Teaching History for Beginners Webinar Series*. London: Historica Association. Retrieved 10 October 2022 from https://www.history.org.uk/secondary/resource/9923/film-an-introduction-to-lesson-planning-parts-1

Gestsdóttir, S., van Boxtel, C., & van Drie, J. (2018). Teaching historical thinking and reasoning: construction of an observation instrument. *British Educational Research Journal 44*(6), 960-81. Retrieved 12 August 2022 from https://bera-journals.onlinelibrary.wiley.com/doi/10.1002/berj.3471

Grande, J. (2022a). #3 This week, in history . . . how I use card sorts (and why I've fallen back in love with them). Retrieved from *Curricular Pasts: Reflections from a History Classroom*, https://curricularpasts.wordpress.com/2022/01/22/3-this-week-in-history-how-i-use-card-sorts-and-why-ive-fallen-back-in-love-with-them/

Grande, J. (2022b). #6 This week, in history . . . why the hinterland is core. Retrieved from *Curricular Pasts: Reflections from a history classroom*, https://curricularpasts.wordpress.com/2022/03/06/6-this-week-in-history-why-the-hinterland-is-core/

Grande, J. (2022c). #7 This week, in history . . . I've been checking 'for' understanding less. This is what I've been doing instead. Retrieved from *Curricular Pasts: Reflections from a History Classroom*, https://curricularpasts.wordpress.com/2022/03/13/7-this-week-in-history-ive-been-checking-for-understanding-less-this-is-what-ive-been-doing-instead/

Hall, L. (2021). The power of teacher talk – Part 2. Retrieved from *Practical Histories*: https://practicalhistories.com/2021/04/the-power-of-teacher-talk-part-2/

Hammond, K. (2014). The knowledge that 'flavours' a claim. *Teaching History 157,* 18-24.

Harris, R., Burn, K., & Woolley, M. (2013). *The Guided Reader to Teaching and Learning History.* Oxford: Taylor & Francis Group.

Haydn, T., & Harris, R. (2010). Pupil perspectives on the purposes and benefits of studying history in high school: a view from the UK. *Journal of Curriculum Studies 42*(2), 241–61, DOI: 10.1080/00220270903403189

Haydn, T., & Stephen, A. (2022). *Learning to Teach History in the Secondary School.* Abingdon: Routledge.

Haydn, T., Stephen, A., Arthur, J., & Hunt, M. (2014). *Learning to Teach History in the Secondary School: A Companion to School Experience* (4th ed.). London: Taylor & Francis Group.

Hibbert, D., & Patel, Z. (2019). Modelling the discipline: how can Yasmin Khan's use of evidence enable us to teach a more global World War II? *Teaching History 177,* 8-15.

Hill, M. (2020). Curating the imagined past: world building in the history curriculum. *Teaching History 180,* 10-20.

Historical Association. (2020). What's the wisdom on enquiry questions. *Teaching History 178,* 16-19.

Historical Association. (2021). What's the wisdom on ... history assessment. *Teaching History 185,* 56-9.

Lemov, D. (2021). *Teach Like a Champion 3.0: 63 Techniques that put Students on the Path to College.* New Jersey: Jossey-Bass.

Mutton, T., Hagger, H. & Burn, K. (2011). Learning to plan, planning to learn: the developing expertise of beginning teachers. *Teachers and Teaching 17*(4), 399-416. DOI: 10.1080/13540602.2011.580516

Phillips, R. (2001). Making history curious: Using Initial Stimulus Material (ISM) to promote enquiry, thinking and literacy. *Teaching History 105,* 19-25.

Richards, H. (2019). Ringing the changes: the power of enquiry questions that both chime and resonate. Retrieved 19 November 2022 from *One Big History Department,* https://onebighistorydepartment.com/2019/07/12/ringing-the-changes-the-power-of-enquiry-questions-that-both-chime-and-resonate/

Riley, M. (2000). Into the Key Stage 3 history garden: choosing and planting your enquiry questions. *Teaching History 99,* 8-13.

Riley, M. (2019). Picturing the past (and the future). *Historical Association London History Forum Workshop.* London: Historical Association. Retrieved 11 December 2022 from https://www.history.org.uk/secondary/resource/9800/film-picturing-the-past-and-the-future

Riley, M., & Byrom, J. (2008). Professional wrestling in the history department: a case study in planning the teaching of the British Empire at Key Stage 3. *Teaching History 112,* 6-14.

Sherrington, T. (2019). *Rosenshine's Principles in Action.* London: John Catt.

Smith, D. (2014). Period, place and mental space: using historical scholarship to develop Year 7 pupils' sense of period. *Teaching History 154,* 8-16.

Whitburn, R. (2022). A Rosenshine Reformation: in search of pedagogy for historical thinking. HTEN Conference, November 2022.

Worth, P. (2018). Here ends the lesson: shaping lesson conclusions as an iterative process in improving historical enquiries. *Teaching History 173,* 58-67.

5 Working with beginning history teachers to support all pupils' learning

Victoria Crooks

Case study 5.1 Simone's new class

Simone glances down the register of the Year 8 class she is about to begin teaching. The first column is populated with a series of codes indicating the special educational needs and disabilities of certain pupils and whether they are the subject of a specific support plan. Further down the register is a cluster of pupils all with a code indicating they are learners of English as an additional language. A couple of pupils have an asterisk next to them indicating they are part of the school's gifted and talented programme. Simone counts 14 pupils who appear as if they might have additional needs from a class of 30 and feels a knot of anxiety. How will she ever do these children justice in the classroom? How can she hope to meet their needs?

Introduction

Preparing to teach pupils of all attainments and backgrounds within a mainstream setting is an aspect of teaching practice that invokes strong reactions from beginning teachers. Usually, these responses are divided between those fuelled by a determination to 'do better' than they experienced in school themselves, and those who feel overwhelmed by the prospect of meeting the needs of all the learners they will encounter.

A rich history education should be a curricular entitlement for all young people, even if they do not go on to study the subject at a higher level; an understanding of history is vital for their participation in society. Yet, school history has often been presented as a complex subject, beyond the reach of some children. It requires children to grapple with the complexities of marshalling substantive knowledge within a disciplinary process and demands multi-perspectivity. History is a discipline that rarely offers simple and definitive answers to questions. It is also a subject that often relies on pupils' literacy, asking children to engage with complex texts and develop their own written arguments. Additionally, for some pupils, history has been a subject where they have felt unrepresented and therefore disenfranchised from the discipline. Enabling all children to access and then thrive in the history classroom is a multi-faceted responsibility and can therefore seem like an insurmountable challenge to beginning teachers.

Supporting all pupils' learning 97

This chapter will seek to explore how mentors can support their mentees to understand their professional responsibility to meet the needs of all their pupils, offering a framework to help them take a more asset-based perspective to this challenge. While it will consider what history teachers need to understand about working with pupils who have special educational needs and disabilities (SEND), this will not be the sole focus of this chapter. Instead, it will reflect on how mentors can help beginning teachers to consider and support all pupils, to understand why it is important to get to know pupils as individuals, and to consider how curriculum design and certain approaches in the history classroom can benefit everyone, regardless of whether they have a SEND need, have English as an additional language (EAL), identify as being from a less represented group, or even have a particular aptitude for the subject. It will seek to establish that it is possible for all learners to access the discipline and make progress in their historical understanding.

Objectives

At the end of the chapter, you should be able to:

- Understand how the needs of different learners can manifest in the classroom and the responsibility teachers have for supporting all learners.
- Develop principles for inclusion at a curriculum, planning, and in-lesson adaptation level.
- Reflect on different models of scaffolding to support the learning of history.
- Design activities which help beginning teachers to think through these principles for inclusion and support them to plan for the needs of all learners in history.

What do beginning teachers need to understand about inclusion?

Establishing an inclusive classroom, in which all pupils are valued and supported to learn and make progress, is a core responsibility for all teachers. Inclusion involves respecting the cultural and individual diversity of all pupils and meeting their needs to allow them to learn and achieve their potential. As Harris (2005) asserts, 'no pupil should feel excluded from learning either as a result of the topic or the nature of work set' (p. 5). Progressing learning for all is an issue of social justice.

It is vital that beginning teachers understand the following forms of inclusive practice (explained in more detail below):

- Supporting learners with a range of special education needs and disabilities.
- Stretching learners who demonstrate aptitude for a subject.
- Supporting bilingual and multilingual learners, especially those who are new to learning English.
- Respecting the individual identity, culture, and background of pupils.

Task 5.1 provides a starting point for considering how to support a beginning teacher to take on a new class including a range of pupils with different needs.

Supporting learners with a range of special educational needs and disabilities

In England it is the statutory responsibility of all teachers to support learners with SEND. Accordingly, teachers 'must make reasonable adjustments . . to ensure that disabled children and young people are not at a substantial disadvantage compared with their peers' (DfE & DHSC, 2015, p. 17), anticipating and mitigating potential barriers that pupils might experience. Despite this legislation, the 2021 Historical Association Survey revealed that around 20% of responding schools still discourage, or even actively prevent, some pupils from continuing to study history beyond Key Stage 3 due to 'current attainment or low levels of literacy . . . (identified as relevant grounds by 13% and 10% of schools, respectively)' (Burn & Harris, 2021, p. 28).

Your mentee therefore needs to be supported to develop approaches which will ensure all the young people they teach, including those with SEND, can access and participate in their history lessons.

Understanding the different SEND needs of pupils

There are four broad areas of need within SEND:

- Cognition and learning needs – including specific learning difficulties such as dyslexia and dyspraxia.
- Communication and interaction needs – including speech and language difficulties and autistic spectrum disorders.
- Social, emotional, and mental health needs – including attention deficit hyperactivity disorder (ADHD), behavioural needs, and attachment disorders.
- Sensory and/or physical needs – including hearing or visual or multisensory impairments.

A common misconception held by beginning teachers is that pupils with SEND are a homogenous group for whom there is a standard toolkit of teaching approaches. In contrast, experienced teachers know that each child, whether they have a SEND diagnosis or not, is a unique individual requiring consideration of their specific situation. For example, a pupil with limited mobility might need their teacher to consider the space and movement required in a role-play lesson to enable them to be fully included in the activity. A pupil with a diagnosis of Autism Spectrum Disorder (ASD) may need the teacher to communicate prior to the lesson how the role-play lesson will differ from their usual experience. Another pupil with an ASD diagnosis may benefit from a particular role being allocated to them to support their participation in the activity. All three pupils have a SEND diagnosis, but require different approaches and support dependent on their individual need.

One challenge beginning teachers on Initial Teacher Education (ITE) programmes often face when beginning to work with pupils with SEND on placement is lack of access to the SEND register and individual support plans for pupils. Schools usually make the decision to withhold or restrict access to this information due to concerns about sharing data. This puts the beginning teacher in a very difficult position. Ideally, mentors should share this information with their mentees, familiarising them with individual support plans of pupils they will be teaching as early as possible in the induction process, and providing regular opportunities to discuss and review their growing understanding of the pupils' needs.

Stretching learners who demonstrate particular aptitude for history

There is little agreement in the policy and practice of the four nations of the UK about what it means for a pupil to be gifted or talented (Loft & Danechi, 2020, pp. 3–4). However, the conclusions of the 2005 NAGTY History Think Tank helpfully identify 'a number of abilities, attitudes and habits of mind characteristic of, or emerging from, high achievement in history' (Chapman, 2006, pp. 2--3). A common misconception held by beginning teachers is that these gifted or higher-attaining pupils cannot be taught alongside their peers. It is true that hastily set extension tasks, intended to occupy quick-finishing high attainers, are not sufficient for nurturing the significant potential of these learners. However, as illustrated by Hammond (1999), with careful planning it is perfectly possible for the highest-attaining pupils to be stretched while still being taught in a mixed-attaining classroom.

Hammond (1999) explored strategies for supporting a talented pupil while not limiting expectations for the rest of the class. These strategies included providing supplementary risky questions, 'that is, questions which have no obvious answer, which the pupil can get significantly wrong and which stimulate high-order thinking', that were 'blended in with a longer sequence of questions tackled by the whole class' (p. 26). In another lesson, key information was removed from a narrative-sequencing task, meaning the pupil needed to draw on their sense of period and their ability to infer in order to make the necessary connections. In the final lesson, the pupil was given additional evidence cards, requiring them to draw on a wider range of evidence when categorising, selecting, and forming judgements in relation to the enquiry question. Hammond concludes that providing higher-attaining pupils with writing frames limits their freedom to demonstrate the breadth and depth of their understanding, urging instead that these higher-attaining pupils are exposed to historical scholarship (Hammond, 1999) – an aspect of practice others have gone on to explore (Foster, 2015; Foster & Goudie, 2016).

Seixas and Morton (2012) identified 'guideposts' for understanding disciplinary concepts and what a 'demonstration of powerful understanding' might look like for each of these guideposts. Developing a breadth and depth of substantive knowledge, a sound command of the historical processes, and an ability to communicate their historical understanding cogently, are also critical elements of a pupil's progression in history. Supporting beginning teachers to develop a good grasp of what progression looks like, so they can create meaningful opportunities for stretch in their lessons, is key if they are to successfully challenge higher-attaining pupils.

Supporting bilingual and multilingual learners, especially those who are new to learning English

Pupils with EAL should not be considered as having special educational needs unless there is sufficient evidence to suggest that they are experiencing difficulties with their learning for reasons other than their linguistic development (DfE & DHSC, 2015). Hearing-impaired pupils who use sign language as their primary form of communication are a good example of pupils who will rightly be identified as having both a SEND and EAL need. Sadly, in some school settings the EAL status of pupils continues to be recorded alongside SEND information, regardless of whether a SEND need has been identified. This not only leads to misconceptions being established in the mind of the beginning teacher, but can also add to their anxiety about supporting these pupils. It is helpful, therefore, if mentors can reframe 'pupils with EAL' as bilingual or multilingual learners for a more asset-based understanding of the richness of cultural experience and linguistic ability these pupils bring to the classroom.

Lack of consensus around issues such as whether the home language should be employed or avoided in the classroom (Arnot et al., 2014) causes further anxiety amongst beginning teachers. It is therefore important that mentees are helped to distinguish the needs of their bilingual and multilingual pupils and understand the varying strategies which can be employed at various stages of language acquisition. It is often reassuring for them to know that 61% of pupils classified as having EAL are at least 'competent' in English (DfE, 2020, p. 3). Indeed, some bilingual or multilingual pupils may, as advanced users of fluent English living in established communities, be rather bemused to discover they are considered to have EAL. Conversely, other pupils with EAL may be 'new arrivals' who are very early on in their language learning journey and may have previously used a logographic alphabet or only have oral competency in their first language. Pupils who are completely new to English will take an average of six years to achieve 'proficiency', and more to become advanced learners of English (Strand & Lindorff, 2021).

Beginning teachers also need to be made aware that while most pupils with EAL will live in families and homes, like their peers, some (for example refugees) may be living in more precarious circumstances due to fleeing their homeland because of war or imminent danger. For some pupils this may be the first time they've encountered formal schooling, and the routines of the institution (even at the level of classroom doors being closed during lessons) can be unsettling. Being cognisant of this diversity of background and experience is particularly important for those beginning history teachers who will teach sensitive and controversial histories, which may be particularly raw for some pupils (see Chapter 8).

Respecting the individual identity, culture, and background of pupils

For some pupils, experience of a narrow history curriculum can 'disenfranchise' and lead to 'feelings of alienation and apathy' (Traille, 2007, p. 37). Children do not arrive in the classroom as a blank slate; 'the interplay between history and identity is . . . dynamic because our sense of who we are may shape how we interpret the history we are taught, but at the same time the history we are taught may shape who we are' (Harris, Burn, & Woolley, 2013, p. 55). Teachers who seek to support the learning of all pupils in their classes therefore need to be cognisant of these issues. Increasing efforts to attend to more representative understandings of the past (Burn & Harris, 2021) by reconceptualising the curriculum as both a window (providing a frame through which the breadth of the society and global communities can be seen) and a mirror (where personal identities can be reflected) (Style, 1996; Traille, 2007), are therefore another important aspect of planning to support the learning of all pupils. Enfranchising pupils in their historical learning involves including a broader range of 'voices', whether those of ethnically diverse communities, women, LGBTQ+ people, people with disabilities, or the working classes (explored further in Chapter 8). The decision to develop a richly, inclusive curriculum, which respects the identities, cultures, and backgrounds of all pupils, can be transformative in supporting the learning of pupils who have traditionally rarely seen themselves represented with agency in school history.

> **Task 5.1 Preparation for teaching a new class**
>
> Return to the vignette of Simone introduced at the beginning of this chapter. As Simone's mentor:
>
> - What preparation work might you need to do with Simone before handing over the register for her Year 8 class?
> - What information and systems might Simone need to be introduced to before meeting this class?
> - What could you do to help Simone's anxiety around being a supportive teacher for these pupils?

Developing principles for inclusion in the history classroom

Kerridge (2017) wrote compellingly about his experience of working with a lower-attaining group under a system of setting 'all, most, some' lesson objectives, explaining, 'I could not look my students in the eye and tell them, "This objective is for you .. but the other two will probably be too hard for you. They are for the top set to think about." How on earth would that help to rebuild their destroyed dignity?' (p. 17). Effective inclusion should therefore seek to have high expectations of all pupils. To that end, more recently the discourse around inclusion has been one of high expectations while teaching to the top and scaffolding to support the other children to achieve the same outcomes (Sherrington, 2019; DfE, 2019a; 2019b).

It is therefore incumbent upon history teachers to develop principles around which they can plan for effective learning that will enable all their pupils to access, succeed in, and hopefully enjoy historical study. Harris (2005, p. 5) proposes the three principles for an inclusive history classroom, which could also form the basis of a discussion with your mentee around why we use enquiry questions:

1. **Make the work engaging**
   History offers wonderful opportunities to intrigue and excite young people, engaging them in historical exploration, in solving an historical mystery, or in wonder at a world which feels so strange and unfamiliar and yet was inhabited by people who had the same motivations and concerns as they do themselves (Dawson, 2018). Where meaningful enquiry questions, which have disciplinary integrity are employed (Riley, 2000), this problematising and sense of purpose can be clearly and simply conveyed.

2. **Make the work accessible but challenging**
   The enquiry question is also key when we prioritise high expectations and teaching to the top, as it allows all pupils to access the outcome, especially when accompanied by a

carefully structured approach to revealing the enquiry that takes account of individual needs (Philpott, 2008, p. 47).

3. **Decide where you place the obstacles**
   The notion of 'placing obstacles' is a critical element in making the work accessible but challenging. Harris (2005) gives several examples of how judicious planning, with a focus on the rationale of each individual lesson task, can help teachers to make decisions about whether certain tasks are enhancing pupils' learning or simply placing an unnecessary 'obstacle' in their way. Conversely, inserting 'obstacles' at certain points could provide some necessary challenges for other pupils (Harris, 2005, p. 9). For example, a writing task acting as a proxy for historical thinking may in fact be erecting an obstacle for pupils whose problematising might be better served by the manipulation of evidence cards in a dialogic paired task. In this case it might be better to save the writing activity for when it has greater purpose.

Drawing on key principles such as these can assist beginning teachers to understand the purpose of taking a scaffolded approach to their planning and teaching, where the historical coherence and purpose of each element of the lesson is carefully considered.

Approaches to support inclusion for learning in history

By revealing to their mentees that planning for an inclusive history classroom takes place at both a curricular and individual lesson level, mentors can support their mentees to actively notice and proactively practise adaptive teaching techniques for themselves.

Planning for inclusion at the curriculum level

In an article in TES, Christine Counsell (1996) recounted the story of 'Melanie', a Year 9 pupil who, having learnt about the rise of 20th-century dictators, developed her own ahistorical hybrid dictator 'Mutlin' from her studies of Hitler, Mussolini, and Stalin. In this scenario, Melanie is destined to give up on history as soon as she is allowed – she might enjoy history, but it all just feels too difficult. Counsell asserts that to avoid this outcome, her teacher needs to take a more selective approach to their curriculum construction, building conceptual understanding over time, to give Melanie 'the most meaningful and memorable experience' (Counsell, 1996).

Beginning teachers therefore benefit from support that allows them to see that inclusion is not just a series of interventions made during a lesson, but rather needs to begin at the stage of curriculum planning (made visible through Task 5.2) and to pay due regard to:

- the sequencing of historical enquiries, which incrementally introduce and build historical knowledge and understanding of substantive concepts in history through a layering of multiple encounters with the same historical 'idea' in different contexts throughout the curriculum (Fordham, 2016) (see Chapters 3 and 4).
- the development of a disciplinary framework for considering the past – both in terms of understanding the second-order concepts (for example, change and continuity) and of procedural disciplinary knowledge (for example the way that sources are used as part of a historical process in order to understand the past; Harris, 2021 (see Chapter 3)).

- the selection of historical enquiries which are representative and coherent and provide opportunities to hear from a range of historical 'voices', ensuring that asset- (rather than deficit-) based perspectives, which reflect the agency of these voices, are presented (Traille, 2007; Wilkinson, 2014; Mohamud & Whitburn, 2016; Hollis, 2021; Woods, 2021). As Mohamud and Whitburn (2014) express it, this is 'giving young people history they would want to take home with pride' (p. 46) (see Chapter 8).

Task 5.2 Exploring the curriculum

During a mentor meeting explore the department curriculum plan with your mentee.

- Can they identify the historical themes being tackled by the curriculum? How do the substantive topic foci combine to create coherence? Is the substantive focus of the curriculum representative of the full range of voices that can be heard in history? Are pupils provided with both mirrors and windows?
- Can they notice certain themes which are introduced and then subsequently developed to 'incrementally' build deeper understanding of this substantive knowledge, so it does not appear as an unrelated 'package' of facts? Can they identify substantive conceptual threads (e.g., revolution, colonialism, autocracy) which will be encountered across the curriculum?
- When and where can they see disciplinary knowledge being introduced? Are enquiry questions used to reveal the process of history making to pupils? What impact do these questions have upon pupils' understanding of history as a means for developing theories, albeit where some theories have more validity than others (Lee & Shemilt, 2004)?
- Discuss the examination specifications selected by the school and identify how these build on the curriculum studied by all pupils earlier in their school career.

Discuss how this big-picture thinking helps to support pupils' accessing the history curriculum. Model an example from your own teaching in which you make a connection with prior learning/future learning to help build this sense of meaningful knowledge with pupils (for example, when teaching Henry VIII's break with Rome, reveal how you make a connection with the pupils' work on the relationship between Henry II and Thomas Becket). What wider curricular links would pupils benefit from the beginning/early career teacher having in mind as they begin teaching the class?

Inclusion at the lesson-planning level

All too often, the planning beginning teachers do to meet the needs of all pupils is relegated to a tokenistic box on the plan which vaguely refers to scaffolding, circulating to give 1-2-1 support, or setting challenge tasks. Truly planning for inclusion requires a more holistic approach. Mitigating potential pressure points and misconceptions enables access, increases motivation in the lesson, and means the beginning teacher can focus upon responding to the ways pupils are making meaning in the lesson itself.

Some aspects of planning which beginning teachers can be helped to see as a vehicle for providing an inclusive approach in history include:

Planning the lesson as part of a sequence seeking to answer an enquiry question.

This helps to provide direction and purpose to the lesson, increasing motivation and resilience. It also helps to give the substantive knowledge acquired in the lesson meaning by reducing the chance that pupils will see their history lessons as presenting a series of disconnected facts. A purposeful enquiry question also provides a clear rationale for the lesson sequence, thereby making decisions about pedagogical approaches and activities easier and helping to avoid tasks which are there simply as a 'time filler'.

Considering how best to 'begin' the lesson.

The beginning of the lesson should give a reason for the pupils to persist in that learning, something which is especially important for pupils who might find things a bit harder to access.

Well-selected initial stimulus material (ISM) (Phillips, 2001) can be an effective 'hook' into the historical thinking required for an enquiry. An ISM, such as an intriguing or richly detailed painting or photograph, story, or piece of music, or even the classic medieval medicine lesson opener where the teacher sips 'urine' (apple juice) to test the balance of the four humours, can be used as a springboard to generate curiosity. These activities are also often more history-appropriate contexts for posing questions that retrieve prior knowledge, establishing the lesson's direction and purpose in historically meaningful ways.

Sequencing the building blocks of historical knowledge

Thinking carefully about the order in which historical knowledge is encountered and used in a lesson helps all pupils, and particularly pupils with additional needs, to access the historical thinking that needs to take place. Beginning teachers tend to think that substantive knowledge needs always to be front-loaded before the pupils begin application tasks. Mentors can supportively challenge their mentee to consider whether acquiring the subject knowledge as part of a task may, in some circumstances, be more supportive of pupils' emerging understanding and help avoid misconceptions developing.

When planning an interpretations enquiry, for example, it is vital for a beginning teacher to understand the building blocks of disciplinary understanding that pupils require to grasp this challenging second-order concept (Lee & Shemilt, 2004). One of the most difficult things for pupils to appreciate, especially those who may be more concrete in their thinking (pupils with ASD for instance) is that history is constructed rather than received. Beginning an interpretation enquiry on 'Why do historians disagree about King John?' with the interpretation of John provided by the Disney film *Robin Hood*, before leaping into the views of 19th-century historian William Stubbs or the contemporary historian Stephen Church, is a good example of the concept-cracking approach, which starts with an easy and accessible route into a big historical idea before building to the more subtle

Planning for routine and repetition

Permeating lessons with clear routines and structure is supportive of all pupils' learning. For students who are neurodivergent or who are beginning to learn English as an additional language, routine and structure can be especially supportive. Having a predictable pattern to the phases of a lesson allows these pupils to navigate the lesson more easily and reduces their cognitive load (Thompson & Walsh, 2020). Clear routines also have a positive impact on behaviour for learning and can contribute to a calm classroom environment, which can be especially helpful for pupils with ASD or anxiety.

Additionally, building in familiar activities, as Collins (2013) did in his 'image-led enquiry', where visual sources were introduced in every lesson during a unit on the Weimar Republic, relieves students of the need to process new ways of working and allows them to focus instead on the new substantive and disciplinary foci.

Planning for explicit instructions

Beginning teachers often benefit from planning how they will give explicit instructions, particularly when they are just starting out. Everyday speech is littered with hesitation and 'filler' words. For new learners of English as an additional language, or pupils with slower cognitive processing, these fillers clutter the speech and make deciphering the teacher's meaning more challenging. The Bell Foundation (www.bell-foundation.org.uk) recommends that teachers giving instructions should 'use a limited range of instruction language and question forms', using 'signposts such as firstly, then' for longer instructions (The Bell Foundation, 2017). Step-by-step instructions accompanied by visual modelling of verbal directions also helps to make instructions more explicit for pupils.

Planning deliberately for historical thinking

Supporting pupils to think historically involves making the abstract ideas concrete before building back up to more abstract conceptualisations (Gestsdóttir, van Boxtel, & van Drie, 2018). It involves designing activities which scaffold the historical thinking required and provide a safe space for students to engage with the 'struggle' of thinking and decision making without the commitment of writing an assessed response (Evans & Pate, 2007). This is something pupils with dyslexia or ADHD may find particularly helpful.

Good examples of this approach are living graph activities that demonstrate the relationship between the complex factors involved in the Arab-Israeli conflict (Stephen, 2005), or the Great Fire of London card-sort activity which allows pupils to reason through, and change their mind about, the relevance of substantive knowledge as new factors are introduced or removed from the enquiry (Counsell, 1997). Activities such as this help pupils better grasp and hone their understanding of the interplay of historical evidence in historical argumentation, making it routine for them to select and apply knowledge to different aspects of an historical question. This often pays greater dividends for longer-term pupil outcomes than endless practice of exam-style responses.

Planning for writing

Extended writing is important in history as it is the primary way in which historical thinking and argumentation is revealed. However, not all writing that takes place in history classrooms is inherently worthwhile. It is always important to consider whether a writing task is necessary to achieve the historical rationale of the lesson.

When writing is included, it needs to be done in ways that advance pupils' historical thinking or allow them to communicate their historical understanding. Beginning teachers therefore need help to see that time is probably better spent with pupils applying information to an historical question rather than simply copying text from information sheets into a table. For pupils who find literacy more challenging or who find the physical act of writing very demanding (pupils with dyspraxia for example), such copying of text can be a laborious and ultimately fruitless process. For those who have a particular aptitude for history, it is a time-consuming step which prevents them from moving into the interesting thinking with which they really want to grapple.

When preparing for extended writing, teachers often turn to writing frames or modelling to provide a scaffold for pupils. Modelling and writing frames, certainly in terms of the provision of sentence starters, can help pupils to get started by giving them a helping hand into the task. However, writing frames and Point, Evidence, Explain, Link (PEEL) paragraph structures also tend to encourage children to view historical writing as a process of matching the correct historical knowledge into a preordained structure (McDermott, 2020). Modelling can be incredibly supportive, but too often in beginning teachers' lessons the good intentions behind it can lead to dependency on the part of the pupils and leave them still struggling to write historically (Evans & Pate, 2007).

Beginning teachers need their mentors to help them think beyond the generic approaches which scaffold writing to consider how better *historical* writing can be achieved. For example, approaches which help to reveal complex disciplinary ideas can be seen in the work of Foster (2013), who explored the use of metaphors for expressing ideas of change and continuity, and Worth (2017), who used shapes as a means of understanding consequence.

Developing language for thinking

Woodcock (2005) argues that we should seek to explicitly teach pupils complex disciplinary vocabulary, not just because it allows them to express their ideas, but because it actually helps them to continue to develop their historical reasoning as they wrestle with the process of historical writing. This principle can be extrapolated to scaffolding the writing of pupils who are in the initial stages of acquiring English as an additional language. EAL pupils will benefit from being encouraged to select the appropriate vocabulary to form whole sentences, or even to write in their first language and translate across into English (Arnot et al., 2014), rather than completing potentially ahistorical gap fills.

Making the lesson conclusion count by making a connection with the enquiry question

Lesson conclusions, which support the learning of all pupils, require careful planning. This should avoid 'reducing the conclusion to a memory test – especially memory of facts or words' (Counsell in Worth, 2018, p. 61). Instead, end-of-lesson plenaries should be used to refocus on the enquiry question to help pupils see how the knowledge they have just learnt combines with, or disrupts, their previous learning to help them answer the enquiry. This is important for pupils as it makes the learning more meaningful and memorable, and therefore also more motivating.

Planning for homework

Homework needs to be both purposeful and achievable without the support of the class teacher on hand – this is especially important when working with pupils who have English as an additional language who may be the sole English speaker in their family. Designing a bespoke 'Meanwhile elsewhere' or 'Meanwhile nearby'-style homework (https://meanwhileelsewhereinhistory.wordpress.com/), focused on the unique backgrounds of pupils in the specific school context, is a good example of how, when carefully constructed, homework can also be an excellent forum for inclusion of a broader range of voices. It can also provide enrichment for those who demonstrate a particular aptitude for the subject, allowing them to spread their wings beyond the bounds of the curriculum. Inclusive homework is a challenge. It requires planning and should not be left to chance at the end of the lesson, not least because for some pupils recording and understanding what the homework requires is another obstacle.

Task 5.3 provides some questions to focus upon as you support your mentee to evaluate their planning and consider the impact it has upon pupils' historical learning.

Task 5.3 Considering planning

Ask your mentee to identify a recent lesson where their evaluation suggested that not all the students had accessed the historical learning that was intended. Using the lesson plan, help them to reflect on their planning process. Begin by asking these key questions:

- Which pupils seemed to have particular challenges in the lesson? What are their needs? How did you try to anticipate and meet their needs at this planning stage?

Help your mentee to work through the plan systematically by asking some of the following questions during mentoring conversations. As you explore each element, return to the key question, focusing on the individual pupils in the class to show how knowledge of their specific needs might change the approach required:

- Does the enquiry question meet the Riley (2000) test: intriguing; historically valid; having a tangible outcome? If not, why might that have created a barrier for pupils in this lesson?
- Is the lesson part of a wider enquiry? Is the rationale for that enquiry evident in each task the pupils were set? Were the expectations of what pupils could learn and do during the lesson high enough to provide sufficient challenge and motivation?

- How did you plan for pupils to be hooked into the lesson? Was the intention to build their confidence or intrigue and motivate them?
- What threshold knowledge did you decide pupils would require for each activity? How did you plan to help them acquire this knowledge – was it prior to or during the task? Do you think the tasks were introduced in the right order to enable pupils to have a good chance of accessing them?
- When and where are you choosing to scaffold tasks? How are you doing this and what was the intention behind providing the scaffold? For whom was the scaffold effective in removing an obstacle? Did the scaffolding prevent any pupils from demonstrating the fullness of their historical thinking?
- How did you plan for the lesson to conclude? Did this link back to the enquiry question? Did you plan enough time for this aspect of the lesson?

Inclusion at the level of in-lesson adaptations

Experienced teachers often 'go off plan', telling seemingly incidental stories, or breaking off into a period of unscheduled questioning or teacher explanation. For the beginning teacher, the numerous micro-decisions that lead teachers to make these adaptations as they check for pupil understanding are a bit of a mystery. Targeted observation of these colleagues, preferably decoded by a mentor through a whispered paired observation, can begin to help them grasp the power of the in-lesson adaptation.

Knowing when to ask questions and what questions to ask to advance pupils' historical understanding

Questioning is primarily used by teachers to check for understanding – to check what prior knowledge pupils have remembered and what they have understood about applying that knowledge – or to support pupils to make meaningful connections between their new and prior knowledge. Knowing when to ask questions and what questions to ask is a real skill. Regular retrieval practice testing is valuable, but beginning teachers need support to understand that pupils demonstrating they have learnt 'isolated facts without connecting them to a deeper understanding of a topic may not benefit students' higher order learning' (Agarwal, 2019, p. 193). This is a particular risk for pupils who are new to English and pupils with SEND needs that impact cognition and learning. Mentors can help their mentee to plan questions that reveal how pupils are making sense of new non-hierarchical substantive knowledge in their existing schema, or how they are reconsidering its meaning by considering a new disciplinary focus. Teachers who have a clear sense of why they are asking questions are usually able to respond more flexibly to the pupils in front of them, scaffolding targeted questions to enable lower-attaining pupils to participate while also building all pupils to more sophisticated understandings (Crooks, 2021). Mixing specific fact-retrieval questions with questions such as 'when have we encountered this before?' or 'how does this source make us think differently about what we've just learnt?', encourages all pupils to reveal 'the

Supporting all pupils' learning 109

understanding [they have] built as a whole' (Grande, 2022) and provides greater challenges for those with a particular interest in and aptitude for the subject. You can explore some of these ideas around questioning with your mentee using Task 5.4.

> **Task 5.4 Thinking about questioning**
>
> Film a lesson and watch back a questioning phase from the lesson. Ask your mentee to write down all the questions they asked pupils. Explore the questions asked more closely.
>
> - Which pupils are answering the questions? Why is this? How could a different approach (e.g., mini-whiteboards or paired discussion of responses) enable a wider range of pupils to be included in these questioning phases? What impact would that have upon expectations of pupil learning? How would that help provide more information about what different groups of pupils are finding hard or how misconceptions are developing?
> - Categorise the questions as:
>   - Questions intended to reveal what information has been remembered.
>   - Questions intended to reveal what pupils have understood.
> - What is the ratio of the two types of question? How is this helping all pupils to learn to think historically?
> - As responses are being given to the questions, how are the responses being used to ask further questions to unpick misconceptions/deepen the historical thinking of pupils?
> - How is pupil understanding influencing decisions about enacting the plan?

Cementing through visualisation

History lends itself to rich visual representation. Images can perform narrative, immersive, descriptive, explanatory, or aesthetic functions in history lessons (Hill, 2021). Choosing to support teacher exposition, storytelling, reading, and even writing with a well-selected image can help make the history instantly more accessible and understandable for pupils, especially those who have additional needs. Selecting an image with a sense of the purpose it is serving can help can support in-lesson judgements around how much to emphasise and dwell upon that image to support pupil understanding.

Meaningful visual representations, not icons, are important for revealing the richness of the past. Developing hinterland knowledge and an awareness of different aspects of the past helps to construct a sense of period, to world-build (Hill, 2020), adding a 'layer of thickness' (Benger, 2020, p. 32) to pupils' understanding. Images such as illustrations of a medieval village depicting everything from strip farming to the looming presence of the Church, maps illustrating the journeys into the American West, and visually arresting photographs of the Brixton riots all convey rich multilayered understandings of the past which help to make the substantive knowledge more relevant and resonant. For those with English as an additional language or with literacy challenges, such images help to pin complex vocabulary to a tangible and concrete idea. Beginning teachers need to be encouraged to go off plan to quickly search for an image or sketch out a map or timeline on the board when it becomes clear pupils would benefit from more concrete illustration of historical ideas. Task 5.5 provides some ideas for exploring with your mentee how they are using images.

Task 5.5 Reviewing visual images

With your mentee review the visual images they are intending to use in an upcoming lesson.

- Ask your mentee to classify the purpose of those images: are they performing a narrative, immersive, descriptive, explanatory, or aesthetic function? Could better images be selected to help pupils to understand the history better?
- Select one of the images performing a narrative, descriptive, or explanatory function. Annotate the image with the core knowledge and hinterland knowledge required to interpret it. Explore questions that could be asked to deepen pupils' understanding of the period/event by making this core and hinterland knowledge visible to pupils. Consider in what order these questions should be asked to enable all pupils to access the historical thinking.

Making it real through storytelling

Willingham (2009) asserts that 'The human mind seems exquisitely tuned to understand and remember stories – so much so that psychologists sometimes refer to stories as "psychologically privileged", meaning that they are treated differently in memory than other types of material' (p. 145). History is the perfect environment for storytelling, whether through the grand sweeping stories presented in scholarship such as *The Silk Roads* (Frankopan, 2016), or the individual and everyday stories of ordinary people, such as Nottingham hero Eric Irons (Gooptar, 2021). Experienced history teachers often infuse their teacher talk with stories – vignettes focused on real people's lives which help the past to acquire shape and meaning for pupils.

Stories ground the past. They make the past memorable for pupils and enable them to make connections between areas of substantive knowledge by providing tangible examples that allow abstract ideas to become concrete. These stories also aid inclusion, presenting opportunities to draw on stories that integrate more diverse histories into the heart of a scheme of work. Thematic units, which require a solid understanding of chronology and developed sense of period, can often be especially challenging for lower-attaining pupils. Stories help pupils to world-build, allowing them to make sense of the past and avoid anachronistic thinking by constructing 'situation models' or 'cognitive representations' of the past (Hill, 2020).

Beginning teachers, however, often feel very anxious about storytelling, due to concerns about taking on the storyteller role and having sufficient subject knowledge to do it well. It is helpful for mentors to encourage their mentees to recognise the power of stories and to practise this skill as part of their training (Task 5.6).

Task 5.6 Storytelling

Identify an enquiry your mentee is due to teach and set them the task of specific subject knowledge development to identify a story which better reveals the historical rationale behind the enquiry. Get them to practise telling the story in a mentor meeting.

Reading together

History is a text-rich discipline and a rich array of texts – written evidence, historical fiction, scholarship, and narrative accounts – can be used to advance pupils' historical thinking, historical consciousness, and their own historical writing (Foster, 2011; Jenner, 2019). In the mixed-attaining classroom, however, texts can also be a significant obstacle. Within a lesson, teachers are confronted by decisions about when and how much to read, and where that reading should take place.

Beginning teachers need guidance with understanding that using text in class involves far more than simply reading aloud. Effective teachers make constant adaptations within their lessons to make texts more accessible for their pupils (Quigley, 2020). These adaptations include:

- Reading text aloud.
- Providing contextual information about the text through teacher talk.
- Defining tier 3 (subject-specific terminology) and tier 2 (uncommon in everyday texts) vocabulary.
- Breaking down the text through activities such as acting out the story or categorising using a key.
- Providing visual support for key episodes, actors, or ideas in the text.

Additionally, symbol texts can be very supportive for pupils with younger reading ages and those who are new to English to scaffold them into reading alongside their peers (Pampoulou & Detheridge, 2007), while guided reading is an example of a strategy which can make complex extended texts, particularly scholarship texts, accessible for pupils. Scaffolding pupils into reading more complex scholarship texts can also provide stretching opportunities for higher-attaining students to explore more complex historical thinking (Croft, 2005; Bellinger, 2008). Whatever the approach, the development of pupils' reading abilities in history needs to be prioritised to support their ongoing learning in the discipline.

Deciding when to introduce and remove scaffolding

The decisions teachers make during a lesson around when to introduce and withdraw scaffolding are a critical element of adaptive teaching and an incredibly difficult skill for beginning teachers to master. Having planned a lesson to ensure pupils experience desirable difficulty (Druckman & Bjork, 1994) rather than pointless struggle, teachers need to prioritise their awareness of pupil learning and the end goal of developing pupils' disciplinary independence. Teachers need to be constantly checking what understanding the pupils have developed to decide whether to stop and reteach an element of the lesson or provide more structural scaffolding into a task. Similarly, they need to be able to read the signs to know when scaffolding should be removed and pupils encouraged into more independent thinking and historical expression. Three-part modelling, or guided practice, in the form of *I do, We do, You do* has become very established in much classroom practice (Lemov, Hernandez, & Kim, 2016, p. 298), but when employed by beginning teachers it can become more of an 'I do, I do and you copy, you do by copying what I've done but inserting a different piece of factual information'. Beginning teachers need to observe how experienced teachers decide when to facilitate growing independence in their students and to have opportunities to practise implementing this in their own classrooms.

Rendering historical thinking and processes visible
As explored previously, modelling is a key aspect of classroom practice. However, too frequently, modelling is reserved for the exemplification of desired outcomes, rather than for the historical thinking and reasoning that needs to take place to achieve that outcome (Gestsdóttir, van Boxtel, & van Drie, 2018). Engaging with this metacognitive process, where the teacher deliberately narrates how they break down the thinking processes through dialogic problematising and rehearsal, is a valuable in-lesson adaptation to support pupils. Similarly, whole-class discussion can provide opportunities for 'eliciting pupils' thinking – making this thinking explicit and open for further discussion' (van Boxtel & van Drie, 2013, p. 51). All pupils benefit from having the disciplinary process articulated; the highest-attaining will quickly be able to recognise the processes underlying historical scholarship and begin to translate this understanding into their own writing.

Case studies to discuss with your mentee

Case study 5.2 Leila's support for a pupil with dyslexia

Leila teaches Danika, a pupil with a dyslexia diagnosis. In a class discussion Danika describes Hitler as being 'an authoritarian ruler of a totalitarian regime'. When she comes to write this down in her work, she simply says that 'Hitler was a bad man'. What does Leila need to do to enable Danika to reveal her understanding?

Case study 5.3 Adeel's targets

For the past three weeks Adeel's mentor has set him the target 'to use more adaptive teaching techniques to help pupils with lower literacy access tasks'. In his most recent lesson, with Year 10, Adeel was disappointed with the pupil responses to the exam-style question he set. He noted that the lower-attaining pupils achieved marks at least one or two grades below their target grade and were not able to do much beyond stating a few key names, despite having been retaught the substantive knowledge just before they attempted the question.

Adeel feels he is building in lots of opportunities for knowledge retrieval and checking pupil understanding. What else does Adeel need to consider?

Case study 5.4 Paul's support of newly arrived refugee children

Several refugee children have recently arrived at Paul's school, having fled from a war-torn country. These pupils are new to English. Some have arrived with their families, others are living with relatives, and some are living in local authority care. Three students are about to join Paul's Year 9 class. The next enquiry is about the Blitz.

What considerations does Paul need to have in mind when planning for these pupils to join his class?

Summary and key points

- Beginning teachers need to be supported to develop inclusive practices in the history classroom to ensure that all pupils can reach their potential.
- Inclusive practice involves adapting teaching to support learners with a range of special education needs and disabilities, stretching learners who demonstrate aptitude for history, supporting bilingual and multilingual learners, especially those who are new to learning English, and also respecting the individual identity, culture, and background of all pupils.
- Planning for inclusive practice needs to take place at the level of curriculum planning, lesson planning, and in-lesson adaptation.
- Understanding pupils as individuals is key to meeting their needs, and beginning teachers need to build a toolkit of approaches from which they can select appropriate strategies to help all pupils to better understand history and engage in deeper historical thinking.

Further reading and resources

- **Chapman, A. (2006). Supporting *High Achievement in History: Conclusions of the NAGTY History Think Tank 28/29 November 2005*. Warwick: gifted talented youth: The National Academy**

  This report explores what it means for a young person to demonstrate a particular aptitude for history and how this can be supported. It can be accessed here: https://

www.academia.edu/19742315/Chapman_A_2006_Supporting_High_Achievement_in_History_Conclusions_of_the_NAGTY_History_Think_Tank_28_29_November_2005

- **Harris, R. (2005) 'Does differentiation have to mean different?'** *Teaching History* **118, and Kerridge, R. (2017) 'Learning without limits',** *Teaching History 168*

    These articles are important reading for beginning teachers considering how to make history accessible and meaningful for all pupils.

- **The Bell Foundation**

    The Bell Foundation aims to overcome the disadvantage experienced by children, adults, and communities in the UK that speak English as an Additional Language (EAL) through language education. Their website contains training support and practical guidance for teaching staff working with pupils who have EAL. Their site can be accessed here: https://www.bell-foundation.org.uk/

References

Agarwal, P. K. (2019). Retrieval practice & Bloom's taxonomy: do students need fact knowledge before higher order learning? *Journal of Educational Psychology 111*(2), 189-209.

Arnot, M., Schneider, C., Evans, M., Liu, Y., Welply, O., & Davies-Tutt, D. (2014). *School Approaches to the Education of EAL Students*. Cambridge: The Bell Foundation. Retrieved 13 August 2022 from https://www.bell-foundation.org.uk/app/uploads/2017/05/Full-Report-FV.pdf

Bellinger, L. (2008). Cultivating curiosity about complexity. *Teaching History 132*, 5-15.

Benger, A. (2020). Teaching Year 9 to argue like cultural historians: recasting the concepts of empathy as historical perspective. *Teaching History 179*, 24-35.

Burn, K., & Harris, R. (2021). *Historical Association Survey of History in Secondary*. London: Historical Association. Retrieved 3 August 2022 from https://www.history.org.uk/secondary/categories/409/news/4014/historical-association-secondary-survey-2021

Chapman, A. (2006). *Supporting High Achievement in History: Conclusions of the NAGTY History Think Tank 28/29 November 2005*. Warwick: gifted talented youth: The National Academy. Retrieved 29 January 2023 from https://www.academia.edu/19742315/Chapman_A_2006_Supporting_High_Achievement_in_History_Conclusions_of_the_NAGTY_History_Think_Tank_28_29_November_2005

Collins, S. (2013). Cunning Plan for placing visual sources at the heart of historical learning. *Teaching History 152*, 42-4.

Counsell, C. (1996, September 13). The march of 'Mutlin'. *Times Educational Supplement*. Retrieved from https://www.tes.com/magazine/archive/march-mutlin

Counsell, C. (1997). *Analytical and Discursive Writing at Key Stage 3*. London: Historical Association. Retrieved 12 August 2022 from https://www.history.org.uk/secondary/resource/1948/analytic-and-discursive-writing-at-key-stage-3

Croft, M. (2005). The Tudor monarchy in crisis: using a historian's account to stretch the most able students in Year 8. *Teaching History 119*, 15-21.

Crooks, V. (2021). *Finding Your Way with Questioning: A Practical Approach for Getting Better at Questioning*. Retrieved 28 January 2023 from *Becoming a History Teacher*, https://uonhistoryteachertraining.school.blog/2021/11/13/finding-your-way-with-questioning-a-practical-approach-for-getting-better-at-questioning

Dawson, I. (2018). *Exploring and Teaching Medieval History*. London: Historical Association. Retrieved 4 August 2022 from www.history.org.uk: https://www.history.org.uk/secondary/resource/9290/exploring-and-teaching-medieval-history-in-schools

DfE. (2019a). *Early Career Framework*. UK Government Department for Education. London: Crown copyright. Retrieved March 2022 from https://www.gov.uk/government/publications/early-career-framework

DfE. (2019b). *ITT Core Content Framework*. Government UK, Department for Education. London: Crown. Retrieved 31 May 2022 from https://assets.publishing.service.gov.uk/government/uploads/system/uploads/attachment_data/file/974307/ITT_core_content_framework_.pdf

DfE. (2020). *English Proficiency of Pupils with English as an Additional Language*. London: Crown. Retrieved 26 January 2023 from https://assets.publishing.service.gov.uk/government/uploads/system/uploads/attachment_data/file/868209/English_proficiency_of_EAL_pupils.pdf

DfE & DHSC. (2015). *Special Educational Needs and Disability Code of Practice: 0 to 25 years*. Department for Education and Department of Health. London: Crown copyright. Retrieved 3 August 2022 from https://www.gov.uk/government/publications/send-code-of-practice-0-to-25

Druckman, D., & Bjork, R. (1994). *Learning, Remembering, Believing: Enhancing Human Performance*. Washington, DC: National Academy Press.

Evans, J., & Pate, G. (2007). Does scaffolding make them fall? Reflecting on strategies for developing causal argument in Years 8 and 11. *Teaching History 128*, 18-29.

Fordham, M. (2016). Knowledge and language: being historical with substantive concepts. In C. Counsell, K. Burn, & A. Chapman, *MasterClass in History Education: Transforming Teaching and Learning* (pp. 43-58). London: Bloomsbury.

Foster, R. (2011). Passive receivers or constructive readers? Pupils' experiences of an encounter with academic history. *Teaching History 142*, 4-13.

Foster, R. (2013). The more things change, the more they stay the same: developing students' thinking about change and continuity. *Teaching History 151*, 8-17.

Foster, R. (2015). Pipes's punctuation and making complex historical claims. *Teaching History 159*, 8-13.

Foster, R., & Goudie, K. (2016). Shaping the debate. Why historians matter more than ever at GCSE. *Teaching History 163*, 17-24.

Frankopan, P. (2016). *The Silk Roads*. London: Bloomsbury Publishing.

Gestsdóttir, S., van Boxtel, C., & van Drie, J. (2018). Teaching historical thinking and reasoning: Construction of an observation instrument. *British Educational Research Journal 44*(6), 960-81. Retrieved 12 August 2022 from https://bera-journals.onlinelibrary.wiley.com/doi/10.1002/berj.3471

Gooptar, C. (2021). Leaders in the community: Eric Irons. Retrieved 13 August 2022 from Nottingham Museums, https://nottinghammuseums.org.uk/leaders-in-the-community-eric-irons/

Grande, J. (2022). #7 This week, in history . . . I've been checking 'for' understanding less. This is what I've been doing instead. Retrieved 12 August 2022 from Curricular Pasts, https://curricularpasts.wordpress.com/2022/03/13/7-this-week-in-history-ive-been-checking-for-understanding-less-this-is-what-ive-been-doing-instead/

Hammond, K. (1999). And Joe arrives . . .: stretching the very able pupil in the mixed ability classroom. *Teaching History 94*, 23-31.

Harris, R. (2005). Does differentiation have to mean different? *Teaching History 118*, 5-12.

Harris, R. (2021). Disciplinary knowledge denied? In A. Chapman (ed.), *Knowing History in Schools* (pp. 97-128). London: UCL Press. doi: 10.14324/111.9781787357303

Harris, R., Burn, K., & Woolley, M. (2013). *The Guided Reader to Teaching and Learning History*. Oxford: Taylor & Francis Group.

Hill, M. (2020). Curating the imagined past: world building in the history curriculum. *Teaching History 180*, 10-20.

Hill, M. (2021). Picturing the past: using historical illustration with clarity and purpose. *Historical Association Conference*. Historical Association. https://www.haconference.com/wp-content/uploads/2021/04/Conference-grid-21-as-of-31-March.pdf

Hollis, C. (2021). Illuminating the possibilities of the past: the role of representation in A-level curriculum planning. *Teaching History 185*, 22-9.

Jenner, T. (2019). Making reading routine. *Teaching History 174*, 42-8.

Kerridge, R. (2017). Learning without limits. *Teaching History, 168*, 16-22.

Lee, P., & Shemilt, D. (2004). 'I just wish we could go back in the past and find out what really happened': progression in understanding about historical accounts. *Teaching History 117*, 25-31.

Lemov, D., Hernandez, J., & Kim, J. (2016). *Teach Like a Champion Field Guide 2. 0: A Practical Resource to Make the 62 Techniques Your Own*. New York: John Wiley & Sons, Incorporated.

Loft, P., & Danechi, S. (2020). *Support for More Able and Talented Children in Schools (UK)*. House of Commons Library Briefing Paper. London: House of Commons Library. Retrieved 3 August 2022 from https://researchbriefings.files.parliament.uk/documents/CBP-9065/CBP-9065.pdf

McDermott, L.A. (2020). Triumphs show: making their historical writing explode. *Teaching History 181*, 68-71.

Mohamud, A., & Whitburn, R. (2014). Unpacking the suitcase and finding history. *Teaching History, 154*, 40-46.

Mohamud, A., & Whitburn, R. (2016). *Doing Justice to History: Transforming Black History in Secondary Schools*. London: Trentham Books.

Pampoulou, E., & Detheridge, C. (2007). The role of symbols in the mainstream to access literacy. *Journal of Assistive Technologies 1*(1), 21-7.

Phillips, R. (2001). Making history curious: Using Initial Stimulus Material (ISM) to promote enquiry, thinking and literacy. *Teaching History 105*, 19-25.

Philpott, J. (2008). Helping pupils with Special Educational Needs to develop a lifelong curiosity for the past. *Teaching History 131*, 44-50.

Quigley, A. (2020). *Closing the Reading Gap*. London: Routledge.

Riley, M. (2000). Into the Key Stage 3 history garden: choosing and planting your enquiry questions. *Teaching History 99*, 8-13.

Seixas, P., & Morton, T. (2012). *The Big Six Historical Thinking Concepts*. Toronto: Nelson College Indigenous.

Sherrington, T. (2019). *The Learning Rainforest: Great Teaching in Real Classrooms*. Melton: John Catt Educational Limited.

Stephen, A. (2005). 'Why can't they just live together happily Miss?' Unravelling the complexities of the Arab-Israeli conflict at GCSE. *Teaching History 120*, 5-10.

Strand, S., & Lindorff, A. (2021). *English as an Additional Language, Proficiency in English and Rate of Progression: Pupil, School and LA Variation*. University of Oxford Department of Education; Unbound Philanthropy; The Bell Foundation. Cambridge: The Bell Foundation. Retrieved 4 August 2022 from https://www.bell-foundation.org.uk/app/uploads/2021/03/University-of-Oxford-Report-March-2021.pdf

Style, E. (1996). *Curriculum as a Window or a Mirror, Social Science Record*. Summit, NJ: Social Science Record. Retrieved 4 August 2022 from https://nationalseedproject.org/Key-SEED-Texts/curriculum-as-window-and-mirror

The Bell Foundation. (2017). *Classroom Support Strategies: Working with EAL Learners in Secondary Settings*. Retrieved 26 January 2023 from The Bell Foundation, https://www.bell-foundation.org.uk/app/uploads/2018/07/Classroom-Support-Strategies-Working-with-EAL-Learners-in-Secondary-Settings.pdf

Thompson, A., & Walsh, K. (2020). *Teacher Handbook: SEND - Embedding Inclusive Practice*. WholeSchool SEND. London: nasen.

Traille, K. (2007). 'You should be proud about your history: They made me feel ashamed': teaching history hurts. *Teaching History 127*, 31-7.

van Boxtel, C., & van Drie, J. (2013). Historical reasoning in the classroom. *Teaching History 150*, 44-52.

Wilkinson, M. (2014). Helping Muslim boys succeed: the case for history education. *Curriculum Journal, 25*(3), 396-431. doi: 10.1080/09585176.2014.929527

Willingham, D. (2009). *Why Don't Students Like School*. San Francisco, CA: Wiley.

Woodcock, J. (2005). Does the linguistic release the conceptual? Helping Year 10 to improve their causal reasoning. *Teaching History 119*, 5-14.

Woods, T. (2021). Diversifying the curriculum: one department's holistic approach. *Teaching History 183*, 62-71.

Worth, P. (2017, 24 September). 'It's like this big, black hole, Miss, that's dragging everything into it.' Year 9 consider the impact of World War I on Russia by playing with the idea of consequence 'shapes'. Retrieved 26 January 2023 from *History Teaching and Learning*, https://lobworth.com/2017/09/24/its-like-this-big-black-hole-miss-thats-dragging-everything-into-it-year-9-consider-the-impact-of-world-war-i-on-russia-by-playing-with-the-idea-of-consequence-shapes/

Worth, P. (2018). Here ends the lesson: shaping lesson conclusions as an iterative process in improving historical enquiries. *Teaching History 173*, 58-67.

6 Developing beginning teachers' reflective practice through lesson observation and feedback

Laura London

Introduction

While the value of high-stakes lesson observation has been challenged (Coe et al., 2014), the fundamental importance of observing beginning teachers as part of a formative process is well established. The process of lesson observation and feedback remains the most obvious method of constructing beginning teachers' learning (Burn, Hagger, & Mutton, 2015). At its best, this process generates a cycle of reflection, whereby beginning teachers are supported to recognise what they are doing and to understand how effective this is, and are given suggestions for how they might adapt their teaching in the future.

Using lesson observations to create space for a professional dialogue between the observer and the beginning teacher is a complicated and challenging approach. The process itself tends to forefront the asymmetrical nature of the relationship between mentors and beginning teachers (Puttick, 2022). It can serve as a reminder of the mentor's role in the assessment of the beginning teacher's ultimate competence. For many beginning teachers, this can cause concern and anxiety (Burn, Hagger, & Mutton, 2015). Therefore, it is important that beginning teachers see observations and feedback as a valuable, formative, two-way process. This can help mediate beginning teachers' anxiety by giving them greater agency and showing them that it is not about getting it 'right or wrong'.

One further aim of this chapter is to emphasise a mentor's role in supporting beginning teachers to further enhance pupils' historical learning. During lesson observation and feedback, there is potential for mentors to overlook the subject-specific dimension in favour of more immediate and generic concerns, especially those relating to pupils' behaviour. This chapter will provide a rationale for a more historically focused approach to lesson observation and feedback and provide practical strategies to support this approach.

Objectives

At the end of the chapter, you should be able to:

- Understand how observation and feedback support beginning history teachers' development.
- Understand how to structure the observation cycle to best support beginning teachers to engage in meaningful reflection and develop their history teaching.

DOI: 10.4324/9781003223504-6

- Engage in effective and meaningful observation and feedback that focuses on the historical purpose of lessons and pupils' historical learning.
- Design subject-specific lesson feedback with a rigorous focus on pupils' historical learning.

Building relationships

It is not unusual for beginning teachers to have fears about their teaching being 'judged' during lesson observations. These fears can be particularly acute if the observer is a tutor from their Initial Teacher Education (ITE) provider or a member of the school's leadership team. It is natural that beginning teachers will want the lesson to go well. Therefore, beginning teachers can approach lesson observation and feedback as an opportunity to anticipate the observers' judgements, rather than as an opportunity to be truly reflective. Observation and feedback are key to empowering beginning teachers (Lofthouse & Wright, 2021), and a dialogic model of mentoring provides beginning teachers with greater opportunities for professional agency.

In a dialogic model, mentors and beginning teachers work together to extend their understanding. A dialogic approach to lesson observation and feedback will involve collaborative, two-way, discussions at each stage of the observation process. Beginning teachers and mentors ask probing questions and value each other's reflections. In this model, mentors are careful to avoid making strong claims. There is a recognition, as there is in the discipline of history, that claims to knowledge are complex and partial. These dialogic, professionally curious conversations can further enable positive relationships between mentor and mentee.

The lesson observation process

The process of lesson observation and feedback should be structured to maximise beginning teachers' development as they begin to navigate the realities of the classroom. The observation cycle can be broken down into three stages:

1. Pre-observation.
2. The lesson observation.
3. Post-observation.

1. Pre-observation

At this point, it is helpful to agree on both a schedule for observation and a focus for the observation with your mentee. It is important that a beginning teacher knows when they will be observed and is clear about how they need to prepare for this. For example, is a lesson plan required? If so, how far in advance should this be given to the class teacher? Answering these questions will make the beginning teacher more comfortable. The focus for the observation will need to be appropriate to the stage of training and the needs of your mentee. For example, a teacher who is very new to the classroom might focus on designing and meeting purposeful lesson objectives, whereas a more confident beginning teacher might focus on establishing criteria for assessing pupils' understanding of the disciplinary concept of historical significance. Your mentee could take the lead in deciding on a focus for the lesson, or you and your mentee could determine this together.

A review of the lesson plan is also an important diagnostic pre-observation activity. Not all schools will ask beginning teachers to produce a full lesson plan for each lesson taught. This, at least in part, reflects understandable concerns over beginning teachers' workload. While increasing attempts to ease the workload of beginning teachers are welcome, there is also a growing belief that beginning teachers do not need to plan their own lessons to be effective (Green, 2018). However, during the early stages of a beginning teachers' career, their lesson plans provide a crucial insight into their planning rationale. In their research exploring how the subject of geography was incorporated into written lesson observation feedback, Healy Walshe, and Dunphy (2020) also 'found that lesson plans were perceived to be an important way of viewing the trainees' approach and underpinning curricular thinking' (p. 20). The authors point out that given the value of lesson plans for 'rendering visible' curricular thinking, their benefit may well outweigh the workload involved (p. 20). For more on lesson planning, see Chapter 4.

Discussing lesson plans with your mentee is an opportunity for a pre-observation conversation about the intended historical learning. As well as offering encouragement, this conversation is also an opportunity to ask your mentee some questions about the lesson plan. For example:

- Is the historical purpose of this lesson clear to the pupils?
- Do the tasks 'match' with the lesson objectives or enquiry question?
- What previous substantive knowledge will this lesson build on?
- Where are the opportunities in this lesson to check for pupils' understanding?
- What historical misconceptions or preconceptions might come up in the lesson? How can these be dealt with?

By following a questioning and dialogic approach at the pre-observation stage, beginning teachers' own reflections are valued. Task 6.1 provides some prompts for reflection to support this process.

Task 6.1 Pre-lesson observation activities for mentors

In your role as mentor think about how you will work with beginning teachers on their pre-lesson activities.

- How will you agree on a focus before the observation?
- What information will you ask for before the lesson? Will you ask for a copy of the lesson plan? How far in advance of the lesson will you want to see this?
- How will you build beginning teachers' confidence in their own reflections?

---

2. The lesson observation

The lesson observation itself provides mentors with the opportunity to take a diagnostic view of a lesson, with a focus on what is (potentially) effective. While it is inevitable that there will be a need to focus on more generic aspects of the lesson like behaviour management, the emphasis should largely be on the historical learning of the pupils. This subject-specific focus does present some challenges. One of these is that subject-specific concerns can be overtaken by more pragmatic and logistical ones during mentoring conversations (Lindgren, 2005). In addition, beginning teachers are educated in a variety of settings. In some settings, this means teachers are educated within cross-curricular groups, with limited subject-specific input. For these beginning teachers, a history-specific focus is arguably even more important to their development. As Brooks (2017) asserts, beginning teachers need mentors who are going to be able to support them to look beyond behaviour and examine the learning that is happening in their classroom.

As an observer it is not possible to 'see' everything in a lesson; however, this chapter aims to support mentors to attend to the historical learning within the classroom and to follow this up with better history-specific conversations after the lesson. The implication is that an increased focus on subject-specific aspects of the lesson is desirable. As beginning teachers progress through their ITE year, they will move from a focus on technical aspects of enaction in the classroom to more difficult and complex conversations about the curricular object and the ways that students contrast meaning in their subject.

> Mentors need to be supported to avoid the 'observation trap' and to help their mentees think beyond these surface level 'symptoms' of the lesson to the actual 'causes' of those symptoms – causes which often reside in their framing of the subject itself and the curricular thinking which underpins the lesson. A good example of this is around questioning. All the wait time and cold calling in the world won't make a questioning phase in a lesson go well if the questions themselves are fundamentally flawed and lacking disciplinary purpose. (Crooks & London, 2022)

While it is not always easy to take a subject-specific approach to observation, it is certainly possible. Expert mentors look past the logistics of the classroom to 'notice' the historical learning taking place. The tutor and mentors working on the History PGCE (Postgraduate Certificate in Education) at the University of East Anglia (UEA) identified a range of 'common' history-specific areas for development amongst trainees. These areas for development went on to inform a set of history-specific questions (Table 6.1) designed to help mentors identify potential areas for development during lesson observation. This list might also be helpful when deciding on a focus for the lesson observation. For each of these areas, there is suggested reading to support beginning teachers' and mentors' future practice. It is not meant as an exhaustive list of features of a 'good lesson'. These suggestions are intended to support and scaffold mentees' learning and to show that mentors and mentees can both develop their teaching by reading and reflecting together. You can use the prompts in Task 6.2 to reflect on the suggestions in Table 6.1.

Table 6.1 Questions to support mentors to focus on historical learning during lesson observations developed drawing on UEA History PGCE course materials (London, 2022)

Question	Rationale	Potential further reading
Is the lesson or lesson sequence structured around a worthwhile enquiry question? Is the enquiry question used during lesson transitions to support pupils' progress and check for understanding?	An enquiry question is a genuine and worthwhile historical question that pupils are required to answer at the end of a series of lessons. When carefully crafted, enquiry questions can capture pupils' curiosity, build pupils' substantive knowledge, and develop pupils' understanding of historical concepts. In this blog post, Hugh Richards has collated examples of enquiry questions that both 'chime and resonate'.	H. Richards. (2019). Ringing the changes: the power of enquiry questions that both chime and resonate. Retrieved 7 December 2022 from https://onebighistorydepartment.com/2019/07/12/ringing-the-changes-the-power-of-enquiry-questions-that-both-chime-and-resonate/.
Does the lesson appreciate the historical 'bigger picture' and make links to previously taught knowledge and concepts?	When pressed for time, beginning teachers can get into the habit of planning one lesson at a time. Given the workload of a beginning teacher, this is understandable, but it will not allow beginning teachers to see how a coherent sequence of lessons is planned. Consider how the lesson shows an awareness of the whole scheme of work and the knowledge and skills previously taught. Think about how this lesson builds on those taught previously and how it builds a broader understanding of the period.	H. Snelson. (2021).Film: lesson sequences. Retrieved 7 December 2022 from Historical Association's History Teaching for Beginners Webinar Series, https://www.history.org.uk/secondary/resource/10060/film-lesson-sequences.
Does the lesson have a clear historical rationale or purpose?	Sometimes, lessons lack a clear historical rationale or purpose because beginning teachers are unsure about why they are teaching a topic. This might be reflected in the lesson as a tendency towards moral judgement rather than historical explanation. For example, beginning teachers might ask pupils 'Was the Treaty of Versailles fair?' leading pupils to make a moral judgement based on their own contemporary understanding. This ignores the historical perspectives of the time; a different question to allow pupils to better understand historical perspectives might be 'Did the Treaty of Versailles "allow the French to have their victory"'? The quotation here is taken from Paula Kitching's 2019 'The Peace Treaties of 1919'.	M. Riley. (2000). Into the Key Stage 3 history garden: choosing and planting your enquiry questions. *Teaching History*, 99, 8-13.

Table 6.1 Cont.

Question	Rationale	Potential further reading
Is the lesson underpinned by historical scholarship?	Excellent teaching is rooted in strong subject knowledge and the benefits of using historical scholarship in the history classroom have been well documented. During the lesson observation, consider to what extent the lesson reflects recent historical thinking and debate. Beginning teachers have many demands on their time and they might find articles from popular history magazines or podcasts helpful for swiftly updating their subject knowledge.	R. Foster. (2011) Passive receivers or constructive readers? Pupils' experiences of an encounter with academic history. *Teaching History*, *142*, 4-13.
Does the lesson prompt genuine historical thinking? Are the 'higher-value' activities given enough time within the lesson?	Consider which activities in the lesson are most successful for developing pupils' historical understanding. In a bid to cover more content in lessons, beginning teachers sometimes spend more time asking pupils to transfer substantive knowledge from one format to another, without asking pupils to use this knowledge to think historically. In England, this is more often observed in GCSE history lessons, possibly because of the increased content in the specifications.	S. Wineburg. (2007). Unnatural and essential: the nature of historical thinking. *Teaching History* 129, 7-11.
Is this a lesson that appreciates different types of historical knowledge and the ways that subject knowledge can be built in history?	Reflect on the balance between substantive knowledge and historical concepts within the lesson. An imbalance is often demonstrated when beginning teachers ask pupils to make a judgement without first establishing that pupils have a secure knowledge base to make this assessment. Consider the extent to which the pupils have the secure 'fingertip' knowledge (Counsell, 2017, p. 81) required to answer a question that requires a reasoned judgement.	C. Counsell. (2017). The fertility of substantive knowledge: in search of its hidden generative power. In I. Davies (ed.), *Debates in History Teaching* (pp. 80-99). Abingdon: Routledge.
Does the lesson provide opportunities for pupils to get better at history?	Consider opportunities within the lesson for pupils to get better at history. This does not only mean the pupils acquiring substantive knowledge. The beginning teacher also needs a clear idea about how pupils will develop their understanding of disciplinary concepts like significance or causal reasoning.	A. Ford. (2014). Setting us free: building meaningful models of progression for a 'post levels' world. *Teaching History, 157*, 28-40.

(Continued)

Table 6.1 Cont.

Question	Rationale	Potential further reading
Does questioning and dialogue extend pupils' historical thinking?	Under the pressure of observation, beginning teachers can sometimes rush through question and dialogue to get pupils back on task. Beginning teachers may also inadvertently accept factually incorrect answers from pupils. In these instances, it is important to make the beginning teacher aware of this in the lesson feedback. This will allow them to make the corrections in future lessons. Consider the extent to which openings are created and taken to check for pupils' understanding. Questioning is a vital chance for the beginning teacher to recognise, explore, and correct pupils' misconceptions.	E. Stevens (2021). How can we improve our use of questioning in the classroom? Retrieved 7 December 2022, from Practical Histories, https://practicalhistories.cm/2021/09/how-can-we-improve-our-use-of-questioning-in-the-classroom/
Can all pupils access the historical learning in the lesson?	Sometimes pupils cannot access the lesson because the unique challenges of teaching history have not been addressed. For example, it might be that pupils cannot access the history-specific terminology required. Alternatively, does the lesson avoid the pitfalls of presentism? It would be very difficult for pupils to appreciate the historical significance of the Black Death if they were to simply assume that people in the Middle Ages were 'stupid' for not understanding the scientific reasons for the spread of the disease.	T. Huijgen & P. Holthius. (2015). Why am I being accused of being a heretic?' A pedagogical framework for stimulating historical contextualisation. *Teaching History 158*, 50–5.

Task 6.2 Mentor reflection: history-specific observations

- Why do you think taking a subject-specific approach to observations is challenging?
- Consider times when you have been observed. Who observed your lessons? How did that impact on the kind of lesson feedback that you received?
- Consider history lessons that you have observed. Have you seen lessons in which these areas for development might have applied?

---

3. Post-observation

The practice of observing lessons and providing feedback has always been a key part of the mentoring process in schools. Research suggests that some mentors are more accomplished in this facet of mentoring than others, and some are more adept than others at supporting mentees to find their own solutions, without coming across as heart-sinkingly hypercritical and demoralising (Hobson & Malderez, 2013). Research has shown the importance of building trusting personal relationships so that beginning teachers can view the mentor not as a 'judge' but as a 'critical friend' (Adey, 1997, p. 132). Research involving mentors working in England and Germany suggested that, while mentors in England place emphasis on 'support', their German counterparts stress the importance of being 'honest' (Jones, 2001, p. 81). This is likely due in part to cultural factors, as in Germany, 'criticism is generally expressed more generously and frankly than in England' (p. 83). However, structural factors also have a role to play. In England, mentors take the role of 'assessor' in ITE and therefore may feel that they need to be more supportive to attempt to alleviate mentees' anxieties because of this (p. 83). While many mentors will err on the side of positivity, it is also important to be honest with beginning teachers about the areas for improvement. Post-lesson conversations can become emotionally charged, especially when a lesson hasn't gone to plan. To defuse tensions, it can help to set aside a specific time for this conversation to take place and to allow beginning teachers some time to gather their thoughts and reflect on the lesson.

The conversation after the lesson

Post-lesson, there will be a variety of ways to give feedback to trainees. During the post-lesson conversation as mentor, you need to be conscious of the potential for judging the beginning teachers (Hobson & Malderez, 2013). This can occur when a mentor reveals 'too readily and/or too often her/his own judgements on or evaluations of the mentee's planning and teaching' (p. 91). Strong advice within lesson feedback can be restrictive and disempowering, and the use of open and probing questions prompts more reflective responses from beginning teachers. You could start by asking the beginning teacher a question like 'What did you think went well today?' followed by 'Is there anything that you might do differently next time?' It is also important to frame feedback in positive terms and consider the positives first. You could then move into a series of questions about the lesson. The aim here is to support your mentee to reflect and come to their own conclusions and decisions for next time. Table 6.2 provides a suggested structure for your post-lesson conversation.

Table 6.2 Structure for feedback conversations following the lesson observation

Stage	Purpose	For example:
Reassure	Make a positive comment so that the beginning teacher feels that you valued their lesson.	'Thank you – I really enjoyed that.' 'It was good to see Yasmin contributing an answer.'
Establishing a dialogue	By finding out how the beginning teacher feels about the lesson, you open up the dialogue as a two-way process. This allows the beginning teacher to value their own reflections. It is important to fully explore the strengths of the lesson as well as areas for development during the conversation.	'How did you think it went? ''What were you most pleased with today?' 'What feedback from last time did you act on in today's lesson?'

(Continued)

Table 6.2 Cont.

Stage	Purpose	For example:
Review & reflect	Ask the beginning teacher specific questions to encourage them to reflect on aspects of their lesson. This creates an opportunity for the beginning teacher to identify for themselves areas for development.	'You said that you thought that the pupils found the living graph activity confusing. How did you know this?' 'How could you model this for pupils next time?' 'I know that you felt that pupils did not have a clear understanding of the concept of "power". When have pupils learnt about this before?' 'How did you tap into what they already knew about this concept?'
Emphasise	At this point, you can confirm (or not) the beginning teachers' suggestions and emphasise the key aspects of the lesson, including strengths and areas for development. Beginning teachers will need help to differentiate minor concerns from more significant areas for development. Decide on specific areas for development.	'Overall, the lesson really sparked pupils' curiosity through the creative task design.' 'The main area for development is to ensure that pupils can access the lesson and understand historical terminology.'
Action steps	The aim is to establish an understanding of the target/s for the next observation. You can then decide together on action steps. The might take the form of a focused observation, specific reading and reflection, or adapting lesson resources. The beginning teacher should be able to explain what their target for development is *and* what they are going to do to meet their target.	'We need to decide where to go with our targets for next lesson. My feeling is either embedding the enquiry or a focus on reading strategies. What are your thoughts?'

Written feedback

There is evidence to suggest that written feedback following lesson observations is valued by beginning teachers (Hobson et al., 2009). Written feedback is important because beginning teachers may only partially remember post-lesson conversations due to the heightened emotions associated with lesson observations and feedback. The written mode of feedback can also be perceived as more formal and final than verbal feedback.

Written feedback is usually given when targets are set and recorded for future teaching. It is not possible or desirable to focus on every area of development from a lesson at once.

Teaching is complex, and expert mentors tend to focus on one or two aspects for development following a lesson to avoid overloading beginning teachers. Judiciously selecting areas for development that are most beneficial to beginning teachers is a skill. The types of targets set for beginning teachers are influenced by a range of different considerations, including the stage of the beginning teacher's career and their strengths and areas for development.

Research on written lesson observation feedback has broadly supported claims that subject-specific aspects of teaching have tended to be given limited consideration during feedback after a lesson observation. In their study of written lesson observation feedback, Puttick and Wynn (2021) found that written feedback is often generic and does not focus on subject-specific advice. Beginning teachers, especially those early on in their ITE programme, will rightly benefit from feedback on their behaviour management; however, as a beginning teacher develops their teaching practice, this feedback should increasingly focus on pupils' historical learning. Healy et al. (2020) consider the valuable opportunities provided by written feedback in geography to 'render visible' curricular thinking and develop beginning teachers as subject specialists. Once mentors forefront historical learning in their written observations, opportunities are created to open up subject-specific dialogue between beginning teachers and their mentors.

Questioning is a good example of this. After a lesson, a beginning teacher might be given a written target to 'develop questioning to include more open questions'. However, this does not support the beginning teacher to ask *high-quality* open questions. In the post-lesson conversation, the mentor can check the beginning teacher's understanding of the written feedback. Does the beginning teacher understand what makes a rigorous open question? During the conversation, the mentor can model examples of the sort of questions that the mentee could use and ask the mentee to plan their open questions for the next lesson with this class. The targets from the previous lesson inform the beginning teacher's planning for future lessons.

This can be difficult, as these kinds of targets are not easy to convert into a form that fits the popular model of the 'SMART' target. Sometimes, targets can be very precise and achievable; however, this is not always the case. It can be helpful to think about a continuum between hard-edged, specific targets and things to think about over a sequence of lessons and a period of weeks and months. The written lesson feedback in Table 6.3 provides an example of one approach. Task 6.3 provides a further opportunity for you to reflect on the value of written lesson feedback.

Table 6.3 Example of written lesson observation feedback

Class: Year 10   Topic: Was the Elizabethan period a 'golden age'?

Lesson question: Did Sir Francis Drake's treasure make him a 'national treasure'?

Please comment on positive evidence of (potentially) effective teaching.

Clear and concise explanation of the lesson objectives, that is well linked to a departmental enquiry question.

You gave a precise explanation of the term 'national treasure' – giving the example of David Attenborough. Sparking pupils' curiosity through relevant examples was a real strength. It allowed you to access their prior learning and address misconceptions, e.g., around 'exploration' – making the point that this was the first *recorded* circumnavigation is so important – by introducing the students to the nuance, you are alleviating misconceptions.

This lesson really fired students' enthusiasm in the following ways:

- Teacher exposition was confident, engaging, and underpinned by detailed subject knowledge.
- Use of images is beginning to build a sense of time and place for the students.
- This is a small class, and you gave real thought as to how to engage the pupils with paired work and movement around the room.

High expectations were evident throughout, as demonstrated by including plenty of tier three vocabulary, e.g., breaking down circumnavigation to show its meaning before beginning reading. Decoding language in this way will help students across subjects.

You are beginning to focus on how pupils can 'get better' at understanding historical interpretations and you built pupils' relevant substantive knowledge before asking them to make a reasoned judgement. You gave a wonderful explanation of what an interpretation is. It was interesting when you asked the class 'Can I just go around saying things?' They responded 'No' and you were able to ask them 'Why not?' This is such an important point. In dialogue together you made the powerful point that historians use evidence to construct their interpretations – this gets to the heart of what a historian does.

Select up to 3 aspects that can be developed and give clear guidance on what the teacher can do to achieve these.

Evaluation of interpretations

You were beginning to think about how pupils might make progress in their understanding of historical interpretations. Do the pupils know how to go about evaluating historical interpretations?

- Consider the questions you want pupils to ask about interpretations. Read 'What's the wisdom on... Interpretations of the past' from *Teaching History*, 177 (Historical Association, 2019), as it has a useful list.
- Create your own list of questions for our next mentor meeting. We will use this to co-plan your Year 8 Cromwell lesson.

Lesson endings

I was pleased to see a plenary (odd one out) included today and I know this has been a focus for you. How did the lesson ending serve your overall enquiry question?

- Consider how your plenary could look 'forwards' to the next lessons in the sequence to set up the learning for next time.
- In your observations this week, make a note of how teachers end lessons and set up the learning for the next lesson. Do lessons all need a 'different' plenary?
- Review your notes from reading Paula Worth's article 'Here ends the lesson: shaping lesson conclusions as an iterative process in improving historical enquiries' in *Teaching History* 174 (2018).

Task 6.3 Mentor reflection: providing subject-specific written feedback

Read the following lesson observation feedback and make a note of your answer to the following questions:

- How effective do you think this lesson feedback is?
- What is the mentor doing well?
- In what ways could this be more useful for a beginning teacher?

Lesson title: What were the causes of the Black Death and how did it spread?

Details of teaching seen, with a focus on what is potentially effective. Take a diagnostic view.

- Calm, settled, and focused start. Register taken.
- The starter clip really engaged the class, who obviously enjoyed it. They enjoyed the card-sorting activity to put the events of the spread of the Black Death into chronological order.
- This was a well-planned, well-resourced lesson.
- Subject knowledge was good today.
- You have an approachable, yet firm manner with the class and use your voice really well to show your enthusiasm. The behaviour today was good, and you were as firm as you needed to be. As needed, use the school system to give warnings and reinforce your high expectation. I know this class are very enthusiastic and like to ask a lot of questions.
- In our feedback, it was good to hear that you had differentiated the lesson for one specific pupil to support his access to the lesson.

Select up to 3 aspects that can be developed and give clear guidance on **what the teacher can do** to achieve these.

- Consider how you can use strategies to deal with all the pupils' questions (maybe by having questions at the end or in the backs of books etc.) You were beginning

to deflect these points more effectively by the end of the lesson and were well justified in doing so.
- Questioning – this is an area where you are already making progress. Continue to ask follow-up questions and 'bounce' questions around the room. Experiment with whole class response systems. For example, mini whiteboards, thumbs up/down etc.

Compare your answers with the comments made about this feedback below.

This feedback has some strengths. The mentor is positive in tone and makes it clear that the pupils were engaged and on task throughout the lesson. The mentor is encouraging in their use of language by asking the beginning teacher to 'consider' and 'think about' rather than providing a crushing list of things to change. However, in places the feedback is too vague, for example what was 'good' about the beginning teacher's subject knowledge? Did it, for example, reflect historical scholarship?

Overall, the focus is on classroom management rather than the historical learning of the students. As a third-party observer, the most significant issue with the lesson was that the majority of the lesson had been spent on a semi-scientific card sort explaining the order of events. The beginning teacher had not really considered the historical purpose of the lesson. With the focus on the gruesome and grisly aspects there was a temptation to trivialise the suffering of the real people afflicted. While engaging, this central activity did not allow pupils to see the significance of the Black Death beyond its being a grisly and interesting story.

The point about questioning is helpful in suggesting different practical strategies for the beginning teacher to try. Some reading for the beginning teacher might support them to better understand the rationale behind effective questioning in history.

Professional conversations and how to approach feedback with struggling trainees

Conversations with beginning teachers do not always go to plan and sometimes beginning teachers struggle both with receiving and with acting on the feedback given. It can be very dispiriting as a mentor when a beginning teacher fails to respond to feedback. Another difficult issue for mentors is the question of how to approach problems that stem from a lack of professionalism on the part of the beginning teacher. Mentoring a beginning teacher who is struggling to make the required progress is tough. All too quickly, mentors can feel overwhelmed with the responsibility of assessing their mentee. If you find yourself in this situation you will need support; this might come from the member of staff in your school with overall responsibility for beginning teachers or from an ITE tutor. Your ITE provider will have processes in place for supporting trainees who are not 'on track' and you will be able to access these. It is also important to raise concerns early and to briefly document them as they occur.

Developing reflective practices 131

Practical advice is also available from other sources. The 'Move Me On' feature in *Teaching History* – the problem page for history mentors – is designed to offer practical help to all those involved in the education of new history teachers. In the blog series *Becoming a History Teacher*, Crooks explores approaches to giving feedback to different 'types' of beginning teachers. While recognising that new teachers will follow different trajectories, Crooks outlines practical strategies to support struggling beginning teachers and their mentors. The blog series is available at: https://uonhistoryteachertraining.school.blog/contents/.

In Task 6.4, we will consider a scenario where a beginning teacher is not responding to the feedback being given, before reading how an experienced mentor would respond to this situation.

Task 6.4 Mentor reflection: what to do if your mentee is not responding to feedback

Read the following mentoring scenario. Consider how you would respond to this scenario.

Scenario

You are mentoring a student teacher. They are at the beginning of their second school placement, and you are finding them very resistant to feedback following lesson observations. For the most part, lessons go reasonably well as pupils are on task and their substantive knowledge is developing. However, lessons are increasingly repetitive, and regardless of how constructive you are with suggestions for lessons there is no evidence that feedback is being acted on. The lessons remain very similar in focus. When you ask your mentee how they feel the lesson went, their answers are very limited and often focus on minor elements of the lesson. For example, 'I forgot to give the worksheets out at the beginning of the lesson as I had planned.' When you ask questions about the rationale for task design or comment on the need to balance substantive content with disciplinary concepts, your mentee responds with comments like 'I thought of that, but I decided not to because I wanted to focus on something else' or 'I didn't try that here as in my last placement I was told not to do group work.' They commented that they had already tried an idea in another lesson and the other class teacher had advised not to try this again. Conversations following lessons are already hard work and you fear that they might soon become more combative.

Comments from an experienced mentor

It sounds like this student teacher finds reflecting on their teaching uncomfortable and I would open up a conversation to (gently) try to find out why this is the case. This discomfort could be linked to anxieties around assessment, or it might be that this mentee is finding it hard to adjust to a new placement and a new set of expectations. If this were my mentee, once I had a better understanding, I would try some of the following:

- Agree a focus for observation for a series of lessons together. This would allow us to focus on the whole planning process. It might involve the student teacher observing me (or an experienced colleague), with a focus on this aspect of teaching, before jointly planning a series of lessons together. We could also complete some shared reading together. This would give observations and feedback a clear focus and hopefully remove some pressure from individual lesson observations.
- Complete a 'whispered observation' (for further details see Chapter 4) with the student teacher to support them to pick out the most pertinent parts of a lesson and model feedback together.
- Discuss with the student teacher why we give feedback to pupils. This might help the mentee to better understand the rationale for feedback after lessons and see that their mentor is on their side, rather than being critical for the sake of it.
- I would use part of a mentor meeting to discuss the ways that teachers 'get better' at teaching. For example, Clarke and Hollingsworth's (2002) model of interconnected professional growth (p. 951) could be a useful starting point for this mentee to reflect on the relative importance of the factors influencing their development.
- I would also contact the student teacher's ITE tutor to share my concerns and get their perspective.

Working with other members of the department

The ideal is to create a mentoring department where the responsibilities of mentors are shared. However, it is inevitable that some members of your department will have other responsibilities or will not be able to take on a mentoring role. It is important to recognise that the way in which you respond to and analyse a lesson may well be different from the way that others would do this. Therefore, beginning teachers should be observed by a range of teachers. Consequently, it is helpful to share some guidance with other classroom teachers to support them to observe beginning teachers. You might wish to use the summary and key points at the end of this chapter as a starting point for this. It is also important that class teachers provide feedback to the mentor on the lessons they observe. This means that this feedback can inform the mentoring conversations in weekly mentor meetings. Task 6.5 provides some questions for reflection.

> **Task 6.5 How to support other members of the department to work with your mentee**
>
> - As a mentor, how will you prepare colleagues working with your mentee to observe their lessons?
> - How will you seek feedback from other colleagues working with your mentee?

Summary and key points

- The purpose of lesson observations is formative and therefore the process of observation and feedback should be on reflection, change, and improvement.
- It is important to recognise the emotionally charged nature of lesson observations and defuse this as far as possible. One way to do this is to establish an agreed focus and process for lesson observations.
- Lesson feedback should be a two-way, collaborative process in which the beginning teacher feels that their own reflections are valued.
- Lesson observation and feedback provide an opportunity for examining the historical learning that is happening in beginning teachers' classrooms. As a subject specialist, your role in giving subject-specific feedback is particularly valuable and important.
- When observing and giving feedback to beginning teachers, it is important to keep history-specific areas for development at the forefront of your mind.
- Even in the most 'open-door' schools, the majority of teachers' time is spent teaching unobserved; therefore beginning teachers need to fully engage in the reflective process and learn to value their own insights. This will allow them to continue the cycle of reflection and improvement throughout their teaching careers.

Further reading and resources

- **Historical Association. (n.d.). Beginning Teachers' Professional Learning www.history.org.uk/secondary/categories/380/module/8767/beginningteachers-professional learning**

    In this section of the website, you will find ideas for setting meaningful, historically focused targets for your mentee, and guidance for supporting your mentee to adopt a reflective approach. There is also advice on tackling specific issues in mentees' teaching as these arise, through links to the 'Move me on' feature.
- **Hobson, A., & Malderez, A. (2013). Judgementoring and other threats to realizing the potential of school based mentoring in teacher education.** *International Journal of Mentoring and Coaching 2*, **89–108**

    A very useful examination of how the mentor can avoid becoming a 'judgementor' and instead support their mentee to value their own reflections. The article also provides a forthright approach to outlining some of the barriers to establishing open dialogue between mentor and mentee.

References

Adey, K. (1997). First impressions do count: mentoring student teachers. *Teacher Development, 1*(1), 123-33.

Brooks, C. (2017). Pedagogy and identity in initial teacher education: developing a professional compass. *Geography 102*(1), 44-50.

Burn, K., Hagger, H., & Mutton, T. (2015). *Beginning teachers' learning*. St Albans: Critical Publishing.

Clarke, D., & Hollingsworth, H. (2002). Elaborating a model of teacher professional growth. *Teaching and Teacher Education 18*(8), 947-67.

Coe, R., Aloisi, C., Higgins, S., & Elliot Major, L. (2014). *What makes great teaching? A review of the underpinning research.* London: Sutton Trust. Retrieved 28 February 2023, from https://www.suttontrust.com/our-research/great-teaching/

Counsell, C. (2017). The fertility of substantive knowledge: in search of its hidden generative power. In I. Davies (ed.), *Debates in History Teaching* (pp. 80-99). Abingdon: Routledge.

Crooks, V., & London, L. (2022, 26 May). Avoiding the observation trap: interpreting generic mentoring approaches through a subject-specific lens. Retrieved 28 June 2022 from *Becoming a History Teacher*, https://uonhistoryteachertraining.school.blog/2022/05/26/avoiding-the-observation-trap-interpreting-generic-mentoring-approaches-through-a-subject-specific-lens/

Ford, A. (2014). Setting us free: building meaningful models of progression for a 'post levels' world. *Teaching History 157*, 28-40.

Foster, R. (2011). Passive receivers or constructive readers? Pupils' experiences of an encounter with academic history. *Teaching History, 142*, 4-13.

Green, M. (2018). *Addressing teacher workload in Initial Teacher Education (ITE): Advice for ITE providers.* London: DfE.

Healy, G., Walshe, N., & Dunphy, A. (2020). How is geography rendered visible as an object of concern in written lesson observation feedback? *The Curriculum Journal 31*(1), 7-26.

Historical Association. (2019). What's the wisdom on . . . interpretations of the past. *Teaching History 177*, 23-7.

Historical Association. (n.d.). Beginning teachers' professional learning. Retrieved 3 March 2023 from *Beginning Teacher*, www.history.org.uk/secondary/categories/380/module/8767/beginning-teachers-professional-learning

Hobson, A., & Malderez, A. (2013). Judgementoring and other threats to realizing the potential of school based mentoring in teacher education. *International Journal of Mentoring and Coaching 2*, 89-108.

Hobson, A., Ashby, P., Malderez, A., & Tomlinson, P. (2009). Mentoring beginning teachers: what we know and what we don't. *Teaching and Teacher Education 25*, 207-16.

Huijgen, T., & Holthius, P. (2015). 'Why am I being accused of being a heretic?' A pedagogical framework for stimulating historical contextualisation. *Teaching History 158*, 50-5.

Jones, M. (2001). Mentors' perceptions of their roles in school-based teacher training in England and Germany. *Journal of Education for Teaching 27*(1), 27-94.

Kitching, P. (2019). The peace treaties of 1919. *The Historian*, Spring, 40-1.

Lindgren, U. (2005). Experiences of beginning teachers in a school based mentoring program in Sweden. *International Journal of Mentoring and Coaching in Education 1*(2), 89-103.

Lofthouse, R., & Wright, D. (2021). Teacher education lesson observation as boundary crossing. *International Journal of Mentoring and Coaching in Education, 1*(2), 89-103.

Puttick, S. (2022). Geography lesson observations at the interface between research and practice. In G. Healy, L. Hammond, S. Puttick, & N. Walshe (eds.), *Mentoring Geography Teachers in the Secondary School* (pp. 173-86). Abingdon: Routledge.

Puttick, S., & Wynn, J. (2021). Constructing 'good teaching' through written lesson observation feedback. *Oxford Review of Education 47*(2), 152-69.

Richards, H. (2019). Ringing the changes: the power of enquiry questions that both chime and resonate. Retrieved 7 December 2022 from *One Big History Department*, https://onebighistorydepartment.com/2019/07/12/ringing-the-changes-the-power-of-enquiry-questions-that-both-chime-and-resonate/

Riley, M. (2000). Into the Key Stage 3 history garden: choosing and planting your enquiry questions. *Teaching History, 99*, 8-13.

Snelson, H. (2021). Film: lesson sequences. Retrieved 7 December 2022 from Historical Association's *History Teaching for Beginners* webinar series, www.history.org.uk/secondary/resource/10060/film-lesson-sequences

Stevens, E. (2021). How can we improve our use of questioning in the classroom? Retrieved 7 December 2022, from *Practical Histories*, https://practicalhistories.com/2021/09/how-can-we-improve-our-use-of-questioning-in-the-classroom/

Wineburg, S. (2007). Unnatural and essential: the nature of historical thinking. *Teaching History 129*, 7-11.

Worth, P. (2018). Here ends the lesson: shaping lesson conclusions as an iterative process in improving historical enquiries. *Teaching History 173*, 58-66.

7 Exploring the relationship between values and history education

Terry Haydn

Introduction

Values in history education are a difficult facet of history teaching for beginning teachers to get to grips with. Although there are values statements in the current and earlier versions of the National Curriculum for history, it is an area where there are differing views. There is disagreement over the extent to which moral and ethical concerns should be part of school history, particularly when dealing with topics such as the Holocaust (see, for example, Kinloch, 2001 and Chapman, 2020). There is also controversy over whether school history should contribute to the development of democratic citizenship, or at least over the way it might approach such an aim (Lee, 1992; White, 1992; Barton & Levstik, 2004). There is also the question of whether values are to be transmitted, or considered and examined (Slater, 1989), as well as disagreements about which values and dispositions should be present and promoted in the history classroom.

The debate over values in the history classroom has been to some extent distorted by the stipulation that all schools and all school subjects should promote 'Fundamental British Values' (DfE, 2014). This was quite a drastic change from previous statements about values in the curriculum (see, for example, DfEE/QCA, 1999). The Chief Inspector of Schools' statement that Ofsted would take into account the teaching of Fundamental British Values (FBV) in their judgements on schools, and that it would not be enough to just put up a few Union Jacks and pictures of the Queen (Spielman, quoted in Bulman, 2017), further heightened the profile of FBV in public and media debate.

The attention given to FBV has perhaps tended to occlude consideration of other values issues. The title of the document which mandated the promotion of FBV in schools was 'Promoting fundamental British values as *part of* [my italics] SMSC in schools' (spiritual, moral, social, and cultural education). Part of the function of this chapter will be to act as a reminder that although FBV is the most high-profile strand of values issues in the history classroom, there are other strands.

It is difficult to find any history education experts arguing that school history should be 'value free'. There does seem to be a consensus that school history should address values issues (amongst many others, see Illingworth, 2008; Peterson, 2011; Harris, 2017; Ammert et al., 2020; Chapman, 2020; Yoon, 2022). However, given that 'values education' is not generally part of assessment and examination systems (and is not easy to ascribe marks to),

DOI: 10.4324/9781003223504-7

there is always the danger that it can get overlooked amidst the struggle to cover curriculum content and prepare pupils for public examinations. Another factor which might contribute to the marginalisation of values issues is the fact that the ethical dimension is not explicitly highlighted in current history curriculum documentation; it is not itemised as a second-order concept. In Canada it is itemised as one of the 'big six' historical thinking concepts. The case for this is summarised on one page of the Historical Thinking Project website (https://historicalthinking.ca/ethical-dimensions). In the words of the late Peter Seixas (n.d.), 'Historians attempt to hold back on explicit historical judgments about actors in the midst of their accounts, but, when all is said and done, if the story is meaningful, then there is an ethical judgment involved. We should expect to learn something from the past that helps us to face the ethical issues of the day'.

The fact that school history can have some influence on the sort of citizens who will emerge from our schools is one of the reasons that countries all over the world have history on the school curriculum (Hobsbawm, 1997). Recent history has shown the validity of Christopher Hill's (1953) argument that 'History, properly taught, can help men to become critical and humane, just as wrongly taught it can turn them into bigots and fanatics' (p. 9).

Objectives

At the end of the chapter you should have:

- Some suggestions for conversations with your mentee which focus on values issues in history education.
- Reminders about the breadth of values issues relevant to history education.
- Ideas for discussing the issue of Fundamental British Values with your mentee.
- Suggestions for resources relating to moral and ethical issues in history teaching which might be helpful for your mentee.
- Suggestions for helping your mentee to address the issue of 'truth' as a value in history education.

How to approach the teaching of 'Fundamental British Values'

Task 7.1 provides a useful starting point for approaching the teaching of FBV with your mentee.

Task 7.1 Discussing the Department for Education's (DfE) advice for promoting Fundamental British Values (FBV) with your mentee

If beginning teachers are to deal with FBV in an informed way, they should read the document which stipulated that all schools and teachers should promote them.
Ask your mentee to read the DfE's guidance on the teaching of FBV (DfE, 2014) and make a point of discussing it at some point in the placement. Explain to your mentee how the department has tried to address the issue of FBV.

Navigating the issue of Fundamental British Values

Controversies over the issue of FBV have arisen out of the way that some commentators have interpreted the document mandating their promotion, rather than considering the document itself. Some have questioned the idea that 'democracy, the role of law, individual liberty and mutual respect and tolerance of those with different faiths and beliefs' are particularly or exclusively British – or even that they are 'values' (Appiah, 2016). However, careful reading of the document (which is only six pages long), explicitly makes the point that these points are only 'part of' SMSC in schools; page 5 of the document reiterates some of the points made in earlier National Curriculum (NC) iterations of values statements on the curriculum, including enabling students to develop their 'self-knowledge, self-esteem and self-confidence . . . distinguish between right and wrong . . . and contribute to the lives of those living and working in the locality of the school and to society more generally' (DfE, 2014, p. 5).

The problem for history teachers is when FBV are construed in a way which is at odds with the historical record. In 2017, Her Majesty's Chief Inspector of Schools stated that 'pupils should learn how we became the country we are today and how our values make us a beacon of liberalism, tolerance and fairness' (Spielman, quoted in Bulman, 2017). Politicians from both left- and right-wing parties have argued that Britain has always welcomed outsiders (see for example, Brown, 2007; Gymiah, 2019; Javid, 2019). Given that one of the important precepts of history as a discipline is that historians (and history educators) are supposed to 'tell the truth' about the past (or as accurate a truth as can be ascertained from the evidence available), this poses problems for history teachers. An examination of the historical record in this field, for example on the treatment of the Jews, Huguenots, and Irish, Caribbean, and Eastern European migrants reveals overwhelming evidence that there have always been large numbers of people in Britain, and some government administrations, that have been hostile to incomers and that Britain has not always been 'a beacon of liberalism, tolerance and fairness' (see amongst many other examples, Phillips & Phillips, 2009; Dorling & Tomlinson, 2019; Gentleman, 2019; Gildea, 2019).

Beginning teachers need guidance as to how to act in the face of dubious claims about Britain's past, and how to approach the idea of distinctive 'British values'. The following suggestions offer some possible ways forward.

- One useful precept is the ethical importance of 'the historical record', which entails asking pupils the question, 'What does the historical record say about this?' and using this as the foundation for an enquiry approach to a historical issue. This means that beginning teachers need to be at least reasonably knowledgeable about the ways in which the issue in question has been approached within the community of practice that represents the discipline and are careful to accurately reflect the balance and range of historiographical views on the issue in question, without feeling obliged to represent the views of those outside the 'respectable' community of professional practice (for example, Holocaust-denial websites). The *Teaching History* feature 'What have historians been arguing about?' (https://www.history.org.uk/secondary/module/8697/teaching-history-regular-features/9163/what-historians-have-been-arguing-about) is an excellent resource in this respect.

- It might be helpful to remind mentees that the current national curriculum for history aims to ensure that all pupils understand 'the methods of historical enquiry, including how evidence is used rigorously to make historical claims, and discern how and why contrasting arguments and interpretations of the past have been constructed' (DfE, 2013, p. 1). In the words of former Lead Inspector for History, HMI (Her Majesty's Inspector or Inspectorate) John Slater (1989), 'The key question may be whether history is for the transmitting and acceptance of values or, primarily, for their examination and understanding'. So, Brown's (2007) claim that Britain is, and throughout history has always been, 'a tolerant, fair and decent country' can be discussed and subjected to the test of evidence, as is common practice in the consideration of historical claims. History HMI inspectors have consistently argued that one of the purposes of school history is to develop the intellectual autonomy and critical acumen or 'information literacy' of young people. If we are concerned to educate pupils about democracy, one of history's main contributions, HMI argue, is history's 'plurality and unpredictability – different historians coming at events and people from different perspectives, using evidence critically and with integrity, and presenting different views. Above all, history needs to provide young people with the ability to make up their own minds' (HMI, 2005).
- Introduce mentees to the concept of 'critical patriotism' (Chua & Sim, 2017), the idea that it is not unpatriotic to be appropriately critical of some aspects of the national past. Barnes (1984) elevates this to a civic duty, arguing that 'the greatest patriotism is to tell your country when it is behaving dishonourably, foolishly, viciously' (p. 131). As I have argued elsewhere, nearly all countries have their 'skeletons' – discreditable incidents, moments of shame, leaders and governments who have behaved dishonourably, instances of failure and decline:

We should remember that history without skeletons is what was served up in the Third Reich and in Stalin's Russia, and remember the nature of the societies of which that was a part. As a country which has not been without its moments of greatness, its share of great men and great women, it should be all the easier to be open and magnanimous about less glorious moments and personnel. A society that can examine its mistakes and failures is more robust and vital than one which retreats into nostalgia and censorship. (Haydn, 1994, p. 22)

- It can be helpful to give mentees some examples of resources which might be useful for addressing FBV in their teaching. You may have other and better examples, but here are just a few suggestions:
    a) Richard McFahn's activity on the experiences of Windrush migrants in London, which draws on testimony from Phillips and Phillips (2009), makes the point that although some migrants suffered hostility and racism, others were welcomed and treated with friendship and kindness. It points out the dangers of simplistic generalisation, and also makes a point about agency.
    https://www.historyresourcecupboard.co.uk/portfolio/black-britain-was-lord-kitchener-right-was-london-the-place-to-be/

- b) Audrey Gillan's (2006) account of 'the day the East End said "No pasaran" to Blackshirts' gives a graphic and quite moving account of the Cable Street Riots of 1936. It makes the point that although there are 'dark pages' in Britain's treatment of outsiders, there are also positive moments and stories to be told.
- c) The now well-known story of Sir Nicholas Winton and his rescue of Jewish children is a powerful example of how individuals can make a difference for the better: https://www.youtube.com/watch?v=PKkgO06bAZk. It does raise the question of why the children's parents were not allowed to come to Britain.
- d) Illingworth (2008) provides examples of 'values' activities related to persecution over time, drawing on several examples from British history.

- Many of the issues raised by FBV and identity issues are inextricably political in nature – including topics such as the British Empire, migration, terrorism, and the use of historical precedents and analogies in the recent Brexit debate. There is evidence to suggest that beginning teachers in the UK and elsewhere are worried about teaching such topics and may be tempted to teach them in a way that avoids some of the difficult questions involved (Maddison, 2020; Conditt, 2021; Cohen, 2022). Such nervousness is understandable in light of recent government pronouncements expressing concern about the political neutrality of teachers (Mountstevens, 2020; Hazell, 2022). Riley argues that one of the first challenges with beginning teachers is to 'avoid avoidance':

Teachers who are avoiders might shy away from teaching about such subjects such as immigration, the legacy of empire and issues of racism and intolerance. It is clear that the starting point for successful teaching is a willingness and confidence to be a 'risk-taking' teacher who allows pupils to study emotive and controversial issues in a safe and supportive context. (Riley, 2007)

Mentees need reassurance that it is part of the NC for history that pupils learn about the challenges of their times, and that it is entirely proper that they should feel able to discuss the issues around FBV with their classes. Former Lead HMI for History Michael Maddison is unequivocal in his view that history teachers have a duty to address contentious issues around British history and identity (for more detailed development of how to handle controversial issues, see Chapter 8):

As history teachers, it is our duty . . . to explain because, if we don't, who will? A sound history education is also the antidote to fake news. As a result, we must engage with the controversial and the contentious to ensure that pupils understand clearly and can more readily sort fact from fiction. We live in difficult times and one undoubted benefit of studying history is that it can help make pupils comfortable with uncertainty and this is of immense importance at this time. So do not hold back – tackle the difficult topics about which pupils need to know, not least for example, the cost of the British Empire for those who were subjugated. Use the latest scholarship here and in relation to the impact of Empire, for example, see William Dalrymple's latest work on India.

(Maddison, 2020)

- Although the matter will almost certainly have been addressed in your mentee's taught course, it does no harm to remind them of the importance of Section 406 of the 1996 Education Act, which forbids the promotion of partisan political views (https://www.legislation.gov.uk/ukpga/1996/56/section/406). Although not everyone agrees with this view, Conditt (2021) advises that when dealing with identity and values issues, teachers should try to centre class discussion on questions, and avoid sharing their own opinions. It can be helpful to reassure your mentee that they can, if they are unsure, run any teaching connected to a particular facet or strand of FBV past you or the class teacher, to be on the safe side.

Understanding the context of the introduction of Fundamental British Values

It can be helpful (both to beginning teachers *and* pupils) to understand the *context* of the move to promote FBV, and the high profile of the idea of 'Britishness'. Many of the beginning teachers we work with may not be aware of the fact that this is (like the presence of 'significance' in the National Curriculum for history) a comparatively recent development. Oborne and Mulla (2022) suggest that 'before its quiet introduction into national discourse by thinktanks and politicians over the past two decades, the phrase ("Britishness") did not exist; there was no shared concept of "British values" as the country fought the Nazis in the Second World War'. They point out that the phrase 'British values' 'was never mentioned in *Hansard* in the 19th century, and only 31 times in the entire 20th century. It only comes into anything resembling regular use in the first decade of the 21st century.' A quick *Ngram* search over the use of the term 'British values', and 'Britishness' in books confirms this view.

Although it was mandated by a Conservative administration in 2013/14, Oborne and Mulla argue that the current state-promoted notion of British values has its roots in Gordon Brown's 2007 Commonwealth Club speech on national identity 'amid mounting alarm about the future of the Union and concerns over Muslim integration' (Oborne & Mulla, 2022).

Although many of our mentees will be aware of the London bombings on 7/7, fewer appear to be familiar with the now hardly mentioned Ajegbo Report (Ajegbo, 2007). The report was commissioned in the light of riots across many northern cities, and the 'discovery' of the extent of social and educational segregation in these cities. History HMI, in their report *History in the Balance*, gave a slightly broader explanation of the emergence of 'British values' as an issue in history education:

> The roots of recent interest in the concept of Britishness lie in concerns about the failure of all young people to understand how the UK works and to appreciate its values, their limited involvement in the community, the impact of migration into the UK, nationalism in the different parts of the UK, the evolution of the European Union, globalisation and the dominance of US culture, and terrorism. (Ofsted, 2007, p. 32)

However, even in the comparatively short time that British values have been part of history education, the discourse around them has evolved. Whereas in the 'earlier period', around 2007 to 2010, the emphasis was on the 'use' of British values to promote social cohesion (Haydn, 2012), more recently, some have argued that it has mutated into a strand of the 'culture wars', which have seen history used to promote partisan political agendas, and to foster division and mistrust, a point succinctly substantiated by Mountstevens (2020). In terms of the implications for history teachers, I think that beginning teachers need to understand, *and be able to explain to pupils,* both the 'social cohesion' aspirations of the FBV agenda, and the 'culture wars' theory about the ways in which the FBV agenda has evolved. Task 7.2 provides suggestions for how beginning teachers can be supported to address FBV in the classroom.

Task 7.2 'Opening up' values issues in the history curriculum

A collection of quotations on the importance of making connections from the past to the present, which might help provide a 'warrant' to give beginning teachers the confidence to address values issues in the history classroom, can be found at https://terryhaydn.co.uk/pgce-history-at-uea/pgce-student-teacher/purpose-of-school-history/linking-the-past-to-the-present/.

At some point in the placement, ask your mentee to look at the NASUWT (2016) document, *Universal Values: Responding Holistically to the Requirement to Promote Fundamental British Values.* This provides the perspective of a major teaching union on the issue of FBV.

Human or 'universal' values in the history classroom

As noted earlier in the chapter, the stipulation that all teachers and schools should promote FBV was only *a part* of the curriculum's duty to promote 'the spiritual, moral, social and cultural (SMSC) development of their pupils' (DfE, 2014, p. 4). The strands or 'components' of these values were spelled out over three pages in the 1999 and 2007 versions of the NC, in a section titled 'The school curriculum and the National Curriculum: values, aims and purposes (see DfEE/QCA, 1999, pp. 10-12). The current version of the National Curriculum (NC) (DfE, 2013) does not 'unpack' or detail these values in the same way that the earlier versions did, but this does not mean that such values are not part of pupils' SMSC development. This elision of the full range of values which it was hoped the curriculum would develop was a comparatively unremarked change in NC specifications, but I think that it is important that beginning teachers should be aware of these values. A 'cut-down' version is provided below:

> Equality of opportunity for all, a healthy and just democracy ... commitment to the virtues of truth, justice, honesty, trust and a sense of duty ... to make a difference for the better ... develop principles for distinguishing between right and wrong ... develop pupils' integrity and autonomy and help them to be responsible and caring citizens capable of contributing to the development of a just society ... enable pupils to challenge discrimination and stereotyping, develop awareness and understanding of, and respect for, the environments in which they live, and secure their commitment to sustainable development at a personal, local, national and global level ... develop their ability to relate to others and work for the common good. (DfEE/QCA, 1999, pp. 10-12)

My former students expressed surprise when the late Professor Richard Aldrich told them that for much of the time that history had been a compulsory school subject, its main purpose was as moral exemplar. This view of the purposes of school history has become unfashionable (there is little trace of it in current curriculum specifications), but as noted earlier in this chapter, this does not mean that history is a 'value-free zone'. At some point in the placement, it can be helpful to remind mentees that there is a moral and ethical dimension to the study of the past, and that there are moments and occasions in history when we should spend some time explaining to pupils that there are people in the past who have done great harm, and some who have done good things that have benefited humanity. This should also involve getting across to pupils that *they* are historical agents and can make a difference to the sort of society we live in by their example. In the words of Wilke et al.:

> Agency is considered a key concept in historical thinking. Understood in a sociological way, it addresses the question of who has the individual or social potential to act purposefully and to effectuate change in society. Teaching about agency is also assumed to influence civic behaviour, as reflection on the various agents in the past and how they contributed to changes in society, can make students aware of their own role in society today. (Wilke, Depaepe, & Van Nieuwenhuyse, 2019, p. 1)

This moral dimension, and the need to go beyond 'the story of our nation state' can also be discerned in the values statement of the International Society of History Didactics:

> History education should have as its goal the development of free individuals capable of independent democratic and socially responsible judgment, rather than overt or covert indoctrination... A new historical awareness is needed today so that we can understand how the world arrived at its present state, how to build bridges across past and present divisions, how to articulate an understanding and appreciation for cultural differences, and how to make the world a better and safer place in which to live. (International Society for History Didactics, 2007)

A more recent development, and one that receives considerable attention in many other countries, is concern for the environment, sustainability, and the rights of future generations. In addition to the values of honesty, wisdom, respect, engagement, justice, and hope, Kitson (2023) asks whether 'environmental values' should be added to the SMSC dimension of values.

Given that many of the 'challenges of our time' are transnational rather than limited by state boundaries, in addition to teaching pupils about 'Our island story', and promoting 'Fundamental British Values', treatment of values issues in the history classroom need to go beyond exclusively national considerations (see Brown, 2007, Haydn, 2012 for a more detailed development of this point).

There are times as a mentor when there is some value in pointing out to your mentee that 'things are done differently' in other countries so that they do not end their training with an insular and narrow vision of history education. In Finland, for example, more emphasis is placed on the human and global dimensions of history rather than a strong emphasis on the national story, and 'national' values: 'The underlying values of basic education are human rights, equality, democracy, natural diversity, preservation and environment viability and the endorsement of multiculturalism. Basic education promotes responsibility, a sense of community, and respect for the rights and freedoms of the individual' (Rautiainen, 2017).

This is not to suggest that pupils should *not* be taught about their own past, or that they should not examine and discuss the values enumerated in the Fundamental British Values document (DfE, 2014), but there is a danger that the controversies evinced by the 'Britishness' debate and the mandating of FBV might lead to other important values issues in history being neglected.

Disciplinary values in the history classroom

Another strand of values in the history classroom relates to the values associated with the discipline of history. As with other academic disciplines, history has its rules, procedures, and conventions relating to the way that historians operate. Part of the value of pupils studying history is that these rules, conventions, and procedures can be useful not just for making sense of the past, but also for making intelligent and well-informed judgements on the many controversies which confront them in their everyday lives. In the words of Peter Lee:

> The reason for teaching history is not that it changes society, but that it changes pupils; it changes what they see in the world, and how they see it ... To say someone has learnt history is to say something very wide ranging about the way in which he or she is likely to make sense of the world. History offers a way of seeing almost any substantive issue in human affairs, subject to certain procedures and standards, whatever feelings one may have. (Lee, 1992, pp. 23-4)

I would argue that this facet of school history has become more important than ever given that pupils are living in 'a world of systematically disseminated untruths and the technology to make those fantasies, conspiracies and untruths instantly, massively and widely available through the internet' (Schama, 2020).

Lee describes the disciplinary values of history (and explains their importance) as 'cognitive ethics':

> If we teach history as history, we will be handing on cognitive ethics (respect for evidence, respect for persons as sources of arguments and so on) ... Historical understanding requires 'rational passions' like a concern for truth and respect for persons. Students who care nothing for the scope or power of an explanation, omit to ask if another account is equally valid, or are happy to ignore evidence, have simply not begun to grasp the discipline of history. (Lee, 2012, pp. xii-xiii)

Given that it is not possible to shield pupils from the dubious and salacious history that is 'out there' on the internet and on social media, it is important to try to get across to mentees that over the course of Key Stage 3, they should look for opportunities to help pupils to discern between 'good' and 'bad' history, between (a) serious, 'respectable' and professionally authored history, (b) history which is primarily for entertainment, and (c) history which attempts to distort the past for political or financial purposes. This means taking time to point out manipulative and cynical presentations of the past, lazy and simplistic analogies, and sweeping generalisations for which there is inadequate evidence. See Task

Values and history education 145

7.3 for an example of how you might approach this with your mentee. The aim is, of course, that pupils will learn to work out the trustworthiness of claims and accounts for themselves, and that they will develop an understanding of 'what games are being played' with the past (Haydn, 2017). Former HMI for History John Hamer points to the urgent need for pupils to be educated about 'bad history':

> It is necessary and valuable, not harmful or subversive, to introduce bad history, unsubstantiated claims, propaganda, etc. into the history classroom. What is important is how they are used in the classroom, not that they are used. Pupils will in any case be exposed to such material and it is far more helpful if they are exposed to them in a rigorous way. (Hamer, 2020)

Task 7.3 What constitutes 'good history'?

These two extracts elucidate some of the characteristics of 'good' history. They also make the point that because of their training and immersion in the discipline, historians have different priorities to other 'actors' who produce history and are trained to place accuracy and concern for truth as cardinal virtues in their work. This is not to say of course, that all professional historians meet these standards. Share these extracts with your mentee and, at some point in the placement, have a discussion with them about how they might try to educate pupils about the differences between 'good' and 'bad' history.

- **Extract from A. Lester (2023) 'The British Empire rehabilitated'**
  Professional historians tend to write with an ethical code in mind, one that we are taught in our undergraduate and postgraduate training. We are of course influenced by our individual dispositions and politics, but we try our best to set these aside and to develop our arguments through finding and reading all the relevant evidence. We tend to be curiosity – rather than politically – driven. We are interested in explaining phenomena, not allocating collective virtue or blame. When we select quotations from a source, we try to set them in the context of that source's overall stance rather than cherry-picking from it to substantiate a pre-determined argument. When we come across evidence that contradicts our general interpretation, we either try to explain the discrepancy or modify that interpretation. We read widely to try to take account of the work that other scholars have done on our topic, and we are grateful for their efforts. In essence we try, even if we do not always succeed, to avoid writing tendentiously. (Lester, 2023)
- **Extract from R. Aldrich (1997). *The End of History and the Beginning of Education***
  If history is regularly used in the promotion of contemporary causes, it is incumbent on the professional historian . . to ensure that such usage is as accurate as possible, both in its representation of the past, and the connections established between past, present and future. Such a position depends upon the further belief that some history as constructed is better than other history, and that the most important criterion for making such a judgement is the extent to which history . . .

> reflects the past as in actually was .. Most historians .. do find more evidence about the past than they imagine or invent, and the quality of that evidence, coupled with the quality of the necessary selection, ordering and presentation of it, is one important distinction between good history and bad (Aldrich, 1997, p. 5).

There is also an affective dimension to the study of history. Echoing Christopher Hill's claim that taught well, history can make people more decent and humane human beings, Paul (cited in MacBeath, 1998) argues that the study of history can help to develop 'a passionate drive for clarity, fair mindedness, a fervour for getting to the bottom of things, for listening sympathetically to opposing points of view, a compelling drive to seek out evidence, a devotion to truth as against self-interest'.

General educational values and dispositions in the history classroom

There are some values and dispositions which we might hope to cultivate in the history classroom which are not specifically related to the discipline of history.[1] Amongst the desirable qualities accepted by most teachers are that pupils are aware that they are not entitled to spoil the learning of others, they should behave with respect to all other members of the class, and to the teacher, and that they should try to do their best to learn. There are some learner characteristics or dispositions which are almost universally considered to be desirable, others which are more problematic. Amongst the latter is the question of whether teachers should attempt to develop the intellectual confidence of their pupils. On the one hand, we probably do want them to be confident enough to contribute to the lesson rather than being entirely passive, and we probably want them to learn, and be confident enough to argue their case and stand up for their beliefs. There is though the danger of becoming inappropriately intellectually confident (https://www.verywellmind.com/an-overview-of-the-dunning-kruger-effect-4160740). As a rule of thumb, most history teachers want their pupils to learn to be appropriately intellectually confident. Task 7.4 provides an opportunity for mentees to consider the attributes that they hope to cultivate in the history classroom.

Task 7.4 The International Baccalaureate learner profile

As far as I am aware, the International Baccalaureate is the only curriculum that explicitly identifies 'open-mindedness' as a desirable attribute of learners. The profile identifies ten (non-subject-specific) characteristics which it considers to be desirable.

If time permits, ask your mentee to glance at the profile (it is only one page, so it is not an onerous task), and just ask them to reflect on the extent to which they feel that these are sensible and appropriate points.

https://www.ibo.org/contentassets/fd82f70643ef4086b7d3f292cc214962/learner-profile-en.pdf

> Together, reflect upon the extent to which these attributes are explicitly or implicitly present in the curriculum of the department. Is this appropriate in relation to: (a) their understanding of the purposes of the history curriculum, (b) the context of the school?

Another 'variable' in the skills of the teacher is the extent to which they can create and sustain a relaxed, positive, and collaborative working atmosphere in the classroom. There are some history teachers who are accomplished at cultivating a 'community of practice' with their teaching groups, in the sense of encouraging a spirit of collaboration and helpfulness amongst the pupils, where all pupils feel valued, the pupils try to help and encourage each other, and they are comfortable and relaxed about working with each other. There are classrooms where pupils who struggle to do well in history try their best and are positive in their attitudes to the challenges involved, and to the other pupils in the group. Some research has suggested that this cooperative and harmonious climate improves pupil outcomes overall, as well as contributing to the extent to which teachers are able to enjoy their work (Wiliam, 2011; Saito et al., 2015).

We also want to develop history teachers who can 'foster and maintain pupils' interest … and promote a love of learning, and pupils' intellectual curiosity' (DfE, 2013, p. 1). We hope that they will be the sort of history teacher who will get pupils to retain an interest in the subject after they leave compulsory education. In the words of Richards:

> History teaches many useful skills – information gathering, problem solving, the public presentation of arguments and assessments. But that should be secondary to the broader objective of discovering how we were and how we got to where we are. It is not my aim to turn out tunnel-visioned computer operators concerned only about where their next Porsche is coming from. I seek to awaken in my students an open minded broad visioned humanity, informed by a love of learning, a love of ideas, a love of books, a love of argument and debate. (Richards, 1989)

Finding time for 'truth' as a value in history education

Perhaps because it is not included in the list of second-order concepts specified in the current NC for history (the word 'truth' is not mentioned in the document), comparatively little attention has focused on the importance of developing pupils' understanding of the concept of 'truth' in the study and practice of history. This is in the sense of the ethical importance of making an honest attempt to provide the most accurate explanation possible from the evidence available. This is in spite of the facts that respect for evidence is of central importance to the discipline of history (see, amongst others, Evans, 2003; Conrad et al., 2013; Fordham, 2015) and that lack of respect for 'truth' and evidence is a major problem in many modern societies (D'Ancona, 2016; Pomerantsev, 2019; Godonis & Jones, 2021; Oborne, 2021; Steinhauer, 2022).

As Walsh (2017) and Wineburg (2018) have demonstrated, there are things that history teachers can do to improve the information literacy of young people. But as well as developing pupils' cognitive skills, history teachers can try to educate pupils about the moral and ethical dimensions of truth as a civic virtue. As I have argued elsewhere:

> Many of the bad things that happen in the world are done by people who are very clever, who did well in history at school, and who often have high-level qualifications in history. They are, at one level, very skilful at handling evidence, in the sense of cleverly manipulating and distorting it for morally and ethically dubious purposes. They are not good at handling evidence in the ethical sense, and this has often had a harmful effect on democratic societies and on life on the planet generally. (Haydn, 2017, p. 174)

In an article in *The Historian* (see suggested further reading), former Secretary of State for Education Sir Keith Joseph wrote that 'the teaching of history has to take place in a spirit which takes seriously the need to pursue truth on the basis of evidence and at the same time accepts the need for give and take in that pursuit and that teaching in that spirit should encourage pupils to take a similar approach' (Joseph, 1984, p. 12). Overall, the article makes an eloquent case for the importance of finding time to talk with pupils about the part that truth should play in learning about the past.

Task 7.5 Finding time for 'truth' in the history classroom

In a short article (four pages) for *Practical Histories*, I tried to provide some suggestions about how history teachers might develop pupils' understanding of the importance of truth and integrity in history. As with attempts to develop pupil understanding of time and chronology, I suggest that this might best be done not in the form of whole, discrete lessons, but occasional and intermittent mentions, asides, and brief opening-it-up discussions where the topics under discussion are relevant to the uncertainties and difficulties of ascertaining an authoritative picture of an event or person, or one of the many contested issues in history. If you do find some time to address the issue of truth with your mentee, the article may provide some ideas for discussion (Haydn, 2021).

It is important that beginning teachers understand that there are different views about why history should be part of the school curriculum, and that this has an influence over what values should be transmitted, considered, or examined as part of the study of the past. It is also helpful if they can get across to pupils that different constituencies (politicians, historians, educationalists) often have differing aims in mind when prioritising values issues in history, whether it be the inculcation of patriotism or promotion of social cohesion, the cultivation of desirable attributes and dispositions (e.g. tolerance, open-mindedness, concern for the common good), or develop the intellectual autonomy and resistance to manipulation and exploitation. A collection of quotations about the various purposes of school history can be accessed at https://terryhaydn.co.uk/pgce-history-at-uea/pgce-student-teacher/purpose-of-school-history/).

Summary and key points

- It is important that mentees are familiar with the DfE guidance on the teaching of FBV.
- They need to know that there are other aspects of values education that are relevant to history teaching.
- It is helpful if mentees are knowledgeable about the *context* in which FBV were introduced to the curriculum and are familiar with recent discourse around the concept of 'Britishness'.
- There might be times when mentees need to be reminded and encouraged to address contentious issues related to values in history. It is not going against FBV guidance to include discussion of 'skeletons' or 'dark pages' in Britain's past. Almost without exception, politicians of all parties have accepted the desirability of a 'warts and all' consideration of the national past.
- Mentees should be reminded of their responsibilities in relation to Section 406 of the 1996 Education Act, which forbids the promotion of partisan political views.
- At some point in the placement, it might be helpful to have a discussion with your mentee about the importance of 'truth' as a value in history education.

Further reading and resources

- Harris, R. (2017). 'British values, citizenship and the teaching of history', in I. Davies (ed.), *Debates in History Teaching*, 2nd edition (pp. 180–90). London: Routledge,
- Haydn, T. (2021). 'Teaching pupils the importance of truth in history', *Practical Histories*. https://practicalhistories.com/author/terry-haydn/. Retrieved 20 March 2023.
- Joseph, K. (1984). 'Why teach history in school?', *The Historian 2*, 10–12.
- Peterson, A. (2011). 'Moral learning in history', in I. Davies (ed.), *Debates in History Teaching* (pp. 161-71). London: Routledge.

Note

1. Values might be thought of as guiding principles or qualities that are regarded as being correct and desirable in life, particularly in terms of personal conduct. Dispositions are habits, tendencies, inclinations, and personal characteristics.

References

Ajegbo, K. (2007). *Diversity and Citizenship Curriculum Review*. Nottingham: DfES. Retrieved 21 March 2023 from https://dera.ioe.ac.uk/6374/7/DfES_Diversity_%26_Citizenship_Redacted.pdf

Aldrich, R. (1997). *The End of History and the Beginning of Education*. London: Institute of Education.

Ammert, N., Sharp, H., Lofstrom, J., & Edling, S. (2020). Identifying aspects of temporal orientation in students' moral reflections. *History Education Research Journal 17*(2), 132-50. Retrieved 20 March 2023 from https://uclpress.scienceopen.com/hosted-document?doi=10.14324/HERJ.17.2.01

Appiah, K. (2016). There is no such thing as western civilisation. Retrieved 20 March 2023 from *The Guardian*, https://www.theguardian.com/world/2016/nov/09/western-civilisation-appiah-reith-lecture

Barnes, J. (1984). *Flaubert's Parrot*. London: Vintage.

Barton, K., & Levstik, L. (2004). *Teaching History for the Common Good*. Mahwah, NJ: Lawrence Erlbaum.

Brown, G. (2007, 27 February). Speech given at the Commonwealth Club. Retrieved 20 2023, from *The Guardian*, https://www.theguardian.com/politics/2007/feb/27/immigrationpolicy.race

Bulman, M. (2017, September 24). Schools must teach British values, says head of Ofsted. *The Independent*. Retrieved 27 March 2023, from https://edition.independent.co.uk/editions/uk.co.independent.issue.240917/data/7963326/index.html

Chapman, A. (2020). Learning the lessons of the Holocaust: a critical exploration. In F.S.A. Pearce & A. Pettigrew, *Holocaust Education: Contemporary Challenges and Controversies* (pp. 50-73). London: UCL Press.

Chua, S., & Sim, J. (2017). Rethinking critical patriotism: a case of constructive patriotism in Social Studies teachers in Singapore. *Asia Pacific Journal of Education, 37*(1), 1-13.

Cohen, R. (2022). Why teachers are afraid to teach history. *The New Republic*. Retrieved 18 March 2023, from https://newrepublic.com/article/165598/teachers-afraid-teach-history

Conditt, S. (2021, 2 February). Should teachers be apolitical? *The Hechinger Report*. Retrieved 18 March 2023 from https://hechingerreport.org/should-teachers-be-apolitical/

Conrad, M., Ercikan, K., Friesen, G., Letourneau, J., & Muise, D. (2013). *Canadians and Their Pasts*. Toronto: University of Toronto Press.

D'Ancona, M. (2016). *Post Truth: the War on Truth and How to Fight Back*. London: Penguin.

DfE. (2013, 11 September). *National Curriculum in England: History Programmes of Study*. London: DfE. Retrieved 2 April 2023 from https://www.gov.uk/government/publications/national-curriculum-in-england-history-programmes-of-study/national-curriculum-in-england-history-programmes-of-study

DfE. (2014). *Promoting Fundamental British Values as part of SMSC in Schools*. London: DfE.

DfEE/QCA. (1999). *The School Curriculum and the National Curriculum: Values, Aims and Purposes*. London: DfEE/QCA.

Dorling, D., & Tomlinson, S. (2019). *Rule Britannia: Brexit and the End of Empire*. London: Biteback.

Evans, R. (2003). Our job is to explain. Retrieved 27 March 2023, from *The Times Higher Education Supplement*, www.timeshighereducation.com/features/our-job-is-to-explain/177421.article

Fordham, M. (2015). Why does truth matter in teaching? Retrieved 26 March 2023 from *Clio et Cetera*, https://clioetcetera.com/2015/07/19/why-does-truth-matter-in-teaching/

Gentleman, A. (2019). *The Windrush Betrayal: Exposing the Hostile Environment*. London: Guardian Faber.

Gildea, R. (2019). *Empires of the Mind: the Colonial Past and the Politics of the Present*. Cambridge: Cambridge University Press.

Gillan, A. (2006). Day the East End said 'No pasaran' to Blackshirts. Retrieved 2 April 2023 from *The Guardian*, https://www.theguardian.com/uk/2006/sep/30/thefarright.past

Godonis, M., & Jones, B. (2021). *History in a post-truth world*. London: Routledge.

Gymiah, S. (2019). *Politics Live*. BBC 1, 8 April.

Hamer, J. (2020). Contribution to the *Historical Consciousness, Historical Thinking, Historical Culture Conference*. University of Graz, 11-14 November.
Harris, R. (2017). British values, citizenship and the teaching of history. In I. Davies (ed.), *Debates in History Teaching (second edition)* (pp. 180-90). London: Routledge.
Haydn, T. (1994). Skeletons. *The Historian 44*, 21-2.
Haydn, T. (2012). History in schools and the problem of 'the nation'. *Education Sciences 2*, 276-89. Retrieved 20 March 2023 from https://www.mdpi.com/2227-7102/2/4/276
Haydn, T. (2017). Truth in history education. In I. Davies (ed.), *Debates in History Teaching (Second Edition)* (pp. 169-79). London: Routledge.
Haydn, T. (2021). Teaching pupils the importance of truth in history. Retrieved 18 March 2023 from *Practical Histories*, https://practicalhistories.com/2021/09/teaching-pupils-the-importance-of-truth-in-history/
Hazell, W. (2022). War on woke teachers as they're told to be 'balanced' over the British Empire and not to back Black Lives Matter. Retrieved 18 March 2023 from *inews*, https://inews.co.uk/news/education/schools-balanced-political-impartiality-teaching-british-empire-government-woke-teachers-1465467
Hill, C. (1953). *Suggestions on the Teaching of History*. Paris: UNESCO. Retrieved 2 April 2023 from https://unesdoc.unesco.org/ark:/48223/pf0000056926
HMI. (2005). *The Annual Report of Her Majesty's Chief Inspector for Schools 2004/5, Section Relating to History in Secondary Schools*. London: Stationery Office Books.
Hobsbawm, E. (1997). To see the future, look at the past. *The Guardian*.
Illingworth, S. (2008). Hearts, minds and souls: exploring values through history. *Teaching History 100*, 20-4.
International Society for History Didactics. (2007). Retrieved 2 April 2023 from https://ishd.co/
Javid, S. (2019, 6 June). We've welcomed people and it's made us stronger. *British Future*. Retrieved 20 March 2023, from https://www.britishfuture.org/sajid-javid-in-conversation-on-identity/
Joseph, K. (1984). Why teach history in school? *The Historian 2*, 10-12.
Kinloch, N. (2001). Parallel catastrophes? Uniqueness, redemption and the Shoah. *Teaching History 104*, 8-14.
Kitson, A. (2023). Climate and history education. *History Teacher Education Network Conference*. 16 November.
Lee, P. (1992). History in schools: aims and purposes and approaches. A reply to John White. In P. Lee, J. Slater, P. Walsh, & J. White, *The Aims of School History: The National Curriculum and Beyond* (pp. 20-34). London: Tufnell Press.
Lee, P. (2012). Series introduction. In M. Carretero, M. Asensio, & M. Rodriguez-Moneo (eds.), *History Education and the Construction of National Identities*. Charlotte, CA: IAP.
Lester, A. (2023). The British Empire rehabilitated? Review of Biggar, N. (2023) *Colonialism: A Moral Reckoning*. London: William Collins. Retrieved 23 March 2023 from *Bella Caledonia*, https://bellacaledonia.org.uk/2023/03/07/the-british-empire-rehabilitated/
MacBeath, J. (1998). Turning the tables. *The Observer*, 22 February.
Maddison, M. (2020). 10 things to remember when teaching history. *Practical Histories 1*. Retrieved 2 April 2023, from https://practicalhistories.com/2020/11/when-teaching-history-remember-to/
Mountstevens, J. (2020). The government's culture war is chilling for curriculum rigour. *Schools Week*. Retrieved 2 April 2023 from https://schoolsweek.co.uk/the-governments-culture-war-is-chilling-for-curriculum-rigour/
NASUWT. (2016). *Universal Values*. Retrieved 2 April 2023 from https://www.nasuwt.org.uk/advice/in-the-classroom/aims-values.html
Oborne, P. (2021). *The Assault on Truth*. London: Simon and Schuster.

Oborne, P., & Mulla, I. (2022). What are British values? *Prospect Magazine*. Retrieved 18 March 2023 from https://www.prospectmagazine.co.uk/essays/what-are-british-values-liberalism-oborne

Ofsted. (2007). *History in the Balance*. London: Ofsted. Retrieved 20 March 2023 from https://dera.ioe.ac.uk/7089/1/History_in_the_balance_(PDF_format).pdf

Peterson, A. (2011). Moral learning in history. In I. Davies (ed.), *Debates in History Teaching* (pp. 161-71). London: Routledge.

Phillips, M., & Phillips, P. (2009). *Windrush: the Irresistible Rise of Multi-racial Britain*. London: HarperCollins.

Pomerantsev, P. (2019). *This is Not Propaganda: Adventures in the War Against Reality*. London: Faber and Faber.

Rautiainen, M. (2017). Finnish school system and teacher education in context. *Meaning, Thinking and Learning in History Conference*. Jyväskylä, 7-8 June.

Richards, J. (1989, April 8). *The Independent*.

Riley, M. (2007). *Introduction: Teaching Emotive and Controversial History at Key Stage 3*. Retrieved 18 March 2023, from https://www.history.org.uk/secondary/categories/487/module/1140/teach-online/1151/31-introduction-teaching-emotive-and-controversi

Saito, E., Watanabe, M., Gillies, R., Someya, I., Nagashima, T., Sato, M., & Murase, M. (2015). School reform for positive behaviour support through collaborative learning: utilising lesson study for a learning community. *Cambridge Journal of Education* 45(4), 489-518.

Schama, S. (2020). On what history can teach us. *Financial Times Podcast*. Retrieved 2 February 2023 from https://www.ft.com/content/464d6a01-fbc5-43b9-ae76-cc7820393e0d

Seixas, P. (n.d.). The Historical Thinking Project. Retrieved 20 March 2023, from https://historicalthinking.ca/ethical-dimensions

Slater, J. (1989). *The Guardian*.

Steinhauer, J. (2022). *History Disrupted*. Cham: Palgrave Macmillan.

Walsh, B. (2017). Technology in the history classroom: lost in the web? In I. Davies (ed.), *Debates in History Teaching (Second Edition)* (pp. 250-60). London: Routledge.

White, J. (1992). The purpose of school history: has the National Curriculum got it right? In P. Lee, J. Slater, P. Walsh, & J. White (eds.), *The Aims of School History: The National Curriculum and Beyond* (pp. 9-19). London: IOE.

Wiliam, D. (2011). *Embedded Formative Assessment*. Bloomington, IN: Solution Tree Press.

Wilke, M., Depaepe, F., & Van Nieuwenhuyse, K. (2019). Teaching about historical agency: an intervention study examining changes in students' understanding and perception of agency in past and present. *Yearbook of the International Society of History Didactics* 40, 53-79.

Wineburg, S. (2018). *Why Learn History (When It's Already on Your Phone)*. Chicago: Chicago University Press.

Yoon, J. (2022). Moral judgment in history education and historical positionality as a moral evaluator. *Theory and Research in Education* 50(4), 530-52.

8 Supporting beginning history teachers to teach controversial and sensitive issues

Laura London and Victoria Crooks

Introduction

This chapter focuses on how mentors can support their mentees to take an historically rigorous and ethical approach to teaching controversial and sensitive issues in history. The benefits of teaching controversial issues in history are well recognised in international scholarship (Barton & McCully, 2007), and this chapter will emphasise the importance of opening up the past to ensure that no topics are considered off limits. For mentors guiding their mentees to teach controversial issues, this presents specific challenges. Many experienced teachers feel 'uncertain and underprepared' when it comes to teaching controversial and sensitive issues, for reasons including concerns about emotional reactions from their pupils, perceived pressures from their school and community, or their own beliefs, values, and identities (Kello, 2016, p. 35). In choosing to address controversial issues teachers make themselves vulnerable and potentially expose themselves to criticism. Beginning teachers, especially those on Initial Teacher Education (ITE) programmes, are under more scrutiny than their fully qualified colleagues and are therefore likely to feel this vulnerability more acutely.

Mentors have an important role to play in supporting beginning teachers to teach controversial and sensitive issues in history confidently and effectively. This chapter will explore what makes an issue in history controversial, so that mentees do not unknowingly stumble into controversial or sensitive territory. It will also present a rationale for teaching controversial and sensitive issues to enable beginning teachers to feel more able to adopt a 'risk-taking' approach (Kitson & McCully, 2005), a rationale which also supports beginning teachers to better explain their curricular and pedagogical choices to pupils, colleagues, and parents. The chapter will also explore why the dialogic approach to mentoring, as outlined in Chapters 1 and 6, is critical to successfully mentoring beginning teachers to plan and teach controversial or sensitive issues. Great history teachers use their considerable professional expertise flexibly as they teach these topics. Much of this expertise is implicit, and great mentors will make their thinking explicit to their mentee. 'Risk taking' (Kitson & McCully, 2005) can only be adopted by mentees with the continued support of a mentor utilising a dialogic model of mentoring, rather than by following an instructional coaching model. Teaching pupils about sensitive and controversial issues in history is complex. The personal and community-based understandings pupils bring to these topics mean there are no easy answers, steps to follow, or universal hard-and-fast rules for how they should be taught.

This chapter has also been influenced by recent efforts to develop evolving principles for teaching history that can be considered controversial or sensitive (Mohamud & Whitburn, 2016; Mohamud & Whitburn, 2019; Elias & Spafford, 2021; Kerridge & Snelson, 2022). These working principles for teaching controversial and sensitive histories provide a very valuable tool for developing beginning teachers' professional expertise alongside their mentors. A range of working principles, accompanied by practical suggestions for resources, are explored later in this chapter. While it is the case that the beginning teacher, at the start of their career, is less likely to feel secure in their expertise, they will also provide a valuable and fresh perspective to their department. Your role, as their mentor, will be to make space for their voice to be heard and to demonstrate to your mentee that you are still learning. This chapter recognises the value of beginning teachers' contributions to the teaching of controversial and sensitive issues.

Objectives

At the end of this chapter, you should be able to:

- Understand why beginning teachers find teaching controversial and sensitive issues challenging.
- Support your mentee to better understand what sensitive and controversial issues are in history, and why it is important to teach about these issues in the history classroom.
- Help your mentee to understand the benefits of considered and supported 'risk taking' (Kitson & McCully, 2005) when teaching controversial and sensitive issues.
- Explore working principles to support your mentee to teach controversial and sensitive issues.
- Suggest practical resources to support your mentee in teaching controversial and sensitive issues in their history lessons.
- Recognise the value of the new perspectives beginning teachers bring to curriculum development.

What are controversial and sensitive issues in history?

There is no agreed definition of a controversial issue in history. Some definitions provide an epistemic criterion, for example:

> ... a matter is controversial if contrary views can be held on it without those views being contrary to reason. (Deardon, 1981, p. 38)

Other definitions provide a social explanation, focusing on societal or community divisions:

> The controversial issues which do tend to pose serious problems for the teacher are those on which society at large (or the local community, or even the school itself) is clearly divided and for which different groups offer conflicting explanations and advocate conflicting solutions based on alternative values. (Stradling, 1984, p. 121)

The Historical Association's *Teaching Emotive and Controversial History* (TEACH) report provides the following useful definition:

> The study of history can be emotive and controversial where there is actual or perceived unfairness to people by another individual or group in the past. This may also be the case where there are disparities between what is taught in school history, family/community histories and other histories. Such issues and disparities create a strong resonance with students in particular educational settings. (Wrenn et al., 2007, p. 3)

This definition is particularly helpful, as it captures not only the nature of the controversy as being rooted in unfairness or injustice but also the importance of family, school, and community contexts. It could be argued that any issue in history has the potential for controversy. Issues can become controversial depending on how they are addressed by the teacher or because of pupils' own positions and interpretations. Children will of course bring the views of their family, their local community, and beyond with them into the classroom. It is perhaps more helpful for beginning teachers to understand that 'there are kinds and degrees of controversiality' (Kello, 2016, p. 36) so that, with support, they can unpick why an issue is controversial. This will help beginning teachers to anticipate pupils' reactions and questions. It is these hard-to-anticipate questions that have the potential to unnerve newer teachers and deter them from teaching controversial or sensitive historical events or issues. When recently asked to define a controversial issue by their PGCE tutor, UEA student teachers settled upon the following shared definition:

> A topic that has high susceptibility of conflicting views, which, if lacking intervention, could lead to disruption.

This definition provides a revealing insight into the perspective of these beginning teachers. The focus here is on the social criterion for controversy and the definition specifically refers to the possible 'disruption' that conflicting views might create in the classroom. Behaviour for learning is often a significant concern for beginning teachers. Mentors have a valuable role in supporting mentees to structure activities around controversial and sensitive issues in order to help begin to alleviate this worry.

Not all sensitive histories are explicitly controversial. Sensitive histories are often considered to be so because they relate to aspects of group identity. These might include race, gender, religion, sexuality, or disability. Aspects of history are also considered sensitive when they relate to dark, difficult, or shameful events in a country's past. They could also be considered controversial because of the methods chosen to study these aspects of the past or the contentious historiographical debate surrounding them. It is important that beginning teachers understand these distinctions. For example, the controversy around teaching the British Empire within public and political debate is often framed around a balance-sheet approach to teaching empire (Martin, 2022; Smyth, 2022). This approach weighs the 'good' against the 'bad' before coming to a 'reasoned judgement'. Supporting mentees to understand the disciplinary and ethical weaknesses of this approach – which were powerfully set out by Benger in his article in *Teaching History* 187 (2022) – is an important part of a mentor's role when preparing beginning teachers to plan and teach this topic.

Beginning teachers also need to understand that controversial or sensitive issues are not fixed. Indeed, the first page of the National Curriculum for History at Key Stage 3 in England (DfE, 2013, p. 1) states that children should understand 'the challenges of their time'. As an example, the events of the pandemic have caused many teachers to rethink their teaching of the Black Death, with certain activities no longer deemed appropriate. Likewise, changes to technology have also required school curricula to adapt. Schools are increasingly concerned about the prevalence of misogyny on social media and the impact of influencers who promote misogynistic rhetoric (PSHE Association, n.d.). While education can only be part of the solution, many schools are responding through their curriculum to safeguard both pupils and staff, and to build resilience to misogynistic narratives. Boyd's 'call to arms' (2009, p. 16) for an inclusive curriculum provides a fascinating insight into how this vision can be practically realised.

The climate emergency has meant that many departments have incorporated an element of 'big history' (Hawkey, 2015) to develop pupils' understanding of humanity's impact on the environment. As Hawkey points out, one of the challenges here is history teachers' subject knowledge, partly due to a lack of available resources. Teaching this topic presents a huge challenge, but as Peter Langdon (2022) states, 'the time for action is indeed now, and it is incumbent on us as history teachers to face these challenges head on, and to begin to develop practical ideas for the classroom'. For practical ideas, Teach Climate History www.notion.so/Teach-Climate-History-4ff7284d696c4de48f423593d5ba5424, and the UCL Centre for Climate Change and Sustainability Education both provide resources and training for teachers.

Disciplinary thinking and sensitive and controversial histories

When planning and teaching about controversial and sensitive issues there is the potential for beginning teachers to take a moralistic approach rather than a more rigorous, disciplinary one. Beginning teachers will need support to see controversial or sensitive issues through a 'disciplinary lens'. Enquiry questions like 'Was the dropping of the atomic bombs justified?' tend to encourage pupils to reach moralistic judgements, rather than engage in disciplinary thinking. To support this disciplinary thinking, enquiry questions that invite students to reach judgements based on the use of evidence and reasoning are more rigorous. In his chapter 'Teaching sensitive and controversial issues', Davies (2017) gives 'What can we say about the Holocaust?' as an example of an enquiry question that allows students to explore evidential thinking. This enquiry 'enables students to use their critical, evaluative engagement with: the archaeology, survivor testimony, perpetrator testimony, and even denial of the Holocaust, in an historically rigorous manner to reach academically and emotionally sophisticated judgements' (p. 264). As a mentor, you could review your curriculum with your mentee with a focus on controversial issues using Task 8.1. This provides a practical opportunity for your mentee to identify controversial and sensitive issues in history, see the value in teaching these topics through historical enquiry, and to understand the curriculum as a 'working' (never finished) document to which they can contribute.

Task 8.1 Exploring your history curriculum with your mentee

Discuss your curriculum with your mentee.

- Identify the controversial or sensitive issues in your curriculum.
- What makes these issues sensitive or controversial?
- Do these issues involve an element of unfairness or injustice? Or are these issues controversial because of disagreements about how they should be taught? Or both?
- Consider why history teachers and historians do not consider some events to be controversial.
- Do you teach about topics in history that involve injustice and unfairness that would not be considered sensitive or controversial?
- How do your enquiry questions encourage disciplinary thinking about sensitive or controversial issues in history?

A rationale for teaching controversial and sensitive issues

When teaching controversial and sensitive issues in history, beginning teachers may feel under additional pressure, perceived or real. This might come from pupils or parents, the school itself, or from the local community. Each school's setting is different. A conversation with your mentee about this context will support your mentee to approach teaching sensitive issues with greater confidence and understanding. As an example, a mentee may be working in a faith school, but not belong to this same faith. In this instance the mentee may have obvious questions about how the faith of the school is reflected in the curriculum and pupils' responses to it. However, it may also be the case that the mentee is unaware of many aspects of the school's ethos and values because these are implicit. Mentors can best support their mentees by not making any assumptions and discussing this openly and honestly.

Another way to support beginning teachers is to discuss a shared rationale for teaching controversial and sensitive issues in history. This encourages beginning teachers to tackle these issues and supports them when they are questioned about their curricular and pedagogical choices by pupils, parents, colleagues, the school community, or inspection bodies.

The benefits of teaching controversial and sensitive histories

Some of the benefits of teaching controversial and sensitive histories are set out below:

- Teaching controversial and sensitive issues provides pupils with opportunities for critical reflection and argument. This is considered to be important to the successful functioning of democratic cultures and democracy (Carr, 2007; Davies, 2017) and has the potential to develop pupils' 'democratic competences' (Council of Europe, 2018, p. 32).

- It is easy to jump to a position on an issue, especially with influence from social media. Handled well, teaching controversial issues allows pupils to reach considered positions and construct reasoned arguments.
- Teaching controversial issues can help pupils to better understand how historical narratives are used by politicians, the media, and the public. For example, history can be used by 'in groups' to promote their own interests or to perpetuate conflict (Bilali & Mahmoud, 2017). History teaching that fosters multi-perspectivity (viewing historical events from a range of perspectives), can help students to understand why conflict occurs (Stradling, 2003). Wanssink et al. (2019) set out a schema as a practical tool to support teachers to deal with controversial remarks and conflict within the classroom.
- Taught well, controversial and emotive issues provide students with the opportunity 'to consider their own loyalties, their multiple interests and identities, and recognise that everyone is both an insider or outsider to something, and that their values can be conflicting and can change' (Wrenn et al., 2007, p. 4).
- For many of our pupils the history classroom is one of very few places where the origins of current conflicts, discrimination, and inequality can be discussed openly and honestly. Controversial and sensitive issues cannot be avoided. If teachers do not raise these issues, then pupils will. Teachers need to take the initiative to ensure they are suitably equipped and prepared to answer the questions that might arise.

Task 8.2 provides some prompts to support your discussions about the rationale for teaching controversial and sensitive issues.

> **Task 8.2 Understanding curricular rationale**
>
> Discuss with your mentee:
>
> - Select one controversial or sensitive issue from your curriculum with your mentee. Discuss the benefits of teaching this using the previous summary. How would you explain your reasons for the inclusion of this issue to:
>   - A parent?
>   - A member of SLT?
>   - A school inspector?
> - What concerns might these stakeholders have about the inclusion of this topic? How can these concerns be addressed in your rationale?

Approaches to teaching sensitive and controversial issues

Once beginning teachers are secure in their rationale for teaching controversial and sensitive issues, they can approach their teaching with greater confidence. As a mentor, one approach you might take with your mentee is to use Kitson and McCully's (2005) continuum of teacher responses to controversial issues. This provides teachers, regardless of their level of experience, with a valuable tool for reflection. Kitson and McCully explored teachers' approaches to teaching controversial issues in their research into history teaching in Northern Ireland. Drawing on their interviews with teachers and students they characterised the teachers' positions on a continuum, ranging from 'avoidance' to 'containment' to 'risk-taking'. Kitson and McCully (2005, p. 35) characterise 'avoiders' as those teachers who 'avoid controversy of any kind' and ignore the social utility of history. These teachers are of the view that history does not have a broader contribution to make to society; for them the point of history is simply to get better at history. Conversely, risk takers 'fully embrace the social utility of history and consciously encourage students to empathise with different perspectives' (p. 35). These teachers are willing to push the boundaries and take hold of opportunities to teach controversial topics. In the centre of the continuum is the position of 'containment'. 'Containers' are teachers who will teach controversial topics but sidestep the most controversial aspects of the topic or might teach 'parallel topics' (p. 35). In the article this is exemplified by a teacher who taught the Battle of the Boyne by exploring sources encompassing different perspectives, but who did not open their teaching with wall murals or the marching season and did not include role-playing during the lesson. Teachers practising containment might also choose to teach topics which share similar themes but do not carry the same emotional charge; for example, teachers in Northern Ireland might opt to teach the Arab-Israeli conflict to learn about a divided society. While the parallels between the conflicts are striking, Kitson and McCully point out it cannot be presumed that pupils will make these connections and transfer their understanding between contexts. They ask: 'can we afford not to stir things up a little from time to time?' (p. 35). With support from their mentors, beginning teachers can start to consider which risks are worth taking in their teaching.

Understanding personal sensitivities

This continuum provides a valuable opportunity for beginning teachers to reflect on their own position on the teaching of sensitive and controversial histories. It is not easy to be a 'risk taker', especially for those beginning their teaching career, but it is not just a lack of experience that might prevent a beginning teacher from adopting a 'risk-taking' approach. In her research into Latvian and Estonian teachers' approaches to teaching sensitive and controversial issues, Kello (2016, p. 49) found that 'hiding or avoiding' and 'finding common ground or smoothing edges' were more noticeable features of teaching when the issue was sensitive for the teacher too. Kello refers to this as the teacher having a 'hot' personal relationship to the issue. Teachers were more likely to 'leave the truth open' when they had a 'cooler' attitude to the issue, meaning it was less personally sensitive for the teacher themselves (p. 49). Supporting your beginning teacher to prepare to teach sensitive and controversial histories requires developing an understanding of the issues that are important to them and their own identity. This is a very important part of relationship building with your mentee and will involve conversations about their 'hot' issues to support their delivery of these in the classroom. Kello's research pointed to the value of reflection, of understanding the importance of the relevant factors, and an awareness of alternative teaching approaches. Task 8.3 provides an opportunity for mentor reflection, and a range of teaching approaches are explored later in this chapter.

> **Task 8.3 Considering your own teaching of controversial and sensitive issues**
>
> - Identify where you are positioned on Kitson and McCully's continuum. See A. Kitson & A. McCully, 2005. '"You hear about it for real in school": avoiding, containing and risk-taking in the history classroom', *Teaching History 120*, September, 32–7, for the full continuum.
> - How do you approach teaching controversial issues in your own teaching? What do you see as the 'social utility' of teaching history? What are your 'hot' issues (Kello, 2016)?
> - Discuss your own responses with your mentee and invite them to share their responses to these questions.

Your department's curriculum

The authors of the Historical Association's TEACH Report highlighted that for controversial issues to be taught effectively, these issues should be part of a broader history curriculum, rooted in the values of inclusion, representation, and diversity (Wrenn, et al., 2007; Wrenn, et al., 2013). Your mentee will be teaching lessons that sit within this curriculum. Supporting your mentee to teach controversial and sensitive issues provides a chance for your department to review the diversity of your own curriculum alongside your mentee.

The Historical Association (2019) have compiled a useful set of questions for history teachers to review the diversity of their curriculum. The checklist asks challenging review questions about the curricular intent of including sensitive and controversial topics in our history teaching, for example asking, 'Does our curriculum help students to understand why some past topics are still highly emotional and sensitive for some groups of people?' A review of the substantive content of your curriculum, and the visibility of marginalised groups included within this, is prompted by questions like 'Do our historical enquiries start and end in the right place in order to understand people as fully human, and to understand their perspectives, even if they were not white, rich, northern European and male?' The checklist also suggests departments review the evidential and scholarship basis of their history curriculum, calling on teachers to consider whether 'When we include the work of historians and other "authority" figures . . . we draw on work from a diverse and representative range of people' (Historical Association, 2019).

At the time of writing, concerns about injustices highlight the racism within society and educational settings in England (Joseph-Salisbury, 2020). It is the responsibility of all history teachers to craft a curriculum that is representative and inclusive, and to recognise that any curriculum is never a finished product but rather a working document that must be open to continual review and development. Beginning teachers are increasingly likely to have significant expertise around more representative, inclusive, and decolonised histories, reflecting recent developments in scholarship and the changing curriculum offer at undergraduate level. Departments should embrace the opportunity to engage in dialogue with their mentee about their own curricular choices (see Task 8.4). The 'Move Me On' feature in *Teaching History* 187 recognises that beginning teachers from minoritised groups often have significant expertise informing questions about curricular representation. It includes advice from teachers about how to support them to do this positively and professionally. This advice includes dedicating department meeting time to the issue of race and the curriculum (Patel in Patel, Skepple, & Garry, 2022), constructive communication (Skepple, 2022 in Patel, Skepple, & Garry, 2022), and viewing fresh perspectives as an opportunity to discuss how to include the wider histories of people of colour, gender, disability, and the LGBTQ+ community (Garry in Patel, Skepple, & Garry, 2022).

Task 8.4 Reviewing curriculum content

With your whole department:

- Use the Historical Association's 'Curriculum review checklist to develop history curricula' (accessed at https://history.org.uk/secondary/resource/9620/how-diverse-is-your-history-curriculum) to review your curriculum with your mentee and your department. Think about how you can make space for your mentee within this conversation and support their perspective.
- Pupil perspectives are also important when grappling with curricular decisions. In the *Teaching History* 179 article 'No more doing diversity: How one department used Year 8 input to reform curricular thinking', Priggs (2020) sets out her approach for exploring pupils' responses to their Key Stage 3 (11-14 years) curriculum. The thoughtful responses of her pupils have the potential to inspire other teachers to also explore how their pupils interact with their curriculum; once taught, the curriculum only really exists in pupils' minds. As a department:

    - Read Priggs' article from *Teaching History* 179 with your mentee and consider what role student voice should play in curriculum design.
    - What do you think the pupils will 'takeaway' from their lessons about controversial and sensitive issues (Cusworth, 2021)?
    - How do pupils understand the 'enquiry ethic' (Mohamud & Whitburn, 2019)? How do you know? How can you find out?

- If your mentee has a practice-based research project to complete as part of their teacher training qualification, could the department support them to undertake an investigation into pupil perspectives on the history curriculum to support the ongoing development of the department? This is a good example of one way a mentee can progress their understanding of the professional agency and responsibility teachers have in developing history curricula, while also making a tangible contribution to the department in which they are training.

Principles for teaching sensitive and controversial histories

The inclusion of these wider histories is one important guiding principle for departments looking to develop their curriculum. In this section we outline some broad working principles for teaching controversial and sensitive issues to support your work with your mentee. For each of these there are practical suggestions for developing beginning teachers' subject knowledge and supporting their lesson planning. This also includes references to publications and resources for discussion of good practice during a mentor meeting. This is not intended as an exhaustive list, and we recognise that there will be other principles that you will want to discuss. Please see this as a potential starting point. At the end of this section, Task 8.6 provides an activity that will allow your mentee to begin to put these principles into practice.

Principle 1: Honouring people who have been dehumanised

A curriculum should be planned with an underlying respect for the dignity of people who have suffered injustice. This is one of several relevant considerations for beginning teachers as they approach teaching the Holocaust. This is a deeply dark and difficult period of history, and we know that it is challenging to teach (Pettigrew et al., 2009). Beginning teachers will want to do justice to this topic, and there may be aspects, such as the respectful use of 'atrocity' images, about which they are unsure. It is important that teachers do not select historical sources simply because they have the potential to provoke an emotional response from pupils (Davies, 2017). IHRA guidelines are also clear that 'using graphic images with the intent to shock and horrify is degrading to the victims and can reinforce stereotypes of Jews as victims' (2019, p. 28). Lenga (2020) explores the use of atrocity images further, finding that the common use of these images is deeply worrying, yet she asserts that 'a blanket ban on their use is also problematic' (p. 217), and suggests that with careful consideration, planning, and unpacking, young people can learn from these images. This is a tightrope that beginning teachers need to learn to walk. They need mentors to provide spaces where they can wrestle with these big questions and develop their confidence in teaching sensitive and controversial histories. Exploring resources together is one way of doing this.

University College London's Centre for Holocaust Education has published a research-informed Holocaust textbook. *Understanding the Holocaust* provides examples of how images of the Holocaust can be used sensitively. This is supported by a range of excellent practical online resources for teaching the Holocaust (Centre for Holocaust Education UCL, 2020). These resources take an enquiry-led approach, with a strong focus on the disciplinary concepts. The textbook also takes care to avoid depicting Jewish people as passive victims, for example by including a chapter titled 'Did the Jews fight back?' (Foster et al., 2020). 'The Forever Project', based at the National Holocaust Centre and Museum (n.d.), and 'The Eye as Witness', a project co-created by the National Holocaust Centre and Museum and the University of Nottingham (n.d.), have also asked important questions about depictions of Holocaust survivors and victims. Moreover, they have explored the role of digital technologies, artificial intelligence, and virtual reality in Holocaust remembrance and education, considering the impact of these technologies on pupil understanding. One important aspect of your work with your mentee will involve encouraging them to consider how technology can be used to support their teaching of sensitive and controversial issues.

Principle 2: Restoring the agency of those who have been oppressed

A focus on resistance to subjugation is one aspect of restoring the agency of oppressed peoples. Justice to History, created and led by Mohamud and Whitburn (2019), have created a series of historical enquiries. These enquiries explicitly consider the ethical dimensions of an historical enquiry. Mohamud and Whitburn set out working principles for teaching any unit of study that engages with teaching about Britain and transatlantic slavery. These principles aim to restore the agency of people who have been oppressed, by focusing on the lives of Africans before they were enslaved, the resistance of enslaved people, and the inclusion of African voices in sources and interpretations. These principles provide a very valuable starting point for anyone teaching about Britain and the transatlantic slave trade, beginning teachers included.

The 'Another History Is Possible' website, created by a London-based head of history, asks the question 'How do we allow the nameless numbers of history to become names with stories to tell?' (Another History Is Possible, n.d.). The website supports teachers by developing and sharing a range of resourced enquiries that tell the stories of the silenced. Enquiries include 'What can we infer from "migrant sources" about the history of the British Isles over the last thousand years?' and 'Was there more change than continuity in British-Jamaican relations between 1760 and 1870?' (n.d.). These shared enquiries are an excellent resource for those departments also working to address the silences in our historical narratives and what these silences reveal about inequalities of power (Trouillot, 1995).

The history of the American West is another aspect of the curriculum which has frequently been presented through the eyes of the 'coloniser', rather than the Indigenous peoples who experience conquest and US expansion. The framing of this topic has often resulted either in deficit presentations of Indigenous people, or in their total absence from the curriculum. Ford (2022) has updated his 2017 Hodder textbook on this topic to address this historic framing. He seeks to reframe US history as settler colonialism and make connections to present-day colonial issues. He considers how conflict in the West is presented when Indigenous perspectives are given greater emphasis and brings more diverse stories and voices into these narratives to support more effective representation of Indigenous peoples (Ford, 2023). This work demonstrates clearly how reframing of established areas of study can restore agency to those who have been oppressed.

Principle 3: Taking an approach which is representative and inclusive

There are many resources available to support your beginning teacher and department to teach a curriculum that is representative and inclusive.

Slotting in

Young people should be able 'to 'see themselves' in the history curriculum' (Priggs, 2020, p. 10). In their *Teaching History* article, Kerridge and Snelson (2022) outline a sequence of lessons about Roma and Traveller history with the aim of allowing children from Gypsy, Roma, and Traveller (GRT) communities to do just this, so that they no longer feel unseen in the history classroom. The article sets out useful links and resources, such as the Roma Stories

Oral History Project (www.romaoralhistory.com) and explores broader principles for teaching about the history of GRT communities. Similarly, Snelson and Lingard (2018) challenged history teachers to consider how people with disabilities have been 'hidden in plain sight' both in history and in our teaching (p. 27). Both articles explain how they developed opportunities to 'slot in' the stories and histories of diverse groups. This is an approach also adopted by YorkClio, a group of history teachers and educators working in and around York. YorkClio's resources are available at their website (https://yorkclio.com). This is also a testament to the powerful potential for history teachers and educators to come together at a grassroots level and to positively contribute to the history-teaching community as a whole.

Rather than creating a separate curriculum 'bolted on' to address these histories, the 'slot-in' approach means integrating these histories into the curriculum that you are already teaching. For example, the enquiry 'How much can we learn about women's suffrage from a statue?' would allow students to explore the similarities and differences between the supporters of women's suffrage whose names are engraved on the Millicent Fawcett statue in Parliament Square. One of these suffragettes, Rosa May Billinghurst, was paralysed by childhood polio and campaigned on a specially adapted tricycle. She used this to charge at the police and was arrested for doing so on Black Friday, 18 November 1910, when women were beaten and sexually assaulted by police as they tried to storm the Houses of Parliament (Lewis, 2021). The inclusion of Billinghurst's story and the stories of other women and men from diverse backgrounds challenges students' assumptions about disability, identity, and the wider suffrage movement. Engaging in a dialogue of this nature with your mentee may involve questioning your views of 'normal', to challenge any assumptions you might inadvertently introduce during lessons.

Avoiding tokenism

In his article 'Beyond tokenism: teaching a diverse history in the post-14 curriculum', Dennis (2016) uses a multidirectional-memory approach to move teachers beyond seeing Black history as separate or as distracting from the examination (p. 41). In the article he tells the stories of three individuals, all linked to frequently taught GCSE History topics in England. These include E. I. Ekpenyon (a former headmaster in Nigeria, who had come to study law in London and served as an ARP warden), Hans-Jürgen Massaquoi (born in 1926 to a Liberian father and German mother, who experienced first-hand the transition from Weimar to Nazi Germany), and Henrietta Lacks (an African American born in the 1920s, who became the unknowing donor of cells from a cancerous tumour). The powerful stories of these three individuals fit within existing schemes of work, but all support students to see beyond conventional narratives of the twentieth century. This can help challenge pupils' and our own assumptions, and open pupils' minds to the complexity of history and the multiplicity of peoples' experiences.

Hollis (2019) asserts that making the most of any opportunity to teach the history of marginalised groups is better than not including these histories at all. In relation to the teaching of LGBTQ+ histories, she stresses that 'in an ideal world there would be better integration of these topics in the curriculum year-round, but with the continual pressure on curriculum time, [LGBT History Month] remains a valuable space for us to introduce stories that would otherwise not be explored'. Beginning teachers need to be supported to understand that utilising an annual occasion to spotlight the history of any under-represented group or sensitive area of history is simply the start of a curricular journey, not the end point. Indeed, to avoid tokenism, 'history months' should be seen as a launch pad for departmental discussion and curriculum review and integration.

Supporting your mentee to understand how such shifts in curricular emphasis can open up and lead to a more diverse and inclusive curriculum is an important part of equipping them to be future curriculum makers. It can also help to build their confidence and help teachers avoid becoming overwhelmed as they start to make significant changes to a curriculum. We should be avoiding tokenism, of course, but understanding how incremental changes can build to result in meaningful longer-term redevelopment of a curriculum, for instance by adopting an approach of 'routine representation' (Hollis, 2021), is an important step towards beginning teachers feeling they have curricular agency and can make meaningful contributions to a department.

Principle 4: Addressing dehumanising language

An important part of all teachers' subject knowledge development is their ability to confidently use appropriate language in the classroom. When teaching aspects of history, where controversial dehumanising terms are likely to arise in the source record and legacy textbooks, teachers are faced with challenging decisions around their approach.

It is not uncommon for history teachers to find themselves standing in front of a class feeling awkward and ill-equipped to handle conversations around enslavement, race, empire, Indigenous peoples, and other historically marginalised peoples. Consequently, in this section of the chapter we ask some important questions around the language used in classrooms and encountered in the historical record, appreciating that attributed meanings are both contested and evolving and that they are highly emotive, for individuals and societies. How teachers can remain faithful to the historical record and create a classroom that humanises dehumanising language is an important issue to discuss with your mentee. Beginning teachers are likely to feel unprepared for such encounters when teaching more sensitive or controversial areas of the curriculum. Mentors should provide opportunities for beginning teachers to explore and understand why such language is so emotive, and how it can be appropriately handled so that mentees do not become 'avoiders' of teaching sensitive and controversial aspects of history (Kitson & McCully, 2005, p. 35).

Balancing safeguarding with historical integrity

Teachers have a professional responsibility to ensure our young people are learning in safe spaces today. Being mindful of our safeguarding responsibilities also has implications which reach into whole-school behaviour, such as antibullying and equality policies pertaining to protected characteristics. As shown by Traille's important research into the school history experiences of students of African-Caribbean descent, it is critical history teachers prepare carefully for the teaching of the histories of race and empire, as

> Certain topics are more sensitive than others, and that does not preclude them from being taught, but they need to be taught 'well' with foresight and some sensitivity. Some teachers are still making careless comments about black people in history. They

are apparently ignorant of the damage they may be inflicting on young minds. (Traille, 2007, p. 34)

To ensure that the classroom is a safe environment for all students, beginning teachers should understand that there is never a place in the classroom for dehumanising language which makes people feel less than those around them. Certain terms are agreed to be extremely offensive, and being a 'risk-taking' teacher does not mean we should use, read aloud, or encourage our students to use these extremely offensive and inappropriate terms (for example explicitly racist or homophobic language) in the classroom, even if they appear in an original historical source or document. As the use of language is constantly evolving, terms which are currently considered contested may very quickly come to be regarded as highly offensive. Mentors therefore need to be prepared to have conversations with their mentees about the appropriateness of this contested terminology, considering the context of the school, wider society, and the teacher's own positionality. These conversations will need to be revisited regularly as our shared understanding of language is constantly evolving.

It might therefore seem a simple decision to avoid using source material which includes any dehumanising terms, or to censor or redact any controversial or sensitive language included in a source. However, while redaction or paraphrase may seem a simple solution at first, it also has implications for pupils' historical understanding and needs to be carefully considered. Levstik's (2008) research highlighted that teachers often seek 'safety in silence' (p. 297) when confronted with such complexity. Students exist in a world where they are constantly confronted by the legacy of these difficult histories in their communities and through their encounters with popular culture. Through these encounters they form their own understandings of how these sensitive and controversial aspects of the past impact upon the present. School history lessons can provide a space where their pre-existing understandings become better informed. Carefully planned lessons can enable pupils to navigate the complexity of how and why these dehumanising terms are still used and have such power in the present. Redaction is therefore not a simple choice. Beginning teachers need support to make distinctions between words that can be usefully recontextualised and that do benefit from teachers being explicit about why certain terminology is more appropriate, and words (such as racial slurs) that breach safeguarding parameters and shouldn't be used (Cusworth, 2021, p. 26).

Considering language and terminology

To illustrate, when considering historical topics centred around race and colonialism, we need to begin by understanding what is so problematic about certain terms relating to race, empire, and enslavement, and how we decide whether a term is dehumanising. It is also important to recognise that some seemingly innocuous terms, commonly used elsewhere in history, acquire loaded and even offensive meanings in particular contexts. For example, a term such as 'rebel', which might be historically accurate and perfectly acceptable in some historical contexts, once used in relation to enslavement, reflects the intention of 'owners of enslaved African people to highlight what was considered to be their (the enslaved's) disruptive, troublesome and terroristic resistance to the system of slavery' (Dawkins, 2021, p. 10).

Teaching controversial and sensitive issues 167

Consequently, we need to ask whether the language used in the teaching of these histories:

- Objectifies and disrespects the people to whom they refer.
- Disregards Indigenous perspectives on the period.
- Reduces individuals to a single term and fails to acknowledge the multiplicity of experience.

In 2020 a team of researchers at the University of Nottingham worked with local teachers to produce a series of culturally sensitive anti-racist educational materials to support teachers' work in this area. The resources included *A Glossary of Terminology for Understanding Transatlantic Slavery and 'Race'*, which explores a range of terminology, indicating the 'appropriateness, meaning, and use of each word and phrase', offering alternative terms where relevant (Dawkins, 2021, p. 7). It also contains a section on questions pupils frequently ask in relation to particular terms and issues relating to race and racism; here we see an example of how teachers may wish to respond to a common question about the use of the n-word in popular culture. It has also inspired another glossary, now adopted by the OCR examination board, which reflects the development of terminology for teaching Native American history and serves to exemplify the agency of teachers to bring about systemic change and make a difference when they use their expertise to be a 'risk taker' (Gosrani, 2021).

Exploring resources like a glossary or textbooks (see Task 8.5) alongside your mentee can provide a scaffold for thinking through the selection of material, the structuring of expositions, and the management of discussion. Importantly, it can enable beginning teachers to have challenging but safe 'risk-taking' conversations with their pupils, especially when encountering racist slurs within historic source material. As illustrated by Gosrani's blog (2021), glossaries can also provide models for how the language used to describe other marginalised groups can be assessed and mediated with young people.

Task 8.5 Reviewing textbook presentations of controversial and sensitive issues

Select a few examples of textbooks which cover a sensitive and controversial topic area from your curriculum and discuss them at a mentor meeting. With your mentee, compare how the textbooks introduce the topic through the text and images used on these pages.

- How do the textbooks depict different people and groups involved and impacted by the historical events (perpetrators, victims, and survivors)?
- Do the textbooks make an effort to confer agency to victims and survivors of events such as the Holocaust, colonialism, and enslavement?
- Is the provenance of images and photographs identified? For example, many Holocaust images used in textbooks are examples of perpetrator photography created for propaganda purposes.

- How could images created by victim survivors as acts of resistance change the narrative and humanise the dehumanised?
- Is there any language used in the text or written sources that objectifies and disrespects the people to whom they refer, disregards Indigenous perspectives on the period, or reduces individuals to a single term and fails to acknowledge the multiplicity of experience? Discuss whether it is appropriate for these terms to be censored/redacted, substituted, or addressed with pupils.
- Explore scenarios where your mentee might have to make decisions about resource selection or how to manage a class discussion where such terms may be encountered.

Principle 5: Understanding that sensitive and controversial histories evolve and often require an understanding of the present context

Sensitive and controversial historical issues are not fixed; rather, what is considered controversial or sensitive will change over time and is shaped by world events. This means that teachers need to strike a delicate balance as events unfold. One recent example of this is Russia's invasion of Ukraine. Students are very likely to come to their teachers concerned and worried, with questions that reflect their anxiety. Beginning teachers will also be teaching children from the countries involved. At this point beginning teachers will need clear guidance and advice from both their mentor and their department. A connection to the history-teaching community is vital at these moments (for more on this see Chapter 10). Social media and 'crowdsourced' information sharing, for example the @SnelsonH Twitter thread and the Padlet hosted by Euroclio (https://padlet.com/EuroClio_Secretariat/13ck4n4khw4voyxq), have collated resources for teaching about the war in Ukraine and were immediate practical sources of support. Educational blogs (Crooks, 2022) and online projects, such as the 'Facing History and Ourselves' website (2022), also offered support and resources for teachers seeking to navigate teaching this contemporarily sensitive issue. Additionally, the HA's podcast series 'Confronting Controversial History' (Historical Association, 2022) led by Todd and Robinson, brings together teacher educators and historians, recognising the dynamic nature of the relationship between the past and the present and reflecting on why topics are considered controversial. The series is also excellent for developing teachers' subject knowledge and could provide a good focus for a purposeful mentoring conversation about the role of subject knowledge for teaching.

Task 8.6 Planning and creating resources for teaching controversial and sensitive issues

Identify a sensitive or controversial area of your curriculum where your mentee could design some new resources, develop a new enquiry, or gather a reading list for colleagues to enhance the teaching of this topic. Encourage your mentee to consider the principles outlined above. Support them in the teaching and reflection cycle using these new resources and discuss whether these resources have reframed the teaching of this area of history.

The following resources could provide useful perspectives for supporting these discussions:

- 'A glossary of terminology for understanding transatlantic slavery and race.' Available at https://nottinghammuseums.org.uk/a-glossary-of-terminology-for-understanding-transatlantic-slavery-and-race/ (Dawkins, 2021)
- *Bristol and Transatlantic Slavery: Origins, Impact and Legacy*, textbook (Kennett et al., 2021)
- *OCR GCSE History SHP: The Making of America 1789-1900*, textbook (Ford, 2022). Please note this recommendation is for the 2022 updated edition where the text has been reframed to emphasise the continuity of Indigenous Presence and the colonisation of North America
- 'Photographing the Holocaust', FutureLearn course (University of Nottingham, 2021)
- *Understanding the Holocaust*, textbook (Foster et al., 2020)

Frequently asked questions

These working principles are designed to support beginning teachers and their mentors, but they can also be challenging in practice. Beginning teachers are very likely to ask difficult questions when they are planning and teaching about controversial and sensitive issues. Boxes 8.1–8.4 include a range of questions that beginning teachers have asked their mentors, with some suggestions from mentors for addressing these issues. There is an opportunity to reflect on these questions and answers in Task 8.7.

Box 8.1 Question 1: disclosing personal views

When teaching about controversial or sensitive issues I am unsure whether, or how, I should disclose my own personal views. What would you advise?

Mentor response: For all teachers this is a challenging question. Certainly, teachers cannot promote their own partisan political views and should 'take such steps as are reasonably practicable to secure that, where political issues are brought to the attention of pupils, they are offered a balanced presentation of opposing views' (DfE, 2022). It seems safe to assume that these 'political issues' relate to ongoing political action and activities. Not all controversial or sensitive issues are 'political issues', far from it. And even so, this does not dictate concealing your own views, just the need to provide a range of additional views. In my teaching, if a student asks my opinion, I acknowledge my own position. After all we are all human, and children are pretty perceptive. They have probably already worked out what I think from my tone and body language. Trying to pretend to be neutral might just make you seem insincere, after all we ask the pupils to give their view and support this with evidence, shouldn't we do the same? In their research into teaching controversial issues in Northern Ireland, Barton and McCully (2007) point out that it would be disingenuous for teachers in this context to pretend that they have no opinions. They point to the potential benefits for students, as 'part of this disclosure may involve teachers in admitting their own doubts, confusions, and uncertainties, so that students can feel safer when they too feel a lack of clarity' (2007, p. 15). I recommend reading this article.

Box 8.2 Question 2: spontaneous controversial remarks

I am nervous about how to react to students' spontaneous controversial remarks. For example, what do I say if a student presents a terrorist act as a hoax or conspiracy theory?

Mentor response: This is a difficult question to answer. It is impossible to anticipate the full gamut of students' questions. You can, however, always challenge students when they make unsupported claims. This means when a student makes a controversial remark like the one suggested above, they can expect to be asked 'what evidence do you have to support this claim?' In this instance a student might reply that they heard it on social media. This would allow a teacher to ask a series of follow-up questions about who had posted this, and what their motives for doing so might have been, to refocus the conversation onto a consideration of provenance in historical study. When setting up discussions around sensitive issues make your expectations clear and allocate pupils to specific roles, including those who might be the listeners in the discussion.

There is always a judgement to be made about pupils' motivations when they make controversial remarks, and this requires the teacher to assess the pupils' intent in that moment. If a comment stems from a lack of awareness, it is a teacher's job to tackle this for the benefit of the whole class. In some cases, it may be appropriate to refocus the class on the substantive issue of the lesson and then follow up the controversial remark with the individual pupil after the lesson. Racist, homophobic, misogynistic, or xenophobic comments should always be challenged and reported according to your school's policies.

Box 8.3 Question 3: the respectful use of photographs and films

How can I use photographs and films to respect the dignity and the diversity of people in the past?

Mentor response: When deciding which photographs or films to use, consider how to promote pupils' historical thinking rather than simply to shock or provoke an emotional response. In his chapter 'Teaching sensitive and controversial issues', Davies gives the example of how a photograph of the English football team giving a Nazi salute in 1938 can be used to prompt historical thinking and achieve the desired outcome (Davies, 2017).

When you use films to teach sensitive histories you need to be clear about your rationale for doing so. There are many films about controversial and sensitive histories and, used well, these films can powerfully engage students. To maintain historical rigour, you will need to use films critically, as an interpretation of events to be unpicked. You also need to be mindful that if you show film extracts in class, children have little choice but to watch them. Films must be age-appropriate and if you are unsure about the appropriateness of a film clip, check with the class teacher or head of department.

Box 8.4 Question 4: developing subject knowledge

I am worried about my subject knowledge of Black British history, as my own school and undergraduate education focused on American civil rights. Is there anything that you suggest?

Mentor response: The skilful teaching of controversial or sensitive issues in history relies on teachers having strong subject knowledge, informed by recent academic scholarship. It is a positive that you have identified this as an area for development. My first recommendation would be to read David Olusoga's (2021) *Black and British: A Forgotten History*. I would also recommend *The Heart of the Race*, by Beverly Bryan, Stella Dadzie, and Suzanne Scafe (2018) to help support your understanding of Black women's experiences in Britain. I know it really helped me to learn about movements in education like supplementary schools. The debates we are having about racism and education now are sadly not new ones. Elias and Spafford (2021) make a number of recommendations in their article in *Teaching History* 185. Also, don't forget about podcasts like the BBC's *What Does Windrush Mean Now?* (2019).

Task 8.7 Mentor reflection: answering beginning teachers' questions about teaching controversial and sensitive issues

Consider the mentee questions and the answers given by their mentors in Boxes 8.1–8.4.

- Would you have answered these differently?
- What aspects of this chapter would you benefit from considering further in relation to your own practice? How can you begin to develop your mentoring practice in this area?
- In what ways will you stimulate your mentee to reflect on their teaching of sensitive and controversial issues in the future?

Summary and key points

- Some issues in history are inherently sensitive and controversial, while others become controversial or acquire sensitivity due to the contemporary context in which they are being taught.
- Mentors need to support their mentees to consider the rationale for teaching these sensitive and controversial aspects of history. Working with a mentee to explore this aspect of history also opens up opportunities for a department to engage in curriculum review discussions.
- Teachers themselves have a range of responses to teaching controversial and sensitive histories. Mentors need to provide opportunities for their mentee to explore these responses in order to build the beginning teacher's capacity to teach these topics effectively and sensitively.
- The suggestions made in this chapter are necessarily tentative because of the complex and dynamic nature of these issues, but we hope to have provided a range of suggestions for high-quality teaching resources that can be explored and utilised by mentors and their mentees.

Further reading and resources

- **Facing History and Ourselves: www.facinghistory.org**
  Facing History and Ourselves is a global organisation that provides resources and training for teachers to teach history that confront our collective histories and the injustices of the past, to support our students to make connections with the past and present. You could explore these pedagogical approaches with your mentee.
- **Kitson, A., & McCully, A., 2005. 'You hear about it for real in school': avoiding, containing and risk-taking in the history classroom, *Teaching History 120*, September, 32-7.**
  This article provides a very useful starting point for discussions with your mentee regarding approaches to teaching controversial issues.
- **The RETEACH website: https://reteach.org.uk/subject/history**
  This website is designed for teachers seeking 'fresh viewpoints, deeper subject knowledge, [and] diverse thinking' and includes a range of resources. Mentors and mentees could explore these resources to inform their discussions about the curriculum.

References

Another History Is Possible. (n.d.). About Another History Is Possible. Retrieved 16 November 2022 from https://anotherhistoryispossible.com/

Barton, K., & McCully, A. (2007). Teaching controversial issues . . . where controversial issues really matter. *Teaching History 127*, 13-19.

BBC. (2019). *Beyond Today What Does Windrush Mean Now? Podcast*. Retrieved 16 November 2022 from www.bbc.co.uk/programmes/p07qcjjq

Benger, A. (2022). Beyond the balance sheet: navigating the 'imperial history wars' when planning and teaching about the British Empire. *Teaching History 187*, 8-19.

Bilali, R., & Mahmoud, R. (2017). Confronting history and reconciliation: A review of civil society's approaches to transforming conflict narratives. In C. Psaltis, M. Carretero, & S. Čehajić-Clancy (eds.), *History Education and Conflict Transformation* (pp. 77-96). Cham: Palgrave Macmillan.

Boyd, S. (2009). From 'Great Women' to an inclusive curriculum: how should women's history be included at Key Stage 3? *Teaching History 175*, 16-23.

Bryan, B., Dadzie, S., & Scafe, S., (2018). *The Heart of the Race: Black Women's Lives in Britain*. Croydon: Verso.

Carr, P. R. (2007). Experiencing democracy through neoliberalism: The role of social justice in democratic education. *Journal for Critical Education Policy Studies 5*(2), 1-21.

Centre for Holocaust Education UCL. (2020). Cutting Edge Classroom Resources. Retrieved 18 November 2022 from https://holocausteducation.org.uk/teacher-resources/

Council of Europe. (2018). *Reference Framework of Competence for Democratic Culture*. Retrieved 16 November 2022 from https://rm.coe.int/prems-008318-gbr-2508-reference-framework-of-competences-vol-1-8573-co/16807bc66c

Crooks, V. (2022, 28 February). Teaching children about sensitive and controversial affairs: Talking to children in schools about the situation in Ukraine. Retrieved 16 November 2022 from *Becoming a History Teacher*, https://uonhistoryteachertraining.school.blog/2022/02/28/teaching-children-about-sensitive-and-controversial-current-affairs-talking-to-children-in-schools-about-the-situation-in-ukraine/

Cusworth, H. (2021). Putting Black into the Union Jack. *Teaching History 183*, 20-6.

Davies, M. (2017). Teaching sensitive and controversial issues. In I. Davies (ed.), *Debates in History Teaching* (pp. 261-71). London: Routledge.

Dawkins, J. (2021). A glossary of terminology for understanding transatlantic slavery and race. Retrieved 16 November 2022 from Nottingham Museums, https://nottinghammuseums.org.uk/a-glossary-of-terminology-for-understanding-transatlantic-slavery-and-race/

Deardon, R.F. (1981). Controversial issues and the curriculum. *Journal of Curriculum Studies 13*(1), 37-44.

Dennis, N. (2016). Beyond tokensim: teaching a diverse history in the post-14 curriculum. *Teaching History 165*, 37-41.

DfE. (2013). *History Programmes of Study: Key Stage 3 National Curriculum in England*. Retrieved 28 January 2023 from UK Government Department of Education, https://assets.publishing.service.gov.uk/government/uploads/system/uploads/attachment_data/file/239075/SECONDARY_national_curriculum_-_History.pdf

DfE. (2022). *Political Impartiality in Schools*. Retrieved 16 November 2022 from UK Government Department of Education, www.gov.uk/government/publications/political-impartiality-in-schools/political-impartiality-in-schools

Elias, H., & Spafford, M. (2021). Teaching Britain's civil rights history: activism and citizenship in context. *Teaching History 185*, 10-21.

Facing History and Ourselves. (2022). Teaching about the Ukrainian refugee crisis. Retrieved 16 November 2022 from www.facinghistory.org/resource-library/teaching-about-ukrainian-refugee-crisis

Ford, A. (2022). *OCR GCSE History SHP: The Making of America 1789-1900*. London: Hodder.

Ford, A. (2023, 20 January). Decolonising and diversifying 19th century US history – resources and links. Retrieved from AndAllThat.co.uk, http://www.andallthat.co.uk/america-1789-1900/decolonising-and-diversifying-19th-century-us-history-resources-and-links

Foster, S., Pearce, A., Karayianni, E., & McCord, H. (2020). *Understanding the Holocaust: How and Why Did it Happen?* London: Hodder.

Gosrani, S. (2021, 3 December). Reflections on teaching Native American history. Retrieved 16 November 2022 from https://www.ocr.org.uk/blog/reflections-on-teaching-native-american-history/

Hawkey, K. (2015). Moving forward, looking back – historical perspective, 'Big History' and the return of the longue durée: time to develop our scale hopping muscles. *Teaching History 158*, 40-6.

Historical Association. (2019). *How diverse is your curriculum?* Retrieved 16 November 2022 from www.history.org.uk/secondary/resource/9620/how-diverse-is-your-history-curriculum

Historical Association. (2022). *Confronting Controversial History* podcast series. Retrieved 16 November 2022 from www.history.org.uk/secondary/categories/607/module/8792/podcast-series-confronting-controversial-history

Hollis, C. (2019). Being ambitious with LGBT history. Retrieved 28 January 2023 from *Fresh Alarums*, https://freshalarums.wordpress.com/2019/01/14/being-ambitious-with-lgbt-history/

Hollis, C. (2021). Illuminating the possibilities of the past: the role of representation in A-level curriculum planning. *Teaching History 185*, 22-9.

IHRA. (2019). Recommendations for teaching about the Holocaust. Retrieved 16 November 2022 from www.holocaustremembrance.com/sites/default/files/2021-09/Recommendations%20for%20Teaching%20and%20Learning%20about%20the%20Holocaust%20-%20IHRA.pdf

Joseph-Salisbury, R. (2020). *Race and Racism in English Secondary Schools*. London: Runnymede.

Kello, K. (2016). Sensitive and controversial issues in the classroom: teaching history in a divided society. *Teachers and Teaching 22*(1), 35-53.

Kennett, R., Thorne, S., Allen, T., Bolam, J., Durbin, E., O'Brien, T., Smee, K., & Stevenson, M. (2021). *Bristol and Transatlantic Slavery: Origins, impact and legacy*. Bristol: Bristol Books CIC.

Kerridge, R., & Snelson, H. (2022). We are invisible! Ensuring Gyspy, Roma and Traveller children do not feel unseen in the history classroom. *Teaching History 188*, 10-18.

Kitson, A., & McCully, A. (2005). 'You hear about it for real in school': avoiding, containing and risk-taking in the history classroom. *Teaching History 188*, 10-18.

Langdon, P. (2022). *We musn't regret a failure to face up to teaching climate change*. Retrieved 28 January 2023, from *One Big History Department*, https://onebighistorydepartment.com/2022/02/02/we-mustnt-wait-to-regret-a-failure-to-face-up-to-teaching-climate-change/

Lenga, R.-A. (2020). Seeing things differently: the use of atrocity images in teaching about the Holocaust. In S. Foster, A. Pearce, & A. Pettigrew, *Holocaust Education: Contemporary Challenges and Controversies* (pp. 195-220). London: UCL.

Levstik, L. (2008). Articulating the silences: teachers' and adolescents' conceptions of historical significance. In L. Levstik & K. Barton, *Researching History Education, 284-305*. (pp. 284-305). New York: Routledge.

Lewis, H. (2021). *Difficult Women: A History of Feminism in 11 Fights*. Dublin: Vintage.

Martin, D. (2022, 20 March). Teach bad and good of empire, says minister. Retrieved 16 November 2022 from *Daily Mail*, www.dailymail.co.uk/news/article-10633779/Teach-bad-good-Empire-urges-minister.html

Mohamud, A., & Whitburn, R. (2016). *Doing Justice to History: Transforming Black History in Secondary Schools*. London: Trentham Books.

Mohamud, A., & Whitburn, R. (2019). Anatomy of an enquiry: deconstructing an approach to curriculum planning. *Teaching History 177*, 28-39.

National Holocaust Centre and Museum. (n.d.). *The Forever Project*. Retrieved 19 January 2023, from https://www.holocaust.org.uk/interactive

National Holocaust Centre and Museum and the University of Nottingham. (n.d.). *The Eye as Witness*. Retrieved 19 January 2023, from https://witness.holocaust.org.uk/exhibition

Olusoga, D. (2021). *Black and British: A Forgotten History*. London: Picador.

Patel, Z., Skepple, A., & Garry, J. (2022). Move me on. *Teaching History 187*, 76-9.

Pettigrew, A., Foster, S., Howson, J., Salmons, P., Lenga, R.-A., & Andrews, K. (2009). *Teaching about the Holocaust in English Secondary Schools: An Empirical Study of National Trends, Perspectives and Practice*. London: Holocuast Education Development Programme.

Priggs, C. (2020). No more doing diversity: How one department used Year 8 input to reform curricular thinking. *Teaching History 179*, 10-19.

PSHE Association. (n.d.). Addressing misogyny, toxic masculinity and social media influence in PSHE educaiton. Retrieved 28 January 2023 from https://pshe-association.org.uk/guidance/ks1-5/addressing-misogyny-toxic-masculinity-and-social-media-influence-in-pshe-education#chapter-1

Smyth, C. (2022, 28 March). Teach pupils the benefits of the British Empire says Nadim Zahari. Retrieved 16 November 2022 from *The Times*, www.thetimes.co.uk/article/teach-pupils-the-benefits-of-the-british-empire-says-nadhim-zahawi-2r6jtssp7

Snelson, H., & Lingard, R. (2018). Hidden in plain sight: bringing the past of people with disabilities into the history classroom. *Teaching History 173*, 24-9.

Stradling, R. (1984). The teaching of controversial Issues: an evaluation. *Educational Review 36*(2), 121-9.

Stradling, R. (2003). *Multiperspectivity in History Teaching: a Guide for Teacher*. Retrieved 16 November 2022 from https://book.coe.int/en/history-teaching/2593-multiperspectivity-in-history-teaching-a-guide-for-teachers.html

Traille, K. (2007). 'You should be proud about your history. They made me feel ashamed': Teaching history hurt. *Teaching History 127*, 31-7.

Trouillot, M. (1995). *Silencing the Past: Power and the Production of History*. Boston: Beacon Press.

University of Nottingham. (2021). Photographing the Holocaust (FutureLearn course). Retrieved 20 January 2023, from Future Learn, https://www.futurelearn.com/courses/photographing-the-holocaust

Wansink, B., Patist., J., Zuiker, I., & Savenije, G. (2019). Confronting conflicts: history teachers' reactions to spontaneous controversial remarks. *Teaching History 175*, 68-75.

Wrenn, A., Wilkinson, A., Webb, A., Gillespie, H., Riley, M., Hartnett, P., Harris, R., & Lomas, T. (2007). *TEACH Teaching Emotive and Controversial History 3-19*. London: Historical Association. Retrieved 16 November 2022 from www.history.org.uk/secondary/resource/780/the-teach-report

Wrenn, A., Wilkinson, A., Webb, A., Gillespie, H., Riley, M., Hartnett, P., Harris, R., & Lomas, T. (2013). *TEACH Online Teaching Emotive and Controversial History*. Retrieved 16 November 2022 from www.history.org.uk/secondary/module/1140/teach-online

9 Supporting beginning teachers' use of ICT in the history classroom

Terry Haydn

Introduction

What does it mean 'to be good at ICT' as a history teacher? How can beginning and early career history teachers learn to make best use of the range of new technologies now available to them? How important is it that they receive at least 'a grounding' in the use of ICT?

Developments in new technology and social media offer opportunities to improve teaching and learning in history. Most of the people reading this chapter will at some point in their career as a history teacher, whether, in their own practice, within their department, or at Historical Association (HA) and Schools History Project (SHP) conferences, have encountered history teachers who have been able to make a point more effectively by using one of a variety of ICT applications or a resource from the internet and social media. Ofsted reports on the use of ICT in secondary history departments found wide disparities in the extent to which history teachers make effective use of new technologies and social media (Ofsted, 2011; 2007). The chapter provides guidance on the psychological and 'confidence' factors influencing beginning history teachers' attitudes to making use of ICT and suggests a range of strategies for getting beginning teachers to explore the potential of new technologies and social media for improving their practice.

What I have to say in this chapter is based to some extent on scholarship and research into the use of ICT in history teaching. But as well as scholarship and research, my ideas have been influenced by my experiences of working with beginning history teachers over a number of years. What follows is, in part, my reflections and observations on working with beginning teachers; the views are my own.

I am aware of the danger that those of you who have experience of working with beginning teachers, or who have a strong interest in the potential uses of new technology to improve teaching and learning in history, may find some of what I have written to be rather stating the obvious, but I hope that there will be at least some points which might be of use or interest.

Objectives

At the end of the chapter, you should have:

- An awareness of the breadth of new technology applications which can be used in history teaching.

DOI: 10.4324/9781003223504-9

Values and history education 177

- Insight into the comparative importance of a range of new technology applications to beginning teachers.
- A range of strategies for developing beginning teachers' use of new technology.
- A sense of the timing, workload, and well-being issues involved in developing beginning teachers' ability to use ICT to improve teaching and learning in history.
- Some strategies for enabling beginning teachers to work autonomously to develop their ability to use new technology effectively in their teaching.

Why bother with ICT?

Under current regulations and competence specifications, the ability to use new technology to improve teaching and learning in school subjects in England is scarcely mentioned. I found it difficult to find any mention of ICT in the current version of the Teachers' Standards, the Core Content Framework for Initial Teacher Training (ITT), or the Ofsted Research Review for history (DfE, 2011; 2019; Ofsted, 2021). Those of you who have mentored for a number of years will be aware that in previous competence specifications for beginning teachers, developing the ability to use ICT effectively was a prominent feature of the stipulations which had to be met if trainee teachers were to be judged fit to be unleashed on generations of children. In the 1998 version of the standards, this amounted to 15 pages of detail, with over 100 competences specified, all of which had to be met if the student teacher were to be allowed to pass the course (DfEE, 1998).

The removal of ICT as an area of relevance to beginning teachers seems paradoxical given developments in communications technology and concerns about the effects that new technologies and social media are having on the teaching and learning of history (Walsh, 2017; Wineburg, 2018; Carretero, Cantabrana, & Parellada, 2022; Steinhauer, 2022). Young people now get more of their information about history from social media sites such as Tik Tok, Instagram, YouTube, and other sources than from those mediated by the history teacher, textbook, or television channel (Carretero, Cantabrana, & Parellada, 2022). This clearly has implications for history education. In the words of Wineburg (2019), 'The internet is sowing mass confusion. We must rethink how we teach every school subject'. If anything, new technology and social media have become more important over the past decade rather than less so. However, such are the vagaries of inspection frameworks. Just because the part ICT plays in the development of beginning and early career teachers is not currently 'fashionable' in the way that it was a few years ago, this does not mean that the ability to use new technology adroitly to improve teaching and learning in history has become irrelevant to the development of effective history teachers.

Using ICT does not automatically improve teaching and learning in history; it depends how adeptly it is used, but in the words of Walsh it does offer opportunities to support and enhance best practice in history teaching:

> In its various forms, ICT offers many different affordances: access to a range of historical source material impossible to access any other way; contexts within which to place historical tasks that give them extra meaning and make them more memorable; and tools to investigate, interpret and manage historical information and to demonstrate

understanding. But, at the risk of labouring the point, these affordances are only valuable if they uphold or even extend the conceptual thinking and rigour already to be found in existing good practice. (Walsh, 2017, p. 255)

What are we hoping to achieve as mentors in the field of ICT?

The proliferation of new developments in the field of ICT in recent years has meant that it has become a vast and sprawling agenda for mentors to address, given the considerable pressure on mentors to address the elements of practice that *are* in the Teachers' Standards, ITT Core Content Framework, and Early Career Framework. As with so many aspects of mentoring, there are difficult judgement calls to be made about how much time and attention to give to helping beginning teachers to make best use of new technology. This is complicated further by the question of how well the beginning teacher is functioning in the early stages of their teaching. If they are still struggling with 'fundamental' issues such as lesson planning, managing pupil behaviour, and being able to teach effectively from the front of the class, it is clearly not appropriate to devote time to the more arcane elements of ICT capability at this stage of the placement. However, there are perhaps some competences and dispositions which might be considered generally desirable over the course of the training year as a whole, if there is mentoring time available after fundamental agendas have been addressed. The following tentative suggestions are just things to keep in mind and consider, and the choice of what to focus on might depend in part on where the beginning teacher stands in their ICT capability (and in their attitude to exploring the possibilities of new technology as a history teacher). In my experience, beginning teachers are very much a 'mixed-attaining group' when they start their course of training. They also vary considerably in their attitudes to ICT; some are already quite accomplished, are early adopters, and are keen to engage with the challenges of how to improve their teaching through the use of new technology. Others are less expert, and less confident, and there are some who feel that they are 'not the sort of person who is good at this stuff' and who may well be reluctant to wholeheartedly explore the potential of ICT to improve their teaching. You may find that you have to adapt your handling of ICT issues to suit the psychology and level of expertise of the beginning teacher you are working with, rather than having a standard programme for all of those in your care. These are some of the areas that you may wish to develop or cultivate with your mentee over the course of the programme:

- It might seem a rather prosaic agenda, but if you are working with a beginning teacher who is lacking in confidence around the use of computers, you can assuage their anxieties by (a) helping them by providing patient and gentle instruction, guiding them through things in some instances, and (b) showing them by example that there are times when we all have to find out things by looking them up on YouTube or Google, and that sometimes a bit of patience and initiative is required. If we lean too much on the former strategy, there is the danger of them lapsing further into 'learned helplessness' and thinking that they are genetically incapable of learning anything about using ICT unless someone takes them through it step by step. It might be helpful to adjust the balance between these strategies as the placement unfolds.

Values and history education 179

- Ensuring that they become aware of the need to become knowledgeable and up to date in their awareness of the range of ICT applications, programs, and resources which can be used to enhance teaching and learning in history. Even if they are not enthusiastic devotees of new technology and social media, we want them to be aware that this is part of developing their subject knowledge (in what ways might new technologies help us to teach history more effectively?). Although some ICT applications are 'generic' in that they are used across subject disciplines (for example, presentation software, the use of the internet to gather useful resources, the use of the visualiser for modelling), there are some aspects of ICT which are subject-specific. Data-logging software is of no interest to history teachers, but history databases (for example the Commonwealth War Graves Commission website at https://www.cwgc.org/, the Centre for the Study of the Legacies of British Slavery at https://www.ucl.ac.uk/lbs/, and England's immigration database 1330-1550 at https://www.englandsimmigrants.com/) are of particular interest to history educators.
- Ensuring that they become aware of the need to learn how to use presentation software effectively (whether it be PowerPoint, Prezi, the interactive whiteboard, or other applications). This is important because presentation software is extensively used by the majority of history teachers, so sooner or later, beginning teachers have to get their heads around how to use it adroitly. There will be few people reading this chapter who have not, at one point or another, been bored and 'switched off' by a poorly executed PowerPoint presentation. There are some history teachers who make very skilful and effective use of presentation software, others less so. A mentor confided in me that at one school, the pupils had banded together to send a petition to the head protesting about the PowerPoints they were extensively subjected to across all subjects (for some examples of 'dos and don'ts' of using presentation software, see Haydn (2013), 'We need to talk about PowerPoint'). It is perhaps worth making the particular point here that dire use of PowerPoint was thought to be most usually a result of beginning teachers not giving sufficient attention and care to the quality of ideas and resources in their slides, rather than their inability to use the advanced features of the application.
- Ensuring that they learn to become well organised and efficient in terms of using ICT to save time in planning and assessment and to organise their personal 'archive' of resources effectively. Again, this last point might sound rather prosaic, but as beginning teachers' experience extends, it becomes harder and harder to keep collections of resources 'under control'. Not being able to locate things and doing things at the last minute can add to the stress of teachers' lives. The sooner they learn to organise their digital resources in an efficient, easily retrievable manner, the more time it will save them. It doesn't matter whether they use the same system as you, whether it is thematic or alphabetical, as long as you signal the importance of 'good housekeeping' with resources.
- Ensuring that they become aware of the importance of being able to *adapt* digital resources so that they are appropriate for the class they are teaching. There are not many resources which come 'cellophane wrapped' in a way that is perfect for any teaching group, without any need for modification. There is sometimes a danger that the mentee,

if tired and pushed for time, might simply get hold of someone else's PowerPoint or 'learning package', and not do the necessary work to think through how to adapt and refine the materials so that the teacher exposition which accompanies the presentation is appropriate and high-quality. Chapter 4 has further detail about PowerPoint issues. By the end of their training, we want beginning teachers to be able to use digitally acquired resources to construct well designed and intellectually rigorous pupil tasks, and also to use them to complement high-quality teacher exposition.

- Ensuring that they learn to make good use of communications technology (history websites, discussion groups, blogs, Twitter etc.) to start to integrate themselves into the 'community of practice' of history teachers, which can be so helpful to history teachers' lives. Showing them some of the best history education sites and Twitter feeds can be a good start, but again, the hope is that they will explore things further, and 'share back' with the department as the placement progresses.
- Stressing the importance of initiative in this field and becoming 'autonomous' in ICT use as they find their feet in the classroom. The exigencies of the Covid-19 pandemic demonstrated that there are times when teachers must 'get their heads around things' quickly, rather than 'waiting for the answer lady to come round'.
- Getting across to beginning teachers that ICT can be a good way of extending learning time in history. One of the main problems that history teachers face is that the subject does not get much time on the school timetable (Harris, 2021), and there is a lot to get through (not just in terms of subject content) if pupils are to receive the best possible historical education in the years that they study the subject. Making good use of ICT can be a way of getting pupils to work outside the confines of taught sessions, often willingly. Given the increase in access to computers over the past decade, there are very few pupils who cannot get access to the internet either at school, at the library, or at home over a period of several days (although Covid lockdowns demonstrated the challenge ICT access poses for particular groups of students). Use of the internet can make it much easier to set worthwhile and meaningful tasks for homework. Giving pupils preparatory homework (sometimes termed 'flipped learning'), where they find out about topics before the lesson, can also make for better discussion and debate in class and more confident pupil performance in general. Beginning teachers need to be aware of the potential of internet-based resources for enhancing learning of particular topics, both as part of their lessons or as an option: 'if you are interested in this topic, try having a look at . . .'. Spend a bit of time in a mentee tutorial discussing Web-based resources and, if possible, share some of the internet resources that you have found to be helpful in teaching particular topics.
- This is a personal view, but in the light of recent developments in social media, and the arrival of what has been termed 'the post-truth era' (D'Ancona, 2017; Kakutani, 2018; Mcintyre, 2018), I think it is important that history teachers address the issue of what Wineburg terms 'civic literacy' (Wineburg, 2018). Given that young people receive more of their information about the past from digital sources than from their history teacher, it is important to educate our pupils about how to discern between the 'good' and 'bad'

history that is 'out there' on the internet, particularly as there is no way that we can stop them accessing versions of history that are malicious, distorted, and manipulative (see Haydn, 'Teaching pupils the importance of "truth" in history' (2021), for further development of this point).

What is there to think about in terms of ICT and history?

Those of you who have been mentoring beginning history teachers for a number of years will remember there was a time when history departments were under a degree of pressure to demonstrate they were making use of the computers and interactive whiteboards that were coming into history classrooms. The 2011 *History for All* report stated that 'whiteboards should be used' (Ofsted, 2011), and there was a time when a question about ICT was a feature of the majority of interviews for newly qualified teacher posts (NQT) in history (Haydn, 2004). However, the range of ICT applications to be considered was comparatively limited. In some schools, this amounted to little more than 'curriculum mapping', to ensure that between them, subject departments covered the range of Microsoft Office applications, with the history department often being responsible for either data handling or desktop publishing (Haydn, 2004). The situation has changed dramatically over the past decade, with the development of a wide range of Web 2.0 applications, various forms of voting technology, timeline and conferencing software, Google Apps, visualisers, film-making software, iPhone apps, YouTube history channels, and a range of social media platforms which can be used to teach and learn history. I have a longstanding interest in the ways in which ICT might be used to improve teaching and learning in history and I find it difficult to keep up with new developments. This means that there are hard choices to be made about what facets of ICT to address with your beginning teachers. There are not enough hours in the day to address everything, and the ICT audit suggested in Task 9.1 will support you to make these choices with your mentee.

Task 9.1 Thinking about what it means 'to be good at ICT' in history teaching

Try to find time to have at least a quick glance through the 'History and ICT audit' page at https://terryhaydn.co.uk/wp-content/uploads/2020/06/quotient16.pdf.

It was designed to get beginning teachers to think about the breadth of ICT issues and applications which might be relevant to improving their teaching. Rather than thinking of it as an 'audit', it is probably more helpful to regard it as a 'What is there to think about?' list. The idea was to make it more like a magazine quiz than a threatening and sinister tool to put pressure on beginning teachers – it was just a way to get them to think about which avenues they might like to explore in the course of their training.

You will notice that some applications and issues attract a higher tariff of points. This is because some facets of ICT are obviously more important than others. I would argue, for example, that it is essential that they can use the Virtual Learning Environment (VLE) of the departments they are working in, that they become competent (and preferably, accomplished) in their use of presentation software, and that they make good use of Web-based resources to try to make their lessons interesting and enjoyable for pupils.

The exigencies of the recent waves of the Covid pandemic have also meant that beginning teachers need to 'get their heads round' the challenges of remote teaching. This is an aspect of ICT capability where direct instruction and modelling has a part to play. As noted above, I think that it is also important that beginning teachers are aware of the importance of the 'civic literacy' element of history education and of enabling pupils to make mature and discerning use of the internet. There are some applications that are probably now obsolete or tangential in terms of their relevance; others might only be of relevance to some, and it might be a matter of which avenues the beginning teacher wishes to explore and develop. It is also important that mentees are aware that it is not enough to be able to place a 'tick' against an ICT competence. They need to be aware that for many of the sections of the questionnaire, there is a continuum between novice and expert levels of competence. This is not just a question of levels of *technical* expertise; it is also about *how well* the beginning teacher is able to use the application in their teaching. This might include matters like the question of how good they are at making their PowerPoint presentations engaging and powerful, or how good their judgement is in using moving-image extracts in their lessons.

You may well disagree with the weighting of the scores in the audit; there may be things that should be there which aren't, and some that are no longer relevant. But there may just be aspects of ICT that you have perhaps not thought about.

Whether you reference the audit or not, at an early stage of the placement you may find it helpful to discuss with your mentee 'where they are up to' in terms of their current expertise and prior experience with ICT, what they have covered on the taught element of their course, and which facets of the ICT agenda they might prioritise or explore in terms of their development as a history teacher.

Some general points

Use of social media, Twitter etc.

Some aspects of this are uncontentious. For example, the need to be explicit about the importance of always behaving in a careful and professional manner when using social media. Although the vast majority of beginning teachers are professional in their use of social media, just occasionally they can get it wrong and, either on Facebook, Twitter, TikTok, Instagram or whatever, post or retweet something that is inappropriate. A colleague of mine makes this warning in a very direct way by looking through the posts of student teachers just starting the course in the first teaching session, when they are all together in a teaching group. Just occasionally, especially in the early days of placement, student teachers sometimes carelessly make critical comments about the school or department they have just joined. I know that some of the teachers responsible for supervising cohorts of beginning teachers do a quick trawl of the social media feeds of the students they will be receiving. Mentees should be aware that some prospective employers ask for all social media usernames to be declared on job applications as part of their 'Safer Recruitment' policy. This can be done in a 'light-touch' way and only requires a quick enquiry or reminder, just to be on the safe side.

Other aspects of social media use are more complicated, especially in view of recent concerns about the use of Twitter. There is no hard-and-fast rule here, but it is worth having a conversation with your mentee at some point to discuss the pros and cons of using Twitter, which has become an influential mode of professional development for many history teachers. The limit on the length of 'tweets' makes it quick to use and follow and retweet the posts of others. A common way of using it is to post a link to 'impact resources', and to bookmark incoming tweets that are useful. A lot of history teachers are very generous in sharing collections of resources that they have developed. An important point to keep in mind is that it can pay to be discerning in terms of who to 'follow', or this can become time-consuming with limited reward. The use of 'lists' can also help you to organise and prioritise incoming tweets. Box 9.1 contains some suggestions for history education feeds from some history teachers and teacher educators who are interested in the use of new technology in history teaching. The use of Twitter also requires good judgement on the part of the mentee about what to ask for advice on, and what to retweet.

Beckingham provides an excellent guide to 'Getting started with Twitter' at: www.slideshare.net/suebeckingham/getting-started-with-twitter-23557615.

Box 9.1 Some Twitter feeds and blogs

Most experienced history teachers will be aware of many of these sites, and these are just a few examples, but just in case there are some which are not familiar territory...

Blogs

https://ahistoryteachershares.wordpress.com/
http://www.andallthat.co.uk/
https://anotherhistoryispossible.com/about/
https://clioetcetera.com/author/mfordham/
https://www.historyresourcecupboard.co.uk/author/richardmcfahn/
https://jcarrollhistory.com/author/jcarrollhistory/
https://lobworth.com/category/history-education-blog/
https://onebighistorydepartment.com/ (Historical Association)
https://uonhistoryteachertraining.school.blog/
https://yorkclio.com/

> ### *History education Twitter feeds*
>
> https://twitter.com/apf102
> https://twitter.com/BearWithOneEar
> https://twitter.com/CitoyenneClaire
> https://twitter.com/History_Ben
> https://twitter.com/HughJRichards
> https://twitter.com/jonniegrande
> https://twitter.com/johnsimkin
> https://twitter.com/michaeldoron
> https://twitter.com/MrsThorne
> https://twitter.com/mrwbw
> https://twitter.com/tenigogo
> https://twitter.com/the_history_man
>
> Readers should be aware that Twitter handles and blog addresses change from time to time; generally, they can be located by searching for the name of the person and 'Twitter', or 'blog'.

ICT and dialogic learning

One of the big 'claims' for ICT was that it offered opportunities for 'interactive' learning (Haydn, 2004) in the sense of enabling new forms of 'many to many' conversations, instead of 'one to many' interactions. The development of a wide range of Web 2.0 applications (Padlet, Pinterest, Mural/ly etc.), not to mention blogs and wikis and social media sites such as Twitter, Facebook etc., offers an increasing number of opportunities for learners to share and refine ideas, whether across a class, between schools, or even internationally (Chapman, 2013). As Richardson (2006) points out, there is something very powerful about easily being able to share resources and ideas with a Web audience that is willing to share back what they thought of those ideas. The development of 'voting software' such as Turning Point, Poll Everywhere, and Mentimeter also offers opportunities for pupils to make contributions and responses to PowerPoint presentations (see Walsh, 2006 and Laffin, 2008 for more information on the use of voting software). However, like most aspects of teaching, strategies and methods for developing dialogic learning can be done well or badly. Walsh makes the point that used maladroitly, voting software can be used to create batteries of multiple-choice tests where learners might lose the will to live, rather than helping to support high-order thinking and discussion in the history classroom. It can be helpful to get the beginning teacher to reflect on how well ICT-led approaches work here, and whether using mini whiteboards, red/amber/green cards, or simply using a 'hands up if . . .' approach might be a more time-effective way of gaining feedback from learners. Boxer's (2022) blogpost 'Keeping the one, losing the many' is a good resource for getting beginning teachers to think about questioning and feedback.

The balance between pressure and support

The vast majority of those mentoring beginning teachers are aware of the difficult judgement calls involved in trying to move them forward as much as possible, without overwhelming them with too many demands, targets, tasks, and criticisms. Almost without exception, my former students spoke very positively about the dedication and care with which they were guided into the profession. But just occasionally, and from understandable motives, mentors might err on the side of putting too much pressure on beginning teachers. I have come across cases where, even when teaching very challenging classes, the worst bit of their working week – the thing the beginning teacher dreaded most – was the weekly meeting with their mentor. Some beginning teachers indicated that at times they felt overwhelmed by being bombarded with 'too much stuff' about ICT, to the extent that it became a source of stress rather than a positive experience (Barton & Haydn, 2006). They also felt that it was helpful if the mentor acted as a sort of role model for inducting them into ICT agendas, encouraging them to explore the possibilities and showing them examples which seemed to have worked well. It was not seen as a question of evangelical fervour on the part of the mentor; 'the trainees talked about the development of their personal confidence, interest and ability to see the possibilities' (Barton & Haydn, 2006, p. 265).

Some of my former students talked to me about the skill with which their mentors framed 'targets' for ICT, couching them in terms of getting them intrigued, interested, and willing to try things out, rather than a hard-edged target on which they might be judged in terms of their capabilities. This 'gentle' and encouraging approach also has the advantage of being more likely to develop a sense of 'agency' in the beginning teacher, and the disposition to continue to explore the possibilities of new technology in their future careers. A 'high challenge – low stakes' approach also means that mentors and mentees can experiment with new technology. Amongst the challenges which trainees reported as finding enjoyable were experimenting with a cut-down version of *Pecha Kucha* when using PowerPoint and getting students to make films for presentation to the rest of the class. 'Distributed mentoring' and working collaboratively on ICT activities were also mentioned by trainees as factors that they found helpful in enabling them to make progress in their use of ICT to improve their lessons.

Judging how much time to allocate to ICT

As noted above, this might depend on how well the beginning teacher is doing in other aspects of their teaching, and how interested they are in, and enthusiastic they are about, the possibilities of ICT. It might also depend in part on the attitudes and expertise within the department. I would argue that it is important that you don't get to the end of the placement and find that, in the general 'busyness' of the mentor's agenda and the struggle to cover all the things that must be covered because they are stipulated in regulatory frameworks, the question of how ICT might help to improve teaching and learning in history has not even been mentioned. Task 9.2 provides some suggestions for reviewing your mentee's progress with the use of ICT in their teaching.

Sometimes the mentor's planning agenda can get overtaken by events and new developments. The need to get to grips with remote teaching applications during the lockdown period was one example of this. The recent development of AI applications such as ChatGPT (https://en.wikipedia.org/wiki/ChatGPT) and Character AI (https://www.futuretools.io/tools/character-ai) clearly has implications for history teachers, but at the time of writing, the potential of these applications has not been extensively explored. The fact that such applications separate the narrative that they have manufactured from the sources used to construct that narrative clearly has serious implications for the practice of history, and these need to be explained to learners.

The potential of virtual reality applications for history classrooms and historical computer games, are other comparatively new developments for beginning teachers to consider (see Chapter 8 for further development). A point to get across to mentees is that it is important to try to keep up to date with developments in new technology, whether through online history forums or more traditional media such as the *Times Educational Supplement*.

Task 9.2 Reviewing the extent to which ICT agendas have been considered in the course of the placement

Towards the end of the placement, ask your mentee whether they would have liked more or less attention focused on ICT issues, and try to tease out which aspects of their experiences with new technology they found helpful and interesting. You might also like to think about where ICT issues cropped up in mentor meetings over the course of the placement. A tentative suggestion is that as a minimum, there has been some discussion of ICT both towards the start and end of the placement.

What do expert practitioners say about developing teachers who are accomplished in their use of new technology?

What can we learn from teachers and teacher educators who are considered to be experts in the use of ICT?

It's not primarily about advanced levels of technological expertise

In an OECD study in 2010, one strand of the project explored the views of 'expert practitioners' who had a well-established reputation for making good use of new technology in subject teaching. Nearly all the expert practitioners who were interviewed suggested that 'being good at ICT' as a teacher was not primarily about levels of technological expertise but about the sophistication of teachers' judgements on the potential benefits (and possible disadvantages) of using various forms of new technology. This was seen as a matter of higher-order thinking, creativity, and good judgement rather than advanced technological expertise.

They also stressed that there was no intrinsic benefit or guaranteed learning 'premium' to be gleaned from using ICT. In the words of one expert teacher, 'I always start off by saying, don't go anywhere near a computer, unless there are these rare occasions where using a computer helps you to be able to do something . . . if you haven't got a good idea in the first place, just shoving up a PowerPoint isn't going to do the job' (Haydn, 2010).

Another argued that although basic levels of technological proficiency were a prerequisite for thinking about how to improve teaching and learning with ICT, this was a necessary rather than sufficient condition for effective use of ICT; of far greater importance was the quality of thinking about what sort of engaging and worthwhile things they could do with the application, rather than what levels of technological sophistication they would develop.

Making mentees aware of the potential of ICT for 'building learning packages'

Walsh (2003) makes the point that one of the biggest advantages of ICT is the facility it offers to quickly and easily build up and organise a range of resources that will provide beginning teachers with a rich archive of high-quality resources on whatever topic they might find themselves teaching. The 'communications' strand of ICT means that it is now much easier to get hold of 'the best analogies, illustrations, examples, explanations and demonstrations as conduits for their subject knowledge to engage and enthuse pupils' (Husbands, 2011, p. 85). Although in the early stages of a placement it is generally considered acceptable for the beginning teacher to draw on the resources of the department, as they develop in confidence and experience, it is important to guide them towards exercising initiative in finding high-quality resources for themselves rather than them becoming dependent on the departmental archive. Most history teachers learn to become good 'scavengers' for resources, and a good mentor can help guide them towards the most propitious sites, links, and social media feeds. These can range from using the digital versions of popular history magazines, to maps, graphs, YouTube clips, animations, and striking prose extracts, image collections, cartoons, and quotations.

Mentors can gently make mentees aware of the importance of *using their initiative* to build up good 'collections' of powerful impact resources on a wide range of topics. Beginning teachers vary in the extent to which they exercise initiative in getting hold of resources that will enable them to teach topics in an engaging and powerful manner. Some can tend to be reliant on the resources which are already 'there' in the departmental archive and on the school's VLE; others are quick to do this without even being told. It can be helpful if the department models this (see Task 9.3). Most history teachers are good at 'scavenging and sharing' resources, whether between colleagues or across social media, but it is good to make sure that beginning teachers are inducted into this culture as soon as possible. It is also helpful to mentees if you can give them an honest view about the comparative usefulness of the wide range of portals which are available to history teachers.

Task 9.3 Guiding mentees towards showing initiative in the harvesting of high-quality resources

At some point in the placement, get your mentee to spend a few days where they are making a conscious effort to 'keep an eye out' for resources on one of the topics that they will be teaching on placement. Stress that this may be from the *Radio Times*, the

188 Terry Haydn

> newspapers, browsing through some history websites, talking with other beginning teachers, glancing through history moving-image sites or Google images, or searching YouTube or Google videos. After giving them a few days to do this, discuss what they have come up with as part of a mentor meeting.
>
> At a later stage of the placement, have a conversation with your mentee about what proportion of the resources that they collect they are actually using in their teaching. There is a real danger of getting obsessed with 'collecting stuff' which never gets processed and deployed in lessons (think about what proportion of the books that you buy, the programmes you 'bookmark', or the articles you file you actually get round to reading).

Teaching mentees about the helpfulness of building up a collection of 'impact' resources

Walsh (2017) and Haydn (Haydn & Stephen, 2022) suggest that although the use of ICT to build up high-quality 'learning packages' is important, it is not just a question of quantity or volume of resources. People who have never been teachers perhaps think of knowledge acquisition as a fairly unproblematic thing, something that is slowly shovelled or siphoned into the pupil over a period of time. Those of us who are teachers are aware that learning is to some extent a hit-and-miss affair, and that some of the things that we try to teach leak away over time; retrieval practice is obviously helpful in preventing this, but effective first teaching is another critical element. By 'impact resource', I mean something that makes a teaching point in a vivid and powerful way; something that stays in learners' minds long after the lesson has gone (sometimes termed 'stickiness' (Brown, Roediger, & McDaniel, 2014; Perkins, 2018). It can be something that disturbs learners' previous understandings, or which 'problematises' the issue or concept in a way that makes learners think further about it. It also encourages 'dialogic' learning, whereby learners are sufficiently interested by the resource that they are willing to clarify and modify their understanding through discussion with others (Alexander, 2020). Impact resources can take various forms. They can be images, graphs, moving-image clips, 'mysteries', pieces of prose, maps, newspaper articles, metaphors, and ideas for pupil activities. I suspect that most people reading this chapter will have curated some impact resources of their own over time, which they enjoy using in their teaching, because they know that they 'work well' (see Task 9.4). The internet is, of course (in particular the use of Twitter for 'tip-offs' and sharing), a very useful tool for identifying resources of this nature.

> ### Task 9.4 Talking about and sharing some impact resources for the history classroom
>
> As part of a mentor meeting, explain the idea of impact resources, and if possible, show some to the student, and ask if they have come across other examples. I used

to say to my cohort of student history teachers that ideally, every lesson would have at least one 'component' that intrigued or interested the pupils, so as to 'get them on board' and interested in finding out more about the topic in question. Using their initiative to build up a collection of impact resources is a useful disposition for beginning teachers to acquire.

Moving away from the 'coverage' model of ICT competence

Several expert practitioners have made the point that 'being good at ICT' in subject teaching is not a matter of how many different applications the teacher can use, in the sense of the 'breadth' of their acquaintance with new technology applications, but the extent to which they can use some things well. Some examples of their testimony are given below:

> 'I don't want them all to have to develop their own website, blog, wiki . . . I would rather they focused on one thing and made it a really good, worthwhile, educationally sound wiki or whatever.'
>
> 'It's not good enough to put a tick, can use PowerPoint, tick, can use Movie Maker . . . it's about how well they can use it . . . Whether they can use it in a powerful and effective way and in different ways, to perhaps do different things.'
>
> 'It's funny because in a skills set sense, I don't have a list . . . I don't think, they must be able to do PowerPoint, they must be able to upload a YouTube video and so on. It's more that when we cover things . . . we consider how various bits and pieces of ICT might help to get the idea or concept across more effectively and they just bump into lots of ICT things along the way.'
>
> 'I've stressed a lot less about coverage than I used to. I pick a relatively small number of areas that I want to focus my attention on. When I see the number of students who are actually using ICT in their teaching and what they're doing with it, it strikes me that's a sensible way to go.'
>
> (quoted in Haydn, 2014, p. 6)

Another strand of 'progression' in the use of ICT was seen as the transition from awareness of the potential of an ICT application to the ability to use the application in terms of personal or private use through to successful classroom use, and even (in some cases) the beginning teacher's ability to get pupils using the application autonomously and usefully. It was also, in part, about a willingness to 'have a go' and cautiously experiment:

> 'If they're creative people then they will have a go and they will look for ways of making it relevant and exciting and interesting, and try things out, even if they don't always work, it's about them thinking about what sorts of things you can do with Twitter, or PowerPoint or whatever.' (Quoted in Haydn, 2014, p. 5)

Other factors bearing on the beginning teacher's ability to make good progress in their use of ICT commonly mentioned by expert practitioners were the mentor's ability and willingness to act as a role model in terms of being keen to explore ICT agendas and their ability to model the effective use of technology in a relaxed and reassuring way. Peer tutoring and collaborative working were also viewed as effective strategies for making progress in ICT. Many respondents had reservations about the 'value for money' offered by some of the more expensive ICT investments, such as interactive whiteboards, e-portfolio software, response technology (voting sets), and one-to-one tablet provision and felt that the ability to make discerning use of the internet was a more important factor in enabling beginning teachers to make progress in ICT. There was also a preference for subject-specific approaches, which made it easier for student teachers to design 'authentic tasks' for their pupils, as opposed to generic ICT training (Haydn, 2010).

Inducting beginning teachers into the use of remote teaching

The unprecedented nature of the coronavirus crisis showed that there are times when teachers have to be adaptable and quick on the uptake to adjust to new developments. Whatever online platform your school uses, it can be helpful for your mentee to become familiar with at least the rudiments of conducting online sessions. Even if there is no lockdown over the course of the placement, such knowledge may well stand them in good stead in the future. There are usually online tutorials which will help your mentee to achieve this, but I think that taking them through it step by step is a more user-friendly way of doing this. If you are not adept and confident in this area, it could be helpful to ask a more experienced colleague (or you could explore the system together with your mentee – the mentor cannot always be an expert on every facet of ICT). If time permits, try to get to a stage where your mentee could do a 'live' session and a prerecorded one (to add a sound commentary to a PowerPoint presentation, see for example, the YouTube clip at https://www.youtube.com/watch?v=Y5dgwwa5XRA), or Crooks' (2021) blog post on 'Finding your feet with remote (and online) teaching' (see Task 9.5).

Task 9.5 Supporting your mentee with remote teaching

Further advice on remote teaching can be gleaned from the following:

- https://uonhistoryteachertraining.school.blog/2020/11/13/from-classroom-to-computer-equipping-training-teachers-to-teach-online/ (Crooks & Burnham, 2020) a blog outlining some of the ways mentors can begin to induct their mentees into online/ remote teaching.
- https://uonhistoryteachertraining.school.blog/2021/01/17/finding-your-feet-with-remote-and-online-teaching/ (Crooks, 2021) a blog considering what teachers should consider when trying to conceptualise how online teaching is related to their usual classroom practice.
- https://onebighistorydepartment.com/2021/02/26/what-could-lemovs-ideas-for-remote-learning-look-like-in-history/ (Fairlamb, 2021). Written for the *One Big History Department* site, this blog has adapted Lemov's advice on remote learning

to the context of history teaching, giving examples of how to ensure that the basic essentials of teaching (situating the lesson within the enquiry, recall, guided practice, interaction, assessment, and feedback) are catered for.
- 2.3.16 History and IT/Teaching for beginners/Historical Association (Historical Association, n.d.). This is a resource developed by the HA's Beginning Teacher resources; this section includes a webinar on blended learning.

Select one of the suggested resources above and ask your mentee to read/watch it for discussion at a mentor meeting.

Summary and key points

- Whatever your level of interest and capability in ICT, don't neglect consideration of new technology just because it is not mentioned in current beginning and early career teacher curriculum specifications. Many history teachers have found that ICT can sometimes help history to be taught more effectively in a variety of ways.
- As well as showing mentees how to make good use of various facets of ICT, try to also develop their confidence and sense of initiative in relation to new technology, so that they will be proactive, open-minded, and willing to experiment with ICT, even after their placement or induction years have ended and they may no longer have a designated mentor to prompt, guide, and encourage them.
- Although part of the ICT agenda is inducting beginning teachers into getting to grips with how to make best use of applications and equipment, such as the data projector, the visualiser, PowerPoint, and the school's VLE and remote teaching platform, research suggests that its most influential strand has been the facility it offers for history teachers to collect and share useful resources and ideas, and to make best use of history teacher networks to discuss and share good practice.
- Try to ensure that mentees are aware of the importance of developing pupils' ability to handle information from the internet and social media in a discerning and intelligent way. School history has an important part to play in developing pupils' civic and information literacy.
- The bottom line is not how much early career teachers use ICT in their teaching, or how broad their areas of expertise in ICT are, but the extent to which they can use new technology to improve both teaching and learning in history.

Further reading and resources

- **Historical Association (n.d.).** ***One Big History Department,*** **https://onebighistory department.com/**
  This is a good example of a site which provides a lot of useful resources for beginning teachers, and which is also invaluable for keeping up to date with new developments in history teaching, whether ICT-related or in general.

- **Walsh, B. (2017). 'Technology in the history classroom: lost in the web?', in I. Davies (ed.), *Debates in history teaching* (pp. 250-60). London: Routledge.**
  A helpful and succinct summary of issues around digital and historical literacy.
- **Wineburg, S. (2018). *Why learn history (when it's already on your phone).* Chicago: Chicago University Press.**
  The sections on 'lateral reading' strategies for evaluating internet sources is particularly useful as a resource for beginning teachers who may not be familiar with the Stanford History Education Group's research and work.

References

Alexander, R. (2020). *A dialogic teaching companion*. London: Routledge.
Barton, R., & Haydn, T. (2006). Trainee teachers' views on what helps them to use ICT effectively in their subject teaching. *Journal of Computer Assisted Learning (22)*, 257-72. doi:doi.org/10.1111/j.1365-2729.2006.00175.x
Boxer, A. (2022). Keeping the one, losing the many. Retrieved 2 February 2023 from *A Chemical Orthodoxy*, https://achemicalorthodoxy.wordpress.com/2022/05/25/keeping-the-one-losing-the-many/
Brown, P., Roediger, H., & McDaniel, M. (2014). *Make it stick: the science of successful learning*. Cambridge, MA: Harvard University Press.
Carretero, M., Cantabrana, M., & Parellada, C. (2022). *History education in a digital age*. Cham: Springer.
Chapman, A. (2013). Using discussion forums to support historical learning. In T. Haydn, *Using new technologies to enhance teaching and learning in history* (pp. 58-73). London: Routledge.
Crooks, V. (2021). Finding your feet with remote (and online) teaching. Retrieved 11 March 2023 from *Becoming a History Teacher* (blog): https://uonhistoryteachertraining.school.blog/2021/01/17/finding-your-feet-with-remote-and-online-teaching/
Crooks, V., & Burnham, S. (2020). From classroom to computer: equipping training teachers to teach online. Retrieved 11 March 2023 from *Becoming a history teacher* (blog) https://uonhistoryteachertraining.school.blog/2020/11/13/from-classroom-to-computer-equipping-training-teachers-to-teach-online/
D'Ancona, M. (2017). *Post truth*. London: Penguin.
DfE. (2011). *Teachers' standards*. London: DfE.
DfE. (2019). *Initial teacher training (ITT): core content framework*. London: DfE.
DfEE. (1998). *Teaching: high status, high standards*. London: DfEE.
Fairlamb, A. (2021). What could Lemov's ideas for Remote Learning look like in history? Retrieved 11 March 2023 from *One Big History Department*, https://onebighistorydepartment.com/2021/02/26/what-could-lemovs-ideas-for-remote-learning-look-like-in-history/
Harris, R. (2021). Disciplinary knowledge denied? In A. Chapman (ed.), *Knowing history in schools* (pp. 97-128). London: UCL Press.
Haydn, T. (2004). The use of ICT in history teaching in England and Wales 1970-2003. Unpublished PhD thesis, University of London.
Haydn, T. (2010). *Case studies of the ways in which initial teacher education providers in England prepare student teachers to use ICT effectively in their subject teaching*. Paris: OECD. Retrieved 12 January 2023 from OECD, https://www.oecd.org/unitedkingdom/45046837.pdf
Haydn, T. (2013). We need to talk about PowerPoint. In T. Haydn (ed.), *Using new technologies to enhance teaching and learning in history* (pp. 95-114). London: Routledge.

Haydn, T. (2014). How do you get pre-service teachers to become 'good at ICT' in their subject teaching? The views of expert practitioners. *Technology, Pedagogy and Education, 23*(4), 455-70. doi:https://doi.org/10.1080/1475939X.2014.892898

Haydn, T. (2021, September 16). *Teaching pupils the importance of 'truth' in history.* Retrieved 12 December 2022 from *Practical Histories*, https://practicalhistories.com/author/terry-haydn/

Haydn, T., & Stephen, A. (2022). *Learning to teach history in the secondary school (5th edition).* London: Routledge.

Historical Association. (n.d.-b). *2.3.16 History and IT.* Retrieved from *Teaching For Beginners* (Historical Association), https://www.history.org.uk/secondary/categories/380/module/8763/teaching-for-beginners/10274/2316-history-and-it

Husbands, C. (2011). What do history teachers need to know? A framework for understanding and developing practice. In I. Davies (ed.), *Debates in history teaching* (pp. 84-95). London: Routledge.

Kakutani, M. (2018). *The death of truth.* London: William Collins.

Laffin, D. (2008). Using remote voting to involve everyone in classroom thinking at AS and A2. *Teaching History 133*, 18-21.

Mcintyre, L. (2018). *Post truth.* Cambridge, MA: MIT Press.

Ofsted. (2007). *History in the balance: history in English schools 2003-07.* London: Ofsted.

Ofsted. (2011). *History for all.* London: Ofsted.

Ofsted. (2021). *Research review series: history.* London: Ofsted.

Perkins, P. (2018). How to make learning stick: top tips from learning psychology. Retrieved 30 January 2023 from *e-Learning Industry*, https://elearningindustry.com/creating-sticky-learning-stick-top-tips-learning-psychology-how-make

Richardson, W. (2006). *Blogs, wikis, podcasts and other powerful webtools for classrooms.* London: Sage.

Steinhauer, J. (2022). *History, disrupted: how social media and the World Wide Web have changed the past.* Cham: Palgrave Macmillan.

Walsh, B. (2003). Building learning packages: integrating virtual resources with the real work of teaching and learning. In T. Haydn, & C. Counsell, *History, ICT and learning in the secondary school* (pp. 109-33). London: Routledge.

Walsh, B. (2006). Beyond multiple choice: voting technology in the history classroom. *Presentation at the E-help Seminar.* 6-7 October, Stockholm. Retrieved 12 January 2023 from http://e-help.eu/seminars/walsh2.htm

Walsh, B. (2017). Technology in the history classroom: lost in the web? In I. Davies (ed.), *Debates in history teaching* (pp. 250-60). London: Routledge.

Wineburg, S. (2018). *Why learn history (when it's already on your phone).* Chicago: Chicago University Press.

Wineburg, S. (2019, 2 December). OPINION: The internet is sowing mass confusion. We must rethink how we teach kids in every subject. Retrieved 21 April 2022 from *USA Today*: https://eu.usatoday.com/story/opinion/2019/02/12/internet-confusion-rethink-education-digital-sputnik-moment-column/2769781002/ucation-digital-sp

10 Continuing Professional Development for beginning history teachers and mentors

Laura London

Introduction

Upon being granted Qualified Teacher Status (QTS), beginning teachers are awarded a passport to teach in any school or academy trust. Many Initial Teacher Education (ITE) providers and induction programmes encourage and enable beginning teachers to engage with the teaching community and wider profession. However, the proliferation of routes into the profession and variation between Early Career Framework (ECF) providers has meant that the extent of subject-specific professional development on offer to beginning teachers varies widely (Ofsted, 2020). Schools and trusts are very likely to have their own priorities for the Continuing Professional Development (CPD) of their teachers and it is not unusual for schools and trusts to take more 'generic' approaches to the provision of CPD (Cordingley et al., 2018; Counsell, 2018). For example, it is popular in many schools in England for whole-school CPD to follow the application of (a version of) Rosenshine's Principles (Rosenshine, 2012) or for school leaders to insist mentors use the instructional coaching manual *Teaching Walkthrus* (Sherrington & Caviglioli, 2020) with all their beginning teachers. While there is much to be learnt from generic approaches, there is also the potential for these to overlook the 'ways of knowing' (Wineburg, 2001) that are so important to the discipline of history. Indeed, the Teacher Development Trust's 2015 review (Cordingley et al., 2015) of the evidence on effective professional development for teachers indicated the importance of focusing on generic *and* subject-specific pedagogy. This chapter will guide mentors through the range of subject-specific CPD opportunities available to beginning teachers and their mentors.

One place that beginning teachers and their mentors can look for subject-specific professional development is their subject community. Even if you and your mentee are part of a very strong department or an academy chain that has excellent CPD provision, there are more opportunities for professional development 'out there' than even the best departments can embrace. Therefore, it is important to look beyond your colleagues in school. The professional discourse of the history teaching community provides fertile ground for beginning teachers as their teaching identity takes shape. One objective of this chapter is to support mentors to connect their mentee to the wealth of expertise held by the history teaching community. This is one important way for a mentor to move their mentee beyond their immediate mentoring relationship. It allows them to support their mentee to be flexible, resourceful, and resilient in adjusting to the challenges of teaching history in future contexts, long after the mentoring relationship has ended. This chapter will also outline practical suggestions for how mentors can support their mentees to secure their first teaching positions.

One positive aspect of recent educational policy in England is the renewed focus on mentoring beginning teachers (DfE, 2019). Indeed, Early Career Teachers (ECTs) in England have welcomed the additional mentor support that is now part of their ECF entitlement. In a recent Teacher Tapp (2022) survey, only 2% of ECTs said that they would drop out of the mentoring support that they receive. Despite the renewed focus of policymakers on mentoring, it is still the case that relatively limited attention is paid to the role and potential for subject communities' involvement in the mentoring process thus far. At the time of writing, the ECF has arguably not yet fully harnessed the power of subject communities. A further purpose of this chapter is to emphasise the opportunities for professional development presented by mentoring a beginning teacher and by establishing and consolidating mentors' connections with the history teaching community. Finally, this chapter aims to suggest practical opportunities for beginning teachers and their mentors to engage with teacher-led, subject-specific professional development in order to strive for answers to pressing curricular questions.

Objectives

At the end of the chapter, you should be able to:

- Connect your mentee to the history teaching community.
- Reflect on, establish, and consolidate your own connections with the history teaching community for your own professional development. See Task 10.1.
- Recognise the potential of the history teaching community for curricular development in history.
- Support your mentee to secure their first teaching post.
- Understand the potential professional development opportunities that are integral to the mentoring role.

Task 10.1 Reflecting on your own Continuing Professional Development (CPD)

- What CPD have you been involved with recently?
- How has it impacted your teaching?
- What proportion of this CPD was subject-specific?

Professional development and the history teaching community

The idea that professional development can lead to improvements in teaching and learning is generally accepted; however, there is no clear consensus as to how this professional development should take place. Teachers' professional development is complex, and models of CPD that assume that teacher development and change happen quickly and easily are likely to fail (Day, 1997). In his explanation of student teachers' professional learning, McIntyre (1995) outlines a process of 'practical theorising' in which student teachers are encouraged to test suggestions for practice against theoretical and practical criteria. More recently, Burn, Mutton, and Thompson (2023) have reasserted that it is this ability to critically evaluate – that is, to understand the rationale and theory behind certain practices – that allows new teachers to determine how to adapt their teaching practices in changing contexts. This is critical for teachers as they move from one school to another.

> Practice alone is not enough; new teachers need a sufficient understanding of the grounds on which that practice is based that they can review its appropriateness and, where necessary, adapt what they are doing in response to particular changes in the context or objectives they are seeking to achieve. (Burn, Mutton, & Thompson, 2023, p. 17)

Chapter 1 sets out a model of teacher expertise in which beginning teachers need to be developed as thinking practitioners who engage with teaching as a professional endeavour (Winch, Oancea, & Orchard, 2015). According to this model, teachers' knowledge is a combination of their own practical experiences of the craft of teaching, subject and pedagogical knowledge, and research literacy. This allows beginning teachers to move beyond viewing their professional knowledge base as inert and unchanging and see it rather as evolving and context-specific. Subject communities have a significant role to play in integrating the dimensions of teachers' professional knowledge (Shulman, 1986).

Associations and networks

The history teaching community has long been involved in the process of curricular theorising, and engagement with this community offers teachers many opportunities to develop their own curricular knowledge (Counsell, 2011; Fordham, 2015). In 1906, the Historical Association (HA) was founded to foster the enjoyment and study of history for all. The HA, as the professional association for history teachers, spans the teaching and academic spheres to support high-quality history teaching for all pupils. The HA has been publishing *Teaching History*, history teachers' professional journal, on a quarterly basis since 1974. The Schools Council History Project (now Schools History Project, SHP) was first established in 1972 as a movement in response to concerns held by the history teaching community over the place and future of history teaching in schools (McDougall, 1976). Its inception certainly marked the beginning of a curricular conversation at grass-roots level in the history teaching community that has endured to this day. Both SHP and the HA have championed the distinctive nature of history education and both are a vital influence on the development of the history curriculum in the UK, providing a highly valued, and much-needed, professional voice for history teachers. For example, in the late 1970s the SHP took on the crucial role of creating and resourcing the History GCSE syllabus to reflect its principles and engage young people with historical enquiry.

The SHP and the HA run national conferences attended by large groups of dedicated history teachers and subject experts. Workshops are led by inspiring and experienced teachers from around the UK, and are packed with practical strategies for teachers to use back home in their own history classrooms. Additionally, attendance is 'good for morale, and it can make you feel that it was a really good decision to dedicate your professional life to being a history teacher' (Haydn & Stephen, 2022).

Subject communities also play an important role in shaping beginning teachers' professional development and professional identity. In her research, Brooks (2017) found the geography teachers involved in her study had a strong sense of teaching purpose, rooted in their subject discipline. These teachers' 'subject story' influenced their teaching identity so profoundly that it had come to act as their 'professional compass'. Brooks defined this as 'a term that describes an ethical perspective on professional practice that stems from a teacher's disciplinary background and knowledge' (2017, p. 46). ITE may initially play an important role in introducing beginning teachers to these ethical perspectives, but the wider subject community also has the potential to shape the fundamental values and beliefs which form a teacher's 'professional compass'. As an example, the SHP's principles are rooted in an ethical approach to history teaching; from a respect for the evidence and people of the past, to a commitment to 'a history curriculum that reflects the continuing social, cultural and ethnic diversity of Britain' (SHP, n.d). In light of the professional challenges facing the teachers in Brooks' study, their connection with their subject discipline was a crucial factor in sustaining them over their careers, even in 'contradictory contexts' (Brooks, 2017, p. 45).

Connecting beginning teachers to their subject communities is one important way in which mentors can contribute to creating inspiring history teachers for the future. That is not to suggest the history teaching community is a homogenous body or is consistently in agreement. Like most communities it is reasonably complex and diverse, and sometimes in conflict. The history community might be best thought of as a series of networks and communities that exist internationally, nationally, and locally, both online and face-to-face, and both officially and unofficially. While there are long established, well recognised, and organised structures like the HA and SHP in the UK, there are also a wealth of more recently established grass-roots, often online, opportunities for history-specific professional development; for example, the BeBold History Network (see Twitter: https://twitter.com/beboldhistory). Many of these valuable opportunities flourished during the Covid-19 pandemic and continue to gather momentum. It is also important not to take an insular approach to CPD. There is so much to be learnt from history colleagues in other countries. For example, Euroclio, the European Association of History Educators, runs projects for history educators and creates resources for its members, as well as organising annual conferences and events for history teachers (see: https://euroclio.eu/association/). As a mentor, it is important to support your mentee to navigate the complexities of the history teaching landscape.

Social media

Facebook provides valuable opportunities for teachers to join subject communities and share ideas and resources. Many teachers have reported that the Facebook groups dedicated to each examination board are particularly useful. At the time of writing, EduTwitter has the potential to provide quick, practical, and accessible advice and connect teachers in an instant. It is also free and accessible to teachers, and many beginning teachers will hear it hailed as the 'best form of CPD'. But Twitter can also feel like a disorientating place, especially to beginning teachers still finding their professional identity. It can also become a difficult place for a beginning teacher who has taken a Twitter misstep. It would be impossible, and undesirable, to guide mentees entirely (after all, they are adults); however, mentors could provide support in this situation by providing some much-needed perspective. It might be that mentors could make tentative suggestions for Twitter opportunities. It might be that your mentee also has recommendations on who to follow or which resources to access. Twitter also provides a valuable 'springboard' or 'access point' (Crooks, 2019) into current educational debates for beginning teachers to pursue. In your role as mentor, you can encourage this and highlight the importance of engaging 'in professional debate in a school-based team, or another community of real-life teachers (such as through an MA or regional network), not just in the Twitter-sphere' (2019). The real point here is the professional, reciprocal conversations between yourself, your mentee, and your department. These are the conversations that have the power to define mentors' and mentees' fundamental values and beliefs about teaching history.

Opportunities for history-specific CPD

Of course, these conversations require time and space. Subject-specific CPD is not always prioritised by school leaders. In the current economic and education context, subject-specific professional development is sometimes viewed as an extravagance. While understandable, this can potentially mean opportunities for teachers' professional development are missed. The Wellcome Trust's *Developing Great Subject Teaching* report (Cordingley et al., 2018) found that 'Schools that are seen to be struggling in terms of pupil outcomes and/or inspection results appear less likely to prioritise subject-specific CPD over more generic school improvement approaches' (2018, p. 2). It might be that the HA's two-day, in-person conference is simply unfeasible for many teachers to attend. However, a department subscription to *Teaching History* and shared monthly reading might be more viable options. There are examples of history-specific CPD that are offered at no financial cost to schools or teachers. One good example is the open-access, flexible online CPD offered by UCL's Centre for Holocaust Education (see: https://holocausteducation.org.uk/core-cpd-courses/). The National Archives also offer a range of flexible CPD opportunities for teachers at no cost (see: https://www.nationalarchives.gov.uk/education/teachers/professional-development/inset-sessions/).

Opportunities for mentors and beginning teachers to access subject-specific professional development vary widely. Therefore, a selection of opportunities for history-specific professional development are outlined below in Table 10.1, with some involving a significantly greater time and financial cost than others. Task 10.2 provides an opportunity for you to reflect on your own involvement with the history teaching community.

Table 10.1 Opportunities for history-specific CPD

	For mentors	For mentees in ITE	For ECTs (1–2 years)	
Opportunities for professional development and subject-knowledge enhancement				
Memberships, clubs, or networks				
HA membership	✓	✓	✓	This includes a monthly subscription to *Teaching History* and online access to all previous issues. This journal contains the Move Me On feature, a problem page for mentors.
History Teacher Educators' Network (HTEN) membership	✓			This network brings together those researching and working in history teacher education. Membership provides access to three online half-day conferences per year.
Practicalhistories.com	✓	✓	✓	Set up to help history teachers improve their practice. Subscription provides free access to an online magazine for sharing good practice.
BeBold History Network	✓	✓	✓	A history teacher-led network, linking academic scholarship with the history classroom.
EuroClio	✓	✓	✓	The European Association of History Educators run projects for history educators and create resources for their members, as well as organising annual conferences and events for history teachers. Membership provides valuable insights into approaches from outside the UK.
Conferences				
The HA Annual Conference	✓	✓	✓	An annual conference, with pathways for primary and secondary education, and for history enthusiasts more generally.
The SHP Summer Conference	✓	✓	✓	An annual conference to develop history teacher subject knowledge and pedagogical understanding.
The SHP New Teachers' Conference		✓	✓	This conference is aimed specifically at those history teachers who are new to the history teaching profession.
Practical Histories Conference	✓	✓	✓	This conference provides history teachers with practical ideas that they can use immediately in the classroom.

(continued)

Table 10.1 Cont.

	For mentors	For mentees in ITE	For ECTs (1–2 years)	
Opportunities to contribute to the history teaching community				
Submit an article for publication, for example, in the journal *Teaching History* or to Practicalhistories.com	✓	✓	✓	First-time and more experienced authors from the history teaching community are invited to contribute an article to *Teaching History*.
Apply to become an SHP regional adviser	✓			The SHP has Regional Advisers whose role is to promote the work of the organisation and support teachers in their region, particularly those teaching the OCR History B course.
Present a session or a workshop at a conference, for example at an HA, SHP, or TM History Icons conference	✓		✓	Depending on the conference, you might share classroom-based action-research or practical ideas for history teaching.
Opportunities to contribute to your local history teaching community				
Join a local branch of the HA or a local records society.	✓	✓	✓	Joining a local branch or society is one way to get more involved with local history.
There are many local professional networks for history teachers: for example, YorkClio https://yorkclio.com or the University of Nottingham History Education Subject Interest Group www.nottingham.ac.uk/education/schools-partnership-gateway/opportunities/teachers/history-group.aspx	✓	✓	✓	Try to find out where local history teacher communities are meeting. You might try asking Twitter or your local ITE subject lead for history.
Build a local history teacher network www.history.org.uk/secondary/categories/487/info/4070/guidance-pack-building-a-local-teacher-network	✓		✓	Building a local teacher network provides the groundwork on which to build strong regional networks for the benefit of history teaching community
Opportunities for recognition of professional development				
Chartered Teacher of History (CTHist) accreditation	✓		✓	A professional accreditation for history teachers or those involved with history teaching education.
HA Teacher Fellowships			✓	This programme aims to bring teachers up to date with historical research and how to apply this in the classroom.
The HA Quality Mark			✓	A recognised award for history departments.

Table 10.1 Cont.

	For mentors	For mentees in ITE	For ECTs (1-2 years)	
Opportunities for recognition of professional development				
The HA's Subject Leader Development Programme (SLDP)	✓		✓	The Subject Leader Development Programme is an online course for developing subject leadership in secondary history teaching.
The HA's Early Career Development Programme (ECDP)			✓	This course is designed as a supportive tool for early career teachers to further help them to teach ambitious and rigorous history.
MA in Education		✓	✓	An MA in Education offers the opportunity to critically reflect on your teaching. Many institutions offer part-time courses designed around teachers' professional commitments.

Task 10.2 A reflection for mentors: the history teaching community

- What does the 'history teaching community' mean to you?
- Where do you get your ideas about history education from?
- In what ways are you involved with the history teaching community?
- How important is this to you and your teaching identity?

Teacher researchers and *Teaching History*

Lawrence Stenhouse (1975) defined the curriculum as 'an attempt to communicate the essential principles and features of an educational proposal in such a form that it is open to critical scrutiny and capable of effective translation into practice' (p. 4). Within this definition the teacher takes on the role of teacher-researcher, turning principles into practice. According to Stenhouse, 'curriculum development translates ideas into classroom practicalities and thereby helps the teacher to strengthen his practice by systematically and thoughtfully testing ideas' (pp. 24-25).

In his study of teacher research, Fordham (2015) theorised that the history teaching community writing for *Teaching History* has 'realised and extended' this vision of curriculum development. Fordham outlines two broad, but not exclusive, traditions of teacher-researchers. The first is described as the 'professional development' tradition, in which teachers 'deploy research tools in order to better understand the context in which they work, with a view to developing their practice accordingly' (2015, p. 137). In the second, the 'what works' tradition, the key issue 'is whether or not the knowledge produced by teachers is transferable beyond particular contexts, and whether such knowledge can inform other teachers about "what works" in practice' (p. 137). The aim is to provide teachers with guidance about 'what works' regardless of context. Fordham contends that both these approaches to teacher research overlook the subject-specific curricular aspect. In his citation analysis of the journal *Teaching History* between 2004 and 2013 he asserts that *Teaching History* is far more than a list of publications; rather, it is an evolving 'published discourse', created by history teacher researchers themselves over time. Fordham uses the example of causal reasoning to illustrate this:

> In all of the articles in this example, teacher-researchers write about their pupils, their lessons and their pedagogy: the overriding concern – and what seems to sustain the conversation over time – is to establish what good causal reasoning might look like in the classroom. The classroom, in this sense, becomes a site in which to theorise about the curriculum. (Fordham, 2015, p. 142)

This 'published discourse' is a collected, powerful, and organised body of professional knowledge that is crucial to the development and autonomy of the history teaching profession. It is likely that beginning teachers will be aware of *Teaching History*. However, they may need support with understanding articles, or they may need to have engagement with the 'published discourse' modelled for them. *Teaching History* provides many examples of practical theorising, but articles are less likely to suggest the 'quick fixes' that might be more attractive to beginning history teachers with many immediate demands on their time. It may be that as a mentor you will, at the very least, need to point your mentee towards a particular article for support. The 'What's the Wisdom' feature provides a helpful starting point for developing teachers' understanding of substantive and disciplinary concepts or for developing their evidential thinking. The *History Education Research Journal* (*HERJ*) is an open-access international journal that covers many aspects of history education and provides abundant opportunities for further reading with your mentee. This could happen in different ways. It might be that you read and discuss articles with your mentee or that your mentee summarises an article for a mentor or department meeting as a catalyst for discussion. Counsell (2011) recognises that while not all history teachers are directly involved with researching the curriculum, the majority are engaged in finding solutions to curricular tensions. Counsell highlights the power of this teacher-led discussion for allowing teachers to resolve curricular tensions and answer problems, stating that 'where practice published as articles or shared through websites and workshops is openly cognisant of others' efforts, it adds up to a coherent discourse of some power' (2011, p. 203).

Curriculum planning as professional development

One way to harness this debate is by involving beginning teachers in the curricular planning process early in their careers. This is an opportunity to initiate beginning teachers into the conversations and debates described in the previous section. Decisions and processes implicit in department planning will need to be made explicit for novice teachers. This process of curricular design (and redesign) is likely to 'look' different in each department, but will probably involve several of the elements outlined in Table 10.2. It will help beginning teachers if their mentors can explain the value of each of these aspects of curricular design and model their thought processes. The stages and questions included in Table 10.2 could provide a useful starting point for conversations with your mentee (see Task 10.3).

Table 10.2 A stepped approach to curricular planning with your mentee

Planning stage	Potential questions for discussion within your department
Reading recent academic scholarship as a department	What has the department already read? Is there a reading list for this? What light does the recent academic scholarship shed on this topic?
Reading about history – specific pedagogies	The HA has a very helpful list of useful and accessible history books, with links to reviews included: www.history.org.uk/secondary/resource/9768/history-teacher-subject-knowledge-reading-list Have teachers already written about teaching this topic or concept in *Teaching History*? How have other departments approached teaching this topic? For other departments' approaches, the OBHD website, www.onebighistorydepartment.com, may be useful.
Reviewing the resources within the department	Do we have the textbooks and resources to be able to teach this? If not, can we source or afford them?
Decisions about knowledge (disciplinary concepts, substantive concepts, substantive knowledge)	What is the purpose of teaching this topic? What are our shared curricular aims? What will be the disciplinary focus of our enquiry? Does this 'fit' with our existing schemes of work?
Decisions about pedagogy	How do our values and beliefs inform our pedagogical choices? How will what we know about the discipline of history inform our pedagogical choices? What will our enquiry 'ethic' be (Mohamud & Whitburn, 2019)?
Devising, designing, and refining the enquiry question/s	Is our enquiry question 'rigorous, challenging and intriguing' (Riley, 2008)?
Sequencing lessons to build knowledge	How can we ensure that our teaching is knowledge-rich, rather than information-rich?
Task design that privileges pupils' historical thinking and learning	What will our learning outcomes for each lesson be? The following websites offer many examples of high value activities for rigorous history teaching: https://thinkinghistory.co.uk/ https://www.nationalarchives.gov.uk/education/ https://www.activehistory.co.uk/ https://sheg.stanford.edu/history-lessons
Decisions about assessment	How can we best assess pupils' historical learning?
Teaching	What is going well? How do we know? How have we adapted our teaching?
Reflection and review	What did pupils learn? How did pupils respond to this scheme of work? How might we refine our enquiry question in the future? Is there any further reading that would support teaching this topic?

> **Task 10.3 Mentor reflection on curriculum planning**
>
> - How do you go about designing a new element of a curriculum?
> - What is your department's 'ideal' way of doing this?
> - Does it always happen this way in practice? Why? Why not?
> - How will you model this process to your mentee so that your thinking is visible?

A graduated approach to CPD for beginning teachers

It may be that you are mentoring a student history teacher who is engaged in ITE, for example completing a PGDE (in Scotland) or a PGCE (in England, Wales, or Northern Ireland). It is equally likely that mentors reading this are mentoring beginning teachers with one-to-three years' experience. For example, in England, ECTs complete their induction period over two years before becoming fully qualified. If you are mentoring in Scotland, it might be that you are mentoring a probationer teacher who is in their first year of employed teaching. The professional development needs of your mentee will depend on the stage of their teaching career and their own level of competency and expertise. For instance, a PGCE student in their first teaching placement is very likely to benefit from a subscription to *Teaching History* (usually provided by their institution) or from attending the SHP New Teachers' Conference. It is unlikely that they would benefit in the same way by building a local teaching network or presenting at a national conference.

Professional development takes place over the long term, and it is important not to overwhelm teachers with opportunities for CPD. As a teacher it is all too easy to feel like you are never doing enough. If you are mentoring a student teacher, you are more likely to take a structured approach to reading; it may be that the institution you are working with has 'set readings' to follow with students. If you have more independence in your work with your student teacher, then you may wish to use the readings set out in previous chapters, on the HA's Beginning Teachers' website pages, or from the pages of *Teaching History*'s 'Move Me On' feature. Beginning teachers will attend department meetings and therefore be involved with curricular theorising and assessment decisions without taking the lead on these. As your mentee comes to the end of their second teaching placement, reminders about joining the HA and other professional teaching communities will become more pertinent. It may also be useful to have a conversation with your mentee about how they can capture, remember, and act on CPD opportunities. This can be done simply and time-effectively using a designated notebook or document. Explain to your mentee that while this might feel like an extra 'thing to do', these reflections will inform conversations with their line managers in school, who will be interested in the 'impact' of CPD on their teaching.

If you are mentoring an ECT in England, then you will be following the two-year programme set out by your ECF provider. The structure of these varies. It may be that you would like to supplement aspects of the programme with subject-specific readings or to critically reflect on the applicability of generic strategies in history with your mentee. This contextualisation of generic CPD was identified by the Wellcome Trust (Cordingley et al., 2018) as an early step in developing effective professional development programmes.

Task 10.4 requires you to consider how you would take a graduated approach to supporting beginning teachers' professional development.

Task 10.4 Supporting a mentee's professional development

Read Case studies 10.1 and 10.2.

As a mentor, how would you support the professional development of these beginning teachers?

Case study 10.1 Theo's subject-specific gaps

Theo is an ECT in your department. It is October and Theo is already competent in the classroom. He is confident in his delivery, and he is using the school behaviour policy to good effect. He has a strong background in history and his subject knowledge is very strong. He is a frequent reader of recent historical scholarship, which he is happy to discuss with you and the department. When you ask Theo about his PGCE he explains that most of his time was spent in mixed-subject groups and that there were only three history-specific teaching days built into the course. Since joining your department as an ECT Theo has completed the training required by his ECF provider; he is now keen to push on in his teaching and asks for your advice about how best to achieve this.

Case study 10.2 Rachel's planning challenge

Rachel is a PGCE student with a school-based ITE provider, who is coming to the end of her second placement. She is highly motivated and completes all the reading suggested by her provider and implements suggestions from this in her teaching. Rachel already has a secure understanding of teaching history, and her lessons are forensically planned to extend and deepen her pupils' historical learning. She is already a member of the HA and has signed up for the SHP annual conference. Rachel will be joining a multi-academy trust that you have worked at previously. It follows a centrally designed curriculum and a very structured approach to CPD. Rachel is really looking forward to joining her new school. Her penultimate mentor meeting has a professional development focus. What sort of suggestions or targets would you set for Rachel?

Supporting your mentee to get a teaching position

Getting an interview

For your mentee to continue with their professional development after ITE, it is crucial that they secure their first teaching post. It is very likely that they will come to you for

Table 10.3 Personal statement checklist

Personal statement checklist	✓
• Does your application showcase your subject knowledge and your love of history? • Have you referred to your qualities, skills, and experience? • Have you included specific examples to support your application? For example, if you say that you are an 'effective planner', how is this exemplified in your statement? • Have you demonstrated that your qualities, skills, and experiences make you a good 'match' for the school you have applied to? • Have you proofread your personal statement carefully? Has anyone else proofread it?	

support with what is a nerve-wracking and competitive process. The first challenge for beginning teachers is to secure an interview, and for most applications this means writing a personal statement. There are many different approaches to doing this. The following short checklist in Table 10.3 might help to support your mentee if they ask for guidance with their personal statement.

If your mentee is consistently not getting shortlisted, they may need further support. It could be that they are making silly mistakes or that there is a more substantial issue with their application. In a blog post, Crooks (2022) deals with this issue and many more, including how to best support your mentee if they are repeatedly unsuccessful at interview. This provides an excellent starting point for a mentor supporting a mentee who is struggling to secure their first teaching job.

The interview day

Interview days will feel like very unfamiliar territory to beginning teachers. Certainly, these days are quite different from the selection days that take place in other sectors. This is partly down to the varied mix of activities that might take place on the day: teaching a lesson; a school tour; a student panel; a formal interview or, increasingly, an 'unseen task'. It is also different because teaching positions are usually offered on the same day as the interview and, if offered the position, a candidate is expected to accept the role promptly, often within 24 hours. A brief conversation with a member of your leadership team would go a long way towards helping your mentee to navigate this territory.

Given the busyness of school life, it may not be possible to organise a mock interview for your mentee each time they are asked for interview. However, by providing your mentee with a list of interview questions you can enable them to plan their answers, with examples, and ask another colleague, friend, or family member to run through the questions with them. The questions in Table 10.4 were compiled with the help of UEA History PGCE mentors and University of Nottingham trainee teachers.

Table 10.4 Potential questions for interview

Potential questions for interview

- What makes a good history teacher?
- How do you assess pupils' *historical* learning in your classes?
- Give an example of how recent academic scholarship has influenced your teaching.
- How would you contribute to a collaborative approach to curriculum development and planning?
- How would you monitor and assess your own delivery of the curriculum?
- What do you feel are the most important issues in history teaching and learning?
- Using specific examples, what principles would you apply when designing resources for classes with mixed levels of prior attainment?
- Describe a lesson you planned and taught that you feel was particularly successful, and explain why.
- If appointed to the post, what evidence might you point to in a year's time to show that you had executed the job description successfully?
- What are your principal strengths and weaknesses as a teacher and how will you ensure that the potential impact of your weaknesses is limited?
- How do you engage the interest and enthusiasm of pupils? Give some examples of ways in which you have done this.
- What can you say to persuade us that you will be successful in securing good results with examination classes?
- In what ways might history teachers use ICT successfully in the classroom? Can you give some examples from your own teaching?
- In what ways will pupils have benefited if they have been in your history lessons from Year 7 to Year 9?
- How did you prepare for today's interview?
- How do you think your lesson went? How would you improve this next time? What would you do in the next lesson?
- There should always be a safeguarding question. For example: 'What does safeguarding mean to you?'

Task 10.5 provides a selection of tasks that your mentee could work through as they prepare for interview.

Task 10.5 Supporting your mentee to do well at interview

Your mentee has been asked for interview. Consider the following tasks, as appropriate.

- Ask your mentee to plan answers, with examples, for three of the questions from Table 10.4. Discuss these answers together.
- Support your mentee to start a conversation with a member of the leadership team around expectations for the interview process and accepting or declining teaching roles.
- The usual planning principles will apply to the interview lesson (see Chapter 4), but the lesson will need to reflect the teaching and learning policy of the school

that your mentee has applied for. Ask your mentee what this is and discuss how this might apply to their lesson plan.
- 'Unseen' written tasks are now a more common feature of the interview day. These are sometimes referred to as 'in-tray tasks' and are usually completed under timed conditions. It is impossible to predict what these might be, but just knowing that these tasks exist and can take several forms will help ensure that mentees are not blindsided. Consider the examples below and discuss how you would approach these.

Example 1. Subject knowledge audit
An applicant is asked to answer the following questions in writing.

- What is your favourite period of history to teach and why do you think it is important to teach it?
- What was the last academic history book that you read and how has it influenced your teaching?
- What were the three most significant events of the twentieth century and how have they shaped the modern world?

Example 2. Lesson planning task
An applicant is given an enquiry question and asked to come up with a brief plan for a series of lessons to answer this. This is then presented to the interview panel.

Example 3. Marking task
An applicant is given some student answers and a mark scheme and asked to grade each answer and provide actionable feedback on each.

Professional development for mentors

Many of the opportunities for professional development suggested in this chapter are relevant both to mentees and to mentors. In their review of the international research literature on mentoring beginning teachers, Hobson et al. (2009) found a 'wealth of evidence' to suggest that mentoring a beginning teacher may have a beneficial impact on mentors' personal and professional development. The review identified many aspects of the mentor experience that had the potential to impact mentors' learning; these included opportunities for critical reflection, participation in mentor training, and opportunities to talk to others about their teaching (2009). In their research into the development of history mentors' subject knowledge, Crooks, London, and Snelson (2021a) found that the university connection supported the development of mentors' disciplinary and substantive knowledge. Interviews with history mentors were conducted across three universities and analysis of the data demonstrated that the university connection was important to mentors' continuing development in the following ways:

1. Working with a beginning teacher enables mentors to prioritise their own subject knowledge development despite the day-to-day pressures of teaching. In some cases, this is the only subject-specific CPD to which they have access.
2. Mentors' own knowledge of the discipline of history is updated and developed by discussions with beginning teachers that are focused on their university-based learning.
3. The university connection supports mentors with access to current scholarship and up to date interpretations of key school topics because beginning teachers have recently studied history, or a related subject, in a university.
4. Mentors revisit their own prior learning of subject knowledge in order to discuss with beginning teachers their learning from university sessions.
5. This process of discussing how to teach history and historical topics with a beginning teacher, enables reflection, creativity and so develops the practice of the mentor.

(Crooks, London, & Snelson, 2021a)

Becoming a mentor with subject-specific providers of ITE is one way to gain immediate access to research and resources (that often sit behind paywalls) via your student teacher. It also provides immediate access to a local mentoring community. This will automatically 'plug' you into a network of history teacher mentors, all working within your local context. The majority of ITE providers run mentor training and there is often a strong subject-specific element within these meetings. Several Higher Education Institutions (HEIs) also offer their mentors further subject enhancement opportunities, for example a subject interest group (SIG). University tutors working within subject-specific HEIs take on an important role developing the criticality and reflection of trainees, with an emphasis on the theoretical underpinnings of teaching history (Crooks, London, & Snelson, 2021b). In this model of ITE the university tutor has the time and space to take the lead in disseminating research to mentors and developing networks to support the development of beginning teachers' and mentors' subject knowledge. This raises an important point regarding teachers' time and workload. Mentors are first and foremost teachers themselves and their priority is, rightly, their pupils. Becoming a mentor, while rewarding, will create another competing demand on your time and, depending on your mentee, your goodwill. Therefore, if you are reading this looking to become a mentor and you have the freedom to choose an institution or training provider to work with, it is absolutely worth asking questions about the opportunities for professional development that come with the role. Given the time and commitment you will invest in being a mentor, there is nothing wrong with asking 'what is in it for me?' The best answers should certainly help persuade you to take up the challenging, but fulfilling, role of mentor.

Summary and key points

- The history teaching community offers a wealth of expertise and professional debate for beginning teachers and their mentors to tap into and contribute to.
- The history teaching community has evolved in complexity over time and is not represented by a single 'official body'. By supporting your mentee to access and navigate these communities and networks, you can positively contribute to their professional development in the long term.

- The extent to which a beginning teacher engages with the history teaching community will be influenced by the extent to which their mentor and department value and engage with the networks and professional conversations of the wider history teaching community.
- The professional development needs of your mentee will depend on the stage of their teaching career and their level of competency and expertise.
- An important opportunity for beginning teachers' professional development is to involve and immerse beginning teachers in the curricular planning process early on their career.
- The role of mentor offers its own opportunities for personal and professional development.

Further reading and resources

- **The beginning teachers' professional learning section of the HA website. Available at:** https://www.history.org.uk/secondary/categories/380/module/8767/beginning-teachers-professional-learning

   In this section you will find ideas, resources, and activities to support the professional learning of colleagues who are engaged in ITE and those in the first and second years of their teaching careers.
- **Crooks, V., 2019. Building your house: Teaching in the long term. Available at:** www.uonhistoryteachertraining.school.blog/2019/07/09/building-your-house-teaching-in-the-long-term/

   This blog post outlines useful opportunities for mentors to support current mentees' future professional development.

References

Brooks, C. (2017). Pedagogy and identity in initial geography teacher education: developing a 'professional compass'. *Geography 104*(1), 44–50.

Burn, K., Mutton, T., & Thompson, I. (2023). *Practical Theorising in Teacher Education*. Abingdon: Routledge.

Cordingley, P., Greany, T., Crisp, B., Seleznyov, Bradbury, M., & Coe, R. (2018). *Developing Great Subject Teaching: Rapid Evidence Review of Subject-Specific Continuing Professional Development in the UK*. London: Wellcome Trust. Retrieved 1 September 2022 from https://wellcome.ac.uk/sites/default/files/developing-great-subject-teaching.pdf

Cordingley, P., Higgins, S., Greany, T., Buckler, N., Coles- Jordan, Crisp, B, . . . Coe, R. (2015). *Developing Great Teaching: Lessons from the International Reviews into Effective professional Development*. Teacher Development Trust. Retrieved 1 September 2022 from tdtrust.org/wp-content/uploads/2015/10/DGT-Full-report.pdf

Counsell, C. (2011). Disciplinary knowledge for all, the secondary history curriculum and history teachers' achievement. *Curriculum Journal* 22(2), 201–25.

Counsell, C. (2018). Senior curriculum leadership 1: the indirect manifestation of knowledge. Retrieved from *The Dignity of the Thing* (blog), www.thedignityofthethingblog.wordpress.com/author/christinecounsell (accessed January 2020)

Crooks, V. (2019). Building your house: teaching in the long term. Retrieved 1 September 2022 from *Becoming a History Teacher,* www.uonhistoryteachertraining.school.blog/2019/07/09/building-your-house-teaching-in-the-long-term/

Crooks, V. (2022). How to support beginning teachers struggling to get their first teaching job. Retrieved 22 November 2022 from *Becoming a History Teacher,* https://uonhistoryteachertraining.school.blog/2022/11/04/pipped-at-the-post-how-to-support-beginning-teachers-stuggling-to-get-their-first-teaching-job/

Crooks, V., London, L., & Snelson, H. (2021a). Reviewing perceptions of the distinct contribution of universities in history initial teacher education. HEIRNET Conference Presentation, 2 September 2021.The History Educators International Research Network.

Crooks, V., London, L., & Snelson, H. (2021b). 'Singing from the same hymn-sheet': exploring school-based mentors' perceptions of the role of HEI subject tutors in ITE partnerships. *TEAN Journal 13*(1), 3-26.

Day, C. (1997). Being professional in schools and universities; limits, purposes and possibilities for development. *British Educational Research Journal 23*(2), 193-208.

DfE. (2019). *Early career framework.* London: HM Government. Retrieved 1 September 2022 from www.gov.uk/government/publications/early-career-framework

Fordham, M. (2015). Realising and extending Stenhouse's vision of teacher research: the case of English history teachers. *British Educational Research Journal 42*(1), 135-50.

Haydn, T., & Stephen, A. (2022). *Learning to Teach History in the Secondary School* (5th ed.). Abingdon: Routledge.

Hobson, A., Ashby, P., Malderez, A., & Tomlinson, P. (2009). Mentoring beginning teachers: what we know and what we don't. *Teacher and Teacher Education, 25*(1), 207-16.

McDougall, H. (1976). A new look at history: schools history 13016. Retrieved 1 September 2022 from www.schoolshistoryproject.co.uk/wp-content/uploads/2015/12/NewLookAtHistory.pdf

McIntyre, D. (1995). Initial teacher education as practical theorising: a response to Paul Hirst. *British Journal of Educational Studies 43*(4), 365-85.

Mohamud, A., & Whitburn, R. (2019). Anatomy of an enquiry: deconstructing an approach to curriculum planning. *Teaching History 177,* 28-39.

Ofsted. (2020). *Building great teachers? Initial education research: phase 2.* Retrieved from www.gov.uk/government/publications/initial-teacher-education-curriculum-research/building-great-teachers (accessed September 2022)

Riley, M. (2008). Into the history garden: choosing and planting your enquiry questions. *Teaching History 99,* 8-13.

Rosenshine, B. (2012). Principles of instruction: research-based strategies that all teachers should know. *American Educator 36*(1), 12-19. Retrieved 1 September 2022 from www.files.eric.ed.gov/fulltext/EJ971753.pdf

Sherrington, T., & Caviglioli, O. (2020). *Teaching Walkthrus: Five-Step Guides to Instructional Coaching.* Woodbridge: John Catt.

SHP (n.d.). Core principles. Retrieved 1 September 2022 from www.schoolshistoryproject.co.uk/about-shp/principles/

Shulman, L. S. (1986). Those who understand: knowledge growth in teaching. *Educational Researcher 15*(2), 4-14.

Stenhouse, L. (1975). *An Introduction to Curriculum Research and Development.* Oxford: Heinemann.

Teacher Tapp. (2022). Early career teachers; the story so far. Retrieved 1 September 2022 from Teacher Tapp, www.teachertapp.co.uk/early-career-teachers-the-story-so-far/

Winch, C., Oancea, A., & Orchard, J. (2015). The contribution of education research to teachers' professional learning: philosophical understandings. *Oxford Review of Education 41*(2), 202-16.

Wineburg, S. (2001). *Historical Thinking and Other Unnatural Acts.* Philadelphia: Temple.

INDEX

Note: Locators in *italic* refer to figures, and **bold** refer to tables; Locators followed by "n" indicate endnotes.

1996 Education Act 141

Africanus, George 78-79, 84-85
agency 143
'Age of Revolution, The' 45
Aldrich, Richard 143, 145-46
all pupils' learning, beginning history teachers to support 96-97; approaches to support inclusion for learning in history 102-12; case studies 112-13; inclusive classroom 97; preparation for teaching new class 101; principles for inclusion in history classroom 101-2; respecting individual identity, culture, and background of pupils 100-1; Simone's new class 96; stretching learners demonstrating aptitude for history 99; supporting bilingual and multilingual learners 99-100; supporting learners with range of SEND 98-99; *see also* beginning teachers
American West history 163
Ashby, Ros 28, 29, 59
assessor, mentor as 5, 125
Attenborough, David 128
Autism Spectrum Disorder (ASD) 98, 104-105

Banham, D. 34
Barnes, J. 139
Barton, K. 170
BeBold History Network 197
beginning teachers 5-6, 11, 18; "cause and consequence" concept 53; "change and continuity" concept 55; helping to deploy subject knowledge 25; historical evidence 59-60; historical interpretations 62; historical significance 63-64; history teaching 39; joint planning with experienced colleagues 74-75; learning deficits 19; practical approaches to support 74; "similarity and difference" concept 57-58; subject knowledge issues 18-19; substantive conceptual knowledge for 41; supporting to understand and teach disciplinary concepts 52; supporting with assessment 90; use of remote teaching 190
Benger, A. 155
'Big Six' concepts: "cause and consequence" concept 52-54; "change and continuity" concept 55-56; historical evidence 59-61; historical interpretations 61-63; historical significance 63-65; "similarity and difference" concept 57-59; *see also* disciplinary concepts
Billinghurst, Rosa May 164
Black and British: A Forgotten History (Olusoga) 171
Boxer, Adam 34, 184
Boyd, S. 156
Brailsford, D. 34
British Empire rehabilitated, The (Lester) 145
British values 136-41, 143-144
Brooks, C. 121, 197
Brown, Gordon 139, 141
Bryan, Beverly 171
Burnham, S. **8**, 46, 89
Burn, K. 34, 196
Byrom, J. 25

Index   213

card-sorting methods 86
Carr, Helen 73
"cause and consequence" concept 52-54
"change and continuity" concept 55-56
Chapman, A. 34, 40, 53
CHATA project 58
ChatGPT 186
Church, Stephen 104
civic literacy 180, 182
Clarke, D. 6, 132
Clarkson 24
Clio et cetera blog site 43-44
cognition: cognitive ethics 144; and learning needs 98
Collins, S. 105
communication and interaction needs 98
'community of practice' 138, 147, 180
concept-cracking approach 104-5
conceptual knowledge 40, *41;* disciplinary 47; first-and second-order 39; *see also* substantive conceptual knowledge
Continuing Professional Development (CPD) 194; associations and networks 196-97; curriculum planning as 202-4; graduated approach for beginning teachers 204-5; and history teaching community 195-96, 201; mentoring beginning teachers 195; opportunities for history-specific 198, **199**-**201**; personal statement checklist **206**; professional development for mentors 208-9; social media 197-98; subject-specific professional development 194, 198; supporting mentee's professional development 205; supporting mentee to get teaching position 205-8; teacher researchers and *Teaching History* 201-2
controversial and sensitive issues in history 153; answering beginning teachers' questions about teaching 171; approaches to teaching 158-59; benefits of teaching 157-58; considering own teaching of 160; definition of 154-56; department's curriculum 160-61; developing subject knowledge 171; disciplinary thinking and 156; disclosing personal views 169-70; exploring history curriculum with mentee 157; planning and creating resources for teaching 168-69; principles for teaching 154, 161-68; rationale for teaching 157; reviewing curriculum content 161; reviewing textbook presentations of 167-68; spontaneous controversial remarks 170; understanding curricular rationale 158; understanding personal sensitivities 159; use of photographs and films 170-71
Cook, R. 66
Counsell, Christine 34, 74, 79, 80, 102, 202
'coverage' model of ICT competence 189-90
critical patriotism 139
Cromwell, Oliver 24
Crooks, V. **8**, 33, 131, 206, 208
'culture wars' theory 142
'Cunning Plan' feature 51
curricular theorising 196
curricular thinking 10, 120
curriculum development 201
curriculum mapping 181
curriculum planning as professional development 202-3; mentor reflection on 204; stepped approach with your mentee **203**

Dadzie, Stella 171
Dalrymple, William 140
data-logging software 179
Davies, M. 156
Dawson, Ian 25, 33, 34, 79, 80
dehumanising language 165; balancing safeguarding with historical integrity 165-66; considering language and terminology 166-67
Dennis, N. 164
Department for Education (DfE): advice for promoting FBV 137; requirements for mentors 9
Developing Great Subject Teaching report 198
dialogic mentoring 7, 119-120, 153-154
dialogic learning, ICT and 184, 188
dinner table test 81
disciplinary concepts: articulation of disciplinary content of own curriculum 49-50; exploration of 65-66; historical disciplinary conceptual knowledge 47; interconnectedness of historical knowledge 50; progression in disciplinary understanding 66-67; relationship between enquiry questions and disciplinary focus 50-52; role of historical disciplinary knowledge 47-48; second-order conceptual 'canon' 48-49; supporting beginning teachers to understand and teach 52; use of enquiry questions 77; *see also* 'Big Six' concepts

disciplinary education 40
disciplinary thinking and sensitive and controversial histories 156
disciplinary values in history classroom 144-46
distributed mentoring 185
domains of mentoring: assessor, mentor as 5; inductor into profession, mentor as 3; pastoral support, mentor as 3-4; teaching discipline, mentor as guide into 4
Donovan, M. 34
'Do Now' retrieval practice tasks 85

Early Career Framework (ECF) 194-195
Early Career Teachers (ECTs) 195, **201**
Ekpenyon, E. I. 164
Elias, H. 171
'eliciting pupils' thinking 112
end-of-lesson plenaries 107
End of History and the Beginning of Education, The (Aldrich) 145-46
English as additional language (EAL) 96-97, 99, 100, 105
enquiry question 101-2; challenges of enquiry questions for beginning teachers 77; history teachers plan using enquiry questions 75-76; identifying and generating effective enquiry questions 78-79; making lesson conclusions count 106-7; sequence seeking to answer 104; teachers design good enquiry questions 76-77
equality of opportunity 142
everyday concepts **42**
expert practitioners' views about developing teachers 186; advanced levels of technological expertise 186-87; inducting beginning teachers into use of remote teaching 190; making mentees aware of potential of ICT 187-88; moving away from 'coverage' model of ICT competence 189-90; supporting mentee with remote teaching 190-91; talking about and sharing some impact resources 188-89; teaching mentees about helpfulness 188
'Eye as Witness, The' project 162

'fingertip' knowledge 80-81
flipped learning 180
Ford, A. 66, 163

Fordham, Michael 24, 33-34, 43-44, 201
Forever Project, The 162
formative assessment 88-89
Foster, Rachel 55, 74, 106
Fullan, M. 18
Fundamental British Values (FBV) 136, 143; approaching teaching of 137; discussion of DfE's advice for promoting 137; navigating issue of 138-41; understanding context of introduction 141-42

Gillan, Audrey 140
Glossary of Terminology for Understanding Transatlantic Slavery and 'Race', A 167
'good' history 145-46
Gosrani, S. 167
Grande, J. 20, 34, 80
Gypsy, Roma, and Traveller communities (GRT communities) 163-64

Haenen, J. 41, *42*
Hamer, John 145
Hammond, K. 47, 80, 99
Harris, R. 49, 97, 101, 102
Hawkey, K. 156
Haydn, T. 188
Healy, G. 127
hearing-impaired pupils 99-100
Heart of the Race, The (Bryan, Dadzie and Scafe) 171
Heller, M. 28
Hibbert, D. 77
Higher Education Institutions (HEIs) 209
Hill, Christopher 137, 146
'hinterland' of historical knowledge 80-81
Historian, The (Joseph) 148
Historical Association (HA) 12, 160, 176, 197
historical discipline 12, 39, 61
historical evidence 59-61, 75
historical interpretations 61-63, 128
historical knowledge: development of 'hinterland' of historical knowledge 80-81; disciplinary conceptual knowledge 47; 'fingertip' and 'residue' knowledge 80-81; interconnectedness with disciplinary concepts 50; sequencing building blocks of 104-5; takeaways as bedrock of planning 79-81

historical learning 48, 85, 127; classroom management 130; disciplinary aspects of 39; enfranchising pupils in 100-1; lesson observation 121; nature of 10-11; planning for summative assessment 89; pre-observation conversation about 120; questions to support mentors to focus **122-24**

historical record 62, 138, 165

historical significance 48, 63-65, 85

historical thinking 76, 77, 87, 89, 112, 170-71; agency in 143; extended writing 106; ISM 104; planning for 105; principles of 65-66; in relation to causation **8;** writing task 102; *see also* 'Big Six' concepts

historical understanding, planning for 11

history-specific feedback 11

history education/classroom: conceptual understanding in 40; principles for inclusion in 101-2; *see also* values in history education/classroom

History Education Research Journal (HERJ) 202

history teaching 23, 39; community 195-96, 201; multi-perspectivity 158; professional discourse of 194; sensitive and controversial topics in 160; use of ICT in 176, 177, 181; values in history education 136

Hobson, A. 3, 208

Hollingsworth, H. 6, 132

Hollis, C. 164

homework, planning for 107

human or 'universal' values in history classroom 142-44

Illingworth, S. 140

immediate post-lesson evaluation **91**

impact resources 188-89

inclusive classroom 97; approaches to support inclusion for learning in history 102; considering planning 107-8; exploring department curriculum 103; inclusion at level of in-lesson adaptations 108-12; at lesson-planning level 103-7; planning for inclusion at curriculum level 102-3; principles for inclusion in history classroom 101-2; rendering historical thinking and processes visible 112

inclusive historical concepts **42**

inductor into profession, mentor as 3

information and communications technology (ICT) 12, 176; balance between pressure and support 185; and dialogic learning 184; expert practitioners' views about developing teachers 186-91; and history teaching 181-82; importance of 177-78; judging allocation time to 185-86; suggestions to develop or cultivate in 178-81; use in history classroom 176; use of social media 182-84

initial stimulus material (ISM) 104

Initial Teacher Education (ITE) 1, 194, 197; challenge facing beginning teachers 98-99; goal of 5; partnership 24

Initial Teacher Training (ITT) 4, 177; *Carter Review of* 4; Core Content Framework 177, 178

in-lesson adaptations, inclusion at 108; cementing through visualisation 109-10; decisions to introduce and remove scaffolding 111-12; questioning advance pupils' historical understanding 108-9; reading historical stories 111; reviewing visual images 110; storytelling 110-11; thinking about questioning 109

'Interconnected Model' of teacher development 6-7

International Baccalaureate learner profile 146-47

internet 188

interview for mentee: getting interview from mentor 205-6; interview day 206; potential questions for **207**; support from mentor 207-8

joint planning with experienced colleagues 74-75

Joseph, Keith 148

judgementoring 7

Kello, K. 159

Kerridge, R. 101, 163

Kitson, A. 143, 158-59, 160

knowledge application 18

Kühberger, C. 43

Lacks, Henrietta 164

Laffin, Diana 32

Langdon, Peter 156

language development for thinking 106

learning 18; to ask historical questions 29-30; deficits 19; flipped 180; historical 10-11; to prioritise subject knowledge enhancement 20-21
Le Cocq, H. 28
Lee, Peter 28, 58, 144
Lenga, R. -A. 162
lesson conclusions 106-7
lesson endings **128-29**
lesson observation and feedback 118, 119, 121; approaching feedback with struggling trainees 130-31; building relationships 119; post-observation 124-26; pre-observation 119-21, 124; professional conversations 130-31; questions to support mentors during **122-24**; response to mentee is not responding to feedback 131-32; working with other members of department 132-33; written feedback 126-30, **127-29**
lesson planning process of beginning teachers: evaluating lessons 90, **91-92**; lesson plan annotation **91**; planning for assessment 88-90; practical approaches to support beginning teachers 74-75; principles of 74; structuring planning process for mentee 82-88; supporting to develop pupils' historical knowledge 79-81; supporting to plan using enquiry questions 75-79; tacit criteria 74
Lester, A. 145
Lévesque, S. 47-48
Levstik, L. 166
Lingard, R. 164
Lomas, Tim 31
London, L. 208
Luff, Ian 33

Maddison, Michael 140
'mapping' concepts 44, *45*
Massaquoi, Hans-Jürgen 164
McCully, A. 158-59, 160, 170
McDonough, F. 39
McFahn, Richard 32, 139
McIntyre, D. 195
'Medicine Through Time' change-and-continuity enquiry 50
mental models of substantive conceptual knowledge 42-43

mentees: aware of potential of ICT 187-88; developing disciplinary subject knowledge 28-29; helping to organise and archive developing subject knowledge 26-27; preparation for career-long development 13; risk taking adopted by 153; teaching mentees about helpfulness 188; teaching to develop substantive historical knowledge 27-28
mentee, structuring planning process for: developing range of subject-knowledge enhancement with 22; exploring history curriculum with 157; pedagogy selection 85-86; planning individual lessons 83-84; planning using existing resources 86-88, *87*; staged process for planning *82*; subject knowledge role in planning process 82-83; worked example of planning process *84*, 84-85
mentoring 1-3; activities 52; balancing demands of 5; domains of mentoring 3-5; preparing mentees for career-long development 13; subject-specific mentoring 9-13; teacher development and approaches of 5-8, **7**
mentors: aware of historical subject knowledge 18; history-specific observations 124; history mentors 12; importance of beginning teachers 24; pre-lesson observation activities for 120; professional development for 208-9; professional wrestling 11; providing subject-specific written feedback 129-30; questions to support during lesson observations **122-24**; recognising complex models of teacher development 7; r mentoring a mentee who is not responding to feedback 131-32; role for career-long development 13
'metahistorical' knowledge 47
Mohamud, A. 163
Morton, T. 48, 66, 99
Mountstevens, J. 142
Mulla, I. 141
multi-perspectivity 96, 158
Mutton, T. 196

National Curriculum in England 24, 27, 47, 48, 57, 136, 138, 139, 142, 156
newly qualified teacher posts (NQT) 181

Oborne, P. 141
Olusoga, David 171
Orchard, J. 6

Palek, D. 47
pastoral support, mentor as 3-4
Patel, Z. 77
Paul, R.146
pedagogical thinking 12
Phillips, M. 139
Phillips, P. 139
placing obstacles 102
Point, Evidence, Explain, Link (PEEL) 106
post-observation 124-25; conversation after lesson 125; structure for feedback conversations **125-26**
post-truth era 180
Postgraduate Certificate in Education (PGCE) 121
PowerPoint presentation 179, 182, 184
practical theorising 1, 196
pre-observation 119-20; activities for mentors 120; history-specific observations 124
Priggs, C. 161
principles for teaching controversial and sensitive histories 154, 161-62; addressing dehumanising language 165-67; honouring dehumanised people 162; representative and inclusive approach 163-65; requiring understanding of present context 168; restoring oppressed people's agency 163
procedural knowledge 47, 49
professional conversations 130-31
professional wrestling in history department 11, 25
progression in disciplinary understanding 66-67
propositional knowledge 40, *41*, 80
published discourse 202
Puttick, S. 127

Qualified Teacher Status (QTS) 194
questions/questioning 127; advance pupils' historical understanding 108-9; to support mentors during lesson observations **122-24**; thinking about 109

reading historical stories 111
Reformation 44; concept categories *45*; 'mapping' concepts 44, *45*

remote teaching 182, 185, 190-91
representative and inclusive approach 163; avoiding tokenism 164-65; 'slot-in' approach 163-64
'residue' knowledge 80-81
'revolution' concept 45
Richards, J. 147
Richardson, W. 184
Riddle, H. 33-34
Riley, Michael 25, 75-76, 79, 107
'risk-taking' approach 153, 159
Robinson 168
Roma Stories Oral History Project 163-64
Rosenshine, B. 194
'routine representation' approach 165
Rüsen 49

Scafe, Suzanne 171
school history 96, 137, 144, 191; lessons 166; purposes of 73, 96, 139, 143; Traille's research into 165; value free 136
school holiday test 81
Schools Council History Project (SCHP) *see* Schools History Project (SHP)
Schools History Project (SHP) 12, 47, 75, 176, 196, 197
Schrijnemakers, H. 41, *42*
second-order concepts *see* disciplinary concepts
secure substantive knowledge 22-23
Seixas, P 48, 66, 99, 137
self-evaluation, detailed **91**
self-observation **92**
Shemilt, D. 58
Silk Roads, The (Frankopan) 110
"similarity and difference" concept 57-59
Slater, John 139
'slot-in' approach 163-64
Smith, D. 80
Snelson, H. 163, 164, 208
'social cohesion' aspirations 142
'social, cultural, religious and ethnic diversity' 48
social, emotional, and mental health needs 99
social media 182-84, 197-98
Spafford, M. 171
special educational needs and disabilities (SEND) 97, 108; areas of need within 98-99; supporting learners with range of 98

spiritual, moral, social and cultural (SMSC) 142
Stanford, M. **8**
Stenhouse, Lawrence 33, 201
'stickiness' 188
storytelling 110-11
subject-specific mentoring 9-10; of beginning and early career history teachers 10; encouraging engagement with scholarship 10; history-specific feedback 11; identifying targets for development 11; inducting into community of history teachers and educators 12; nature of historical learning 10-11; spiral approach to **8**; thinking about planning for historical understanding 11; understanding purposes and relevance of historical discipline 12; *see also* mentoring
subject interest group (SIG) 209
subject knowledge: assessment and progression issues 31; developing mentees' disciplinary 28-29; helping beginning teachers 25; helping mentees to organise and archive 26-27; about how pupils learn in history 34; importance of footnotes and references 29; importance of strands 24; issues with beginning teachers 18-19; learning to ask historical questions 29-30; learning to distil 25-26; role in planning process 82-83; suggested readings on assessment 32; teaching approaches in history lessons 32-34; teaching mentees to develop substantive historical knowledge 27-28; teaching mentees to 'open up' historical topics 30-31
subject knowledge enhancement: checking pupils' subject-knowledge starting points 19-20; developing range with mentee 22; learning to prioritise 20-21; materials selection 22; modelling 20; setting targets 21-22
subject-specific written feedback 129-30
substantive conceptual knowledge 40, *41*; concept mapping 46; conceptual expositions 41; evolving concepts 45-46; importance of 47; key substantive concepts 43-44; mental models 42-43; planning for understanding 44-45; substantive concepts identification 42; taxonomy for **42**
substantive knowledge 40, *41*

summative assessment 89-90
summative judgements 89

tacit criteria 74
takeaways 80; as bedrock of planning 79; test 81
Tarr, Russel 33
Taylor, T. 31
teacher development and mentoring approaches 5-6, **7**; 'Interconnected Model' of teacher development 6-7; spiral approach to subject-specific mentoring **8**; supported reflection and mentoring cycle 7
teacher researchers 201-2
Teacher Tapp 195
Teaching and Assessing Historical Understanding (Lomas) 31
teaching approaches in history lessons 32-34
teaching discipline, mentor as guide into 4
Teaching Emotive and Controversial History (TEACH) report 155
Teaching History journal 201-2
thematic units 110
Thinking Historically (Lévesque) 47
Thompson, I. 196
Times Educational Supplement 186
Todd 168
tokenism 164-65
Traille, K. 165
Twitter 182-84

Understanding the Holocaust 162
unique historical concepts **42**

value-free zone 143
values in history education/classroom 136, 149n1; approaching teaching of FBV 137-42; characteristics of 'good' history 145-46; disciplinary values in 144-46; educational values and dispositions in the history classroom 146, 147; finding time for 'truth' as value in 147-49; human or 'universal' values in 142-44; International Baccalaureate learner profile 146-47; values issues in 137, 142
van Boxtel, C. 46
van Drie, J. 46
Vella, Y. 28

Virtual Learning Environment (VLE) 182
virtual reality applications 186
voting software 184

Walsh, B. 148, 177, 187, 188
Wansink, B. 158
Web 2.0 applications 184
What Is History, Now? (Carr) 73
whispered observation 75
Whitburn, R. 163
Wilberforce 24
Willingham, D. 34, 110

Winch, C. 6
Wineburg, S. 18-19, 29, 148, 177
Winton, Nicholas 140
work scrutiny **92**
Worth, P. 85, 106
writing, planning for 106
written lesson observation feedback 126-27; example of **127-29**; research on 127; subject-specific written feedback 129-30
Wynn, J. 127

YorkClio 164

For Product Safety Concerns and Information please contact our EU
representative GPSR@taylorandfrancis.com
Taylor & Francis Verlag GmbH, Kaufingerstraße 24, 80331 München, Germany

www.ingramcontent.com/pod-product-compliance
Lightning Source LLC
Chambersburg PA
CBHW080613230426
43664CB00019B/2873